HEALED WITHIN

HEALED WITHIN

Susan James

with

Merrilyn Williams

HODDER AND STOUGHTON
LONDON SYDNEY AUCKLAND TORONTO

In order to preserve confidentiality, names have been
changed where appropriate.

The quote on page 219 comes from 'Majesty' by Jack
Hayford published by Rocksmith Music administered by
Leosong Copyright Services Limited, London NW1 0AP.

British Library Cataloguing in Publication Data
James, Susan
  Healed within.
  I. Title II. Williams, Merrilyn
  248.4

  ISBN 0-340-53824-4

*Published by Hodder and Stoughton, a division of Hodder and Stoughton Ltd,
Mill Road, Dunton Green, Sevenoaks, Kent TN13 2YA. Editorial Office: 47
Bedford Square, London WC1B 3DP.*
Photoset by Medcalf Type Ltd, Bicester, Oxon.
Printed in Great Britain by Cox & Wyman Ltd, Reading.

Foreword

Susan James has been a Resident of Douglas House Cheshire Home since 1972. She has been confined to a wheelchair for the past eighteen years, but she has not allowed that to curb her determination to get things done. At various times, she has run a greetings card shop at Douglas House, taken up French and been both Secretary and Chairman of the Residents' Association. She has given talks to schools, Rotary Clubs and Women's Institutes about the concept of the Cheshire Homes and the particular needs of Douglas House. She has been featured on *Songs of Praise*, published a booklet of poetry and, in 1990, attended the Church and Disabled Congress in Michigan.

This book, the story of her life, is a further and most meaningful testament to the source of her inner strength – her joyful Christian faith and her manifest belief in the love of a compassionate God.

I hope that it will reach out to touch other lives, and that it will bring hope and faith and comfort wherever they are most needed.

LEONARD CHESHIRE
7th November, 1990

Preface

WHY?

'At present we do not see everything subject to Him. But we see Jesus . . .'

Hebrews 2:8–9

I have a tiny prison, and paralysis holds me there,
Yet Jesus is perfect freedom: my spirit flies in this wheelchair.

In Africa a mother sits crying, her starving child at her breast;
She has no hope for tomorrow, and feet so weary, finding no rest.

In a city an old man lies dying, the whisky and wine take their toll;
In streets painted people are lonely, sad crazy eyes plead their role.

In this complex world, so oft unfair it can seem as if God doesn't really care.
Why is there hardship in some lifespan? through man's inhumanity to man?

In amazing love, Jesus came to die, the Father's sacrifice for you and I
Help all, we pray, to understand the grace and truth of the heavenly plan.

Why is there famine and why is there war? why the wealthy? why the poor?
Yet I know the battle has been won; while we were yet sinners God gave His Son.

From the four corners of this world may the message of Jesus
be clearly heard;
''Love your neighbour'' is His command; only in love shall none
be harmed.

Till our world passes out of sight in Your amazing shining light
We know Your love, we know Your care, let us Your righteous
armour wear.

Lord, help all peoples to understand and take Your Gospel to
every land;
For every creature, large and small, God is Love, and Love is all.

Acknowledgements

With thanks to my friend, Hugh C. Rae, for his editorial help and advice.

Merrilyn Williams

I thank Merrilyn for her patience in sorting through my partially sighted typing with its mistakes and for coping with such love and patience with my terrible memory.

My thanks also to my dear Aunty Ann and in memory of my beloved parents and Uncle Ricky, who all suffered with me yet were a source of love during the time of my brain tumour.

Thanks also to the care of doctors and nurses in Freedom Fields and to other hospitals since then who have put up with my difficulties. To the Cheshire Foundation and to many friends who deserve to be mentioned by name and who enable my life to be so full; and to friends who have disappeared in and out of my life and particularly those who have encouraged me greatly in my love of the Lord.

To Peter Larkin who helped so much with my desire to write my first book, albeit poetry. To Joni Eareckson Tada for her inspiration in *Joni*.

To Lesley Sampson for her help with my letters and for sharing with me Lamentations 3:22–26 with its Promise of New Every Morning.

Susan James

Contents

PART
ONE

1

Revolution

'Two thousand dollars, please.' I smiled, in what I hoped was a dazzling fashion at the oily cashier behind the grille in the Bank of South America's plush concourse. During my twenty-seven years I'd often been told that I could charm most men with my elfin face and petite figure. I'd no reason to suppose that the cashier might be an exception.

He stared back at me, unblinking, unimpressed.

'Two thousand,' I said again. 'Dollar bills?'

Still there was no response.

The delay was making me nervous; nervous and impatient. I'd been unsettled since early morning when Rosita, our maid, had burst into the bedroom with the news that there had been a revolution. The atmosphere in the foyer was tense, almost frenzied. Cashiers dashed about behind the grilles and customers scurried in and out of doors. But the cashier before me remained silent and scowling. I was tempted to turn on my heel and get out of the place. Through the window I could see sunshine in the street and I longed to be outdoors, free of the synthetic odour of air conditioning, back home in the rarefied freshness of the mountains.

'No dollars,' the cashier said. 'You cannot have so large a sum of dollars.'

My Spanish, though good, was hardly adequate for an altercation. I couldn't understand why my request for dollars was being refused by this insolent little man.

Should I report him to his superior, or would this cause further delay? It wasn't as if we had nothing in our account. David was well paid and, despite our affluent lifestyle, we had no shortage of funds.

Shouting infiltrated from the street. I glanced behind me then repeated my request. 'Two thousand dollars?'

He shook his head.

'But I need it,' I told him. 'I need it urgently.'

His eyes narrowed with hostile pleasure. 'Instructions from the army. We cut back on the withdrawal of dollars.'

I stared at him, confused and helpless, then, with a shrug of his shoulders, he tugged open a drawer, took out a sheaf of banknotes and began to count them. Slowly. Insolently.

He glanced up, his jaws working over the inevitable wad of chewing gum. 'I give you the dollars,' he said. 'But it is forbidden to take them out of Ecuador.'

'But why?'

His self-importance had become insulting. He sneered at my ignorance. 'There has been an emergency. Perhaps you had not heard?'

After Rosita's outburst it had not taken David long to discover that the Revolution had started quietly but had quickly spread. Early in the night the army had entered the government buildings and had wrested power from President Velasco.

David and I had been in Ecuador for a couple of years and knew that, in such an unstable republic, revolutions and counter-revolutions were commonplace, with constant friction between army and president. In fact, this was the third occasion on which Velasco had been deposed. As an employee of the Anglo-Ecuadorian Oilfield Company, David had been warned not to stray into downtown Quito at any time and we'd often seen student riots and demonstrations.

To my mind their protests were justified. Police, postal workers and other government employees often went unpaid. At such times the *Policia* were not above pouncing on innocent motorists and slapping on a fine simply to procure enough hard cash to buy food for their families or, more likely perhaps, drink for themselves. Postal workers, too, were driven to theft and it was always advisable to secure one's letters firmly with sellotape in order to protect the contents.

Even so, the idea of being involved in a revolution, the first that David and I had experienced personally, was not without its excitements. It was somewhat inconsiderate of the army, however, to stage it just as I was about to return to England on holiday and needed cash for the journey.

I felt a strange sense of foreboding, something that lay below the anxieties caused by the current political upheaval. I looked behind me again, through the plate-glass window into the street. Soldiers were stationed at every corner. Rifles and machine guns glinted menacingly in the morning light. But I wasn't really afraid of the bayonets and the guns, which seemed more inconvenient than threatening. I could not explain the sense of dread that came over me but, in a moment, it passed and I was left, instead, with more trivial concerns, tonight's *despedida*, my farewell dinner party, among them.

I watched the bank official casually continue to count out my money and, now that the crisis seemed to be resolved, fretted about other things. Had my parents received my letters informing them that I was returning home ahead of David? What if they hadn't? And how would they interpret the news? Come to that, what would our friends here in Quito make of it? I was always out to give a good impression to them and to David's colleagues and had acquired quite a reputation as a cook since we'd lived in Ecuador. I'd planned an ambitious menu for tonight, including a special cream and liqueur sauce for the fruit salad which was to be served on pineapple shells.

If I was honest with myself, however, I had to admit that it was neither fruit salad nor guns in the streets of

Quito that were causing my underlying anxiety. I had my own revolution to contend with; a revolution in my heart and in my marriage.

My marriage; that was the real problem.

Although David and I had never spoken of our troubles to anyone, the tension between us affected the whole household, from the servants right down to the dog. I was surprised that the expatriates in Quito had not got wind of our disharmony, for ours was a close-knit community and servants were dreadful gossips. We could not openly admit that our marriage was not all that it should be for we were generally regarded as a perfect couple. Outsiders could not know of the days when David and I could find nothing to say to each other, or of the long, sad silences of the nights.

We'd gone on like that for months, never acknow-ledging, even to each other, that a problem existed. I'd hoped, when I'd suggested that I should return to England on furlough ahead of him that my absence would cause him to miss me. Only now did it occur to me that I'd given no thought to whether or not I would miss him.

'Susan? Everything okay?'

I started as David touched my arm just as the teller pushed the dollar bills unceremoniously through the grille at me.

'Is that all of it?' David asked.

'Yes.'

'Pick it up then, and let's go.'

I followed him out of the building. We stepped over the prostrate body of an Otovalan Indian who was snoring off a drunken binge on the steps of the bank, and walked down the street.

The sight of snow-capped mountains soaring above the city's highrise skyline lifted my spirits a little. Set nine thousand feet up in the Andean range, Quito was a cosmopolitan city, a blend of colonial splendour and American-style modernism in which extremes of wealth and poverty met and mingled. I had grown to love the capital and would be sorry to leave, even for a holiday.

How different had been its effect on me when I'd first arrived in South America, a nervous girl, fresh from England. It had frightened me then, before I learned how to cope with the cultural differences, and with the high-flying social life of our compatriots and Ecuadorian dignitaries.

David steered me towards the Fiat 125, ushered me into the passenger seat, and set off over the potholes, heading for our home in the foothills.

'The man in the bank,' I said. 'Did you see how he treated me? He behaved like a little tinpot dictator.'

David did not answer. He frowned and concentrated on negotiating the heavy traffic.

I smoothed down the skirt of my cotton sundress. 'He told me I couldn't take the money out of the country.'

'I'm not surprised.' David sounded brisk but not unduly dismayed. 'But you'll have to risk it, Susan. Otherwise you'll have no dollars at all. This particular spot of trouble may last for some time, so I've heard at the office. Restrictions of all kinds will be imposed. It won't be easy on the company.'

I listened, but not attentively. The company and its problems were David's concern, not mine. My thoughts had turned to the dinner party once more, a good deal of preparation still remained to be done and servants were never totally reliable. Besides, I wanted to try on the new dress I'd had specially made.

With a deftness born of experience, David avoided a stray mongrel and swung the Fiat into the approach to El Quiteno where we lived.

El Quiteno Libre – translated 'Freeman of Quito' – was a highly desirable and attractive residential area. Unlike other suburbs which relied on the ramshackle water-carrier trucks, with their exorbitant, fluctuating prices, and their endless calls to attract trade, it was favoured with a constant water supply and was, therefore, a much sought-after vicinity.

Our home was ultra-modern, and very spacious; ideal for entertaining, with its bar, twin lounges, bedrooms and bathrooms en-suite. The views were breathtaking. To the rear was the glory of Cotopaxi, the famed volcano, now extinct, whose snowcapped tip blushed a soft rosy hue in the morning light. The house overlooked the city and we had a fine close-up view of a smaller companion mountain called Pinchincha. This was craggy at its summit, and occasionally a little cloud would lovingly alight on the peak, then disappear, leaving behind what seemed, to our eyes, a tiny top-knot of snow. How I loved it all!

'You do realise, Susan, that the bankteller was right,' David said. 'Under the circumstances, the authorities will never let you legally take that load of dollars out of the country.'

Cotopaxi, pretty dresses and liqueur sauce went out of my head for a moment; I could think only of my holiday, of getting away for a while, back to my parents' home in England, and the fact that the revolution might stop me.

'But what can I do?' I said, plaintively.

David grinned. 'Beat them at their own game.'

'What do you mean?' I asked.

'Smuggle it out,' said David.

The days passed swiftly and I was hard pressed to be ready to leave on time. I packed simply, with just enough holiday clothes for my six weeks' absence from Ecuador. Fortunately, as it was summer in England, and the other countries in which I was travelling would be hot, I would need only light-weight garments.

By Tuesday 21st July, the day of my departure, I'd finally ticked off every item on my lists of arrangements and preparations, bade farewell to friends and instructed the servants. With the cases downstairs, I waited for David to take me to the airport.

'Why you go before Señor David, Señora?' The maids were puzzled.

I waved a hand airily and glanced briefly at David who had appeared in the hall. 'Oh, I'm sure you'll look after the Señor very well. It'll do him good to be without me for a while. Maybe we'll have a second honeymoon when he joins me . . .' I raised an eyebrow and tried to catch his eye.

David ignored my remark. 'You ready?' he asked and, without waiting for a reply, picked up one of my suitcases and strode towards the front door. The girls followed suit, gathering up the remaining luggage and falling in behind, whilst I cast a last look around and then took up the rear. David reached the door and stopped. The whole entourage came to an abrupt halt.

Before us, my dog, Goliat, barred the way. All morning he had followed me around; now he lay on the mat before the door, his head on his front paws, ears down, and his eyes regarding me soulfully.

'Come on Goliat,' David poked him, his hand-stitched pigskin shoe stirring the dog's midrift in an attempt to get him on to his feet. 'Up you get. There's a good boy.'

The dog lay inert, his eyes still upturned.

David's foot explored the animal's hindquarters in a less gentle fashion. 'Up!' he said peremptorily. 'Come on! Move!'

Still the dog would not budge. In exasperation David threw down the case and grabbed him by the collar. The collie continued to resist.

'This is ridiculous!' David stormed. 'What's got into the animal.' He half-dragged, half-carried the supine beast across the polished floor.

'David, don't hurt him,' I cried angrily. I ran to the aid of my pet, and crouched beside him.

'There, there,' I crooned, disregarding the scratch marks left in the parquet flooring by the dog's claws. I glared at David's retreating back.

'Will you miss me, Goliat?' I whispered into the dog's long silky ears. 'I'll miss you; but I'll soon be home again.'

With moist eyes I followed my husband out and climbed into the car.

It had begun to rain, a steady, gentle pitter patter, as it did most afternoons. David flicked on the wipers, and with a wide, slow sweep they licked across the windscreen, back and forth, back and forth with a tiny flat plopping sound at the end of each stroke.

'Got everything?' he enquired. I nodded, then he reversed out of the drive and pointed the bonnet in the direction of the airport. I turned my head and stared out of the window, blinking rapidly to disperse the brimming tears. The suburbs through which we were passing swam before my eyes. In the garden of one large house a sprinkler had been left on. The water jets mingled with the rain, played softly on green lawns and hung in silver droplets from the dark foliage of fir trees.

An image of Goliat, prostrate before the door, was printed indelibly in my mind. Was I being fanciful, or had he really been trying to prevent my leaving? They say dogs are intuitive. Did he know something I did not? Could it be possible that my collie, in some mysterious way, sensed that this was to be our last farewell? Not for the first time I wondered what had possessed me to make that fateful decision to go ahead of David.

The rain stopped and I glanced upward. The sky rose, a clear blue dome high above the mountain range. Only Pinchincha's peak was hidden; obscured behind a grubby daub of grey cloud.

David kept his eyes fixed firmly on the road ahead and had little to say, other than to check the whereabouts of my money.

'I hope the dollars are well concealed?'

The idea of smuggling a foreign currency out of the country had seemed exciting from the security of home, and I'd been filled with an air of bravado when I'd told my friends. Now that I was on my way that was fast beginning to evaporate.

'I've hidden *volution* clothes,' I replied

'You do realise ggage, amongst my under- government orders t that it's directly against at present? Customs a dollars out of the country more vigilant than usu gration are bound to be

I nodded. What I was d flying right in the face of authority, and you never hich way they would jump. We expats all knew uador needed the services of British oilmen, but t to a jumped-up, under-paid Ecuadorian excise n ough I was only vaguely aware of the ramificatio uld I be caught, the prospect was, nonetheless, ala The muscles of my stomach tightened with sick a nsion. For a moment I considered my position ension. indignation supplanted my fear.

'It's our money anyway,' I burst out e're quite justified in doing what we want with it. do they think they are making rules to prevent us ta what's ours out of the country?'

Nevertheless, my heart was in my mouth w n we arrived at the airport and, by the time David had ked the car then carried my suitcases through the conc rse and joined the queue at the checkout counter, my ner s were taut with anxiety. I fiddled with my airline ticket flicking them rapidly back and forth through my fingers, as if they were the dollars themselves. The queue moved on and David shuffled the suitcases forward, closer to the weighing machine and conveyor belt which would take them straight into the customs hall. My heart lurched. I'd be on my own then. I drew a deep breath.

At last we stood before the desk and I placed my tickets on the high counter. A pair of dusky brown eyes flickered over my suitcases, my hand baggage.

'This all your luggage?' The clerk began to copy out my name and flight details on to the luggage labels and boarding pass.

I swallowed. 'Yes.'

*Hea*ales.

'Put it on.' She indic   s. Suddenly, my heart
David stooped to lif   re overweight? Would I
stood still. Supposing   e? In front of everyone? I
then have to open th   ed at David's arm to steady
caught my breath a   a look of enquiry and hissed,
myself. He turned,   or goodness' sake relax.' He
'Whatever's the r   ne platform.
placed my lugga   hen steadied. With barely more
The needle sh   ne airline official secured the labels
than a cursory   each piece of baggage, handed me
around the h   ickets and with deadpan face wished
boarding pas
me a good f   me to Departures. 'You'd better go
David w   . Not long till they call your flight. Now,
through,   do, don't panic.' He leaned forward and
whatever   iftly. 'Safe journey.' He turned on his heel
kissed n   ut a backward glance, strode off.
and, w   ension of a different nature filled my breast.
App   regretted my impulsiveness in suggesting that
Again   n to England ahead of David. For a moment I
I re   ied his retreating figure. Then I turned and,
wa   ching my hand luggage firmly in one hand and
cl   ssport, ticket and boarding pass in the other, set off
r customs.

Sound seemed to be absorbed in the huge hall so that
an uncomfortable hush hung over the proceedings. I
produced my luggage labels and was directed to an
official, before whom lay my suitcases. I walked towards
him, certain that every eye was upon me, that at any
moment my guilty secret would be discovered. It was
difficult to differentiate between the loud, staccato beat
of my heels on the floor and the irregular thump inside
my chest.

The customs man took my luggage labels and checked
them against those on my cases. 'This all?'

I nodded, then as an afterthought put my hand luggage
on the table. 'And this.'

'Why you leave Ecuador?' He peere
pressing its contents to each side in or
bottom.

'Holiday,' I blurted out. Was he going
the cases? 'My husband's with the Anglo-Ecuadonian Oil
Company. His leave starts in a couple of weeks. I'm going
ahead.'

'Open please.' He indicated my handbag and I passed
it over. 'This is all the money you have?' He flapped open
my wallet.

I swallowed hard. A great lump seemed to be stuck in
my throat.

'That and travellers' cheques.'

My voice sounded false. He must know I was lying.
He replaced the wallet, put the bag on the table, then
crossed his arms. I picked up the bag. He watched me
closely. At the next table a woman was being questioned,
restrained, led away. Loudly, she protested her
innocence. That could be me. Panic set in. That could be
me. That could be me!

'Okay. You go.'

'Yes?'

I could scarcely believe my luck. With a good deal more
panache than I felt, I picked up my hand luggage – and
fled.

Once we had taken off, I reflected with satisfaction upon
my first successful attempt at smuggling. In retrospect
it was an exhilarating experience and I could well
understand how others were lured into a career of
contraband. The emerald ring on my finger had been
smuggled. Like much of the jewellery David had bought
me when we'd first moved to the Ancon Peninsula it had
been brought into Ecuador illicitly, over the border from
Colombia. It was a lovely stone, its rich depths of colour
reminiscent of the sea that lapped the edge of the coas*
and over which we would soon be flying.

I craned forward in my seat. Beneath the aircraft

o, and, as I watched through the portal, my house
came into view. David, Goliat, and the two maids who
were waving up at the plane, were clearly visible in the
garden. Foolishly, knowing full well that they had no
hope of seeing me, I waved frantically back. And then
they were gone, out of sight as the aircraft slowly climbed.

My eyes blurred with tears as the last mountain
disappeared behind a cloud. This country had become
my home, a part of me. Here I'd known sadness, but also
much happiness. And there were friends; dear friends
like Greg . . .

Angry with myself, I dashed a hand across my eyes.
This was ridiculous. It wasn't as if I wouldn't be
returning. This holiday would be over all too soon. And
I was going to enjoy it, every moment! I settled back in
my seat and closed my eyes. A vision of Goliat arose in
my mind: Goliat prancing on the beach, Goliat's sad,
reproachful face as he lay on the mat and barred the way
out. And, I had to admit, I shared his apparent
apprehension.

It wasn't the holiday that disturbed me, but the manner
in which it had come about. And the way in which it
might affect the future.

What lay ahead? Would I ever have left Quito quite so
willingly in that summer of 1970 had I known in advance
all that was to befall me? The broken relationships,
unfinished endings, and devastating encounters with
illness? Almost with death. Where had it all begun?

The aircraft levelled off at 35,000 feet, and droned on
northwestward, following the sun into a new day. I cast
my mind back to days of hope and happiness, back to
the beginnings of romantic dreams, back to a time before
they'd begun to falter, back to the autumn of 1965 when
everything had been so new and full of promise.

PART
TWO

2

New Beginnings

After the clamour of summertime activity in Devon's seaside resorts, autumn could be something of an anti-climax, herald of a long, slow somnolent season before spring brought the first influx of visitors. The autumn of 1965 was different! For me, at least, life in the village of Kingskerswell, just outside Torquay, held no such gloomy prospects. New beginnings were in the air. And in the stillness of early morning on Saturday 9th October, the alarm from my bedside clock was a shrill reminder of the pleasures that lay before me.

Anxious to waste not one precious moment, I rolled over in bed and silenced it swiftly, then wriggled back beneath the blankets to indulge in a half-hour of nostalgia and happy anticipation. The permissive society of the swinging sixties had done nothing to diminish my dream of wedded bliss. And this was my wedding day!

My wedding. The day on which I, Susan Rosemary Hill, would become the wife of Mr David Anthony James. I picked up the invitation which stood on my bedside table and ran my fingers over embossed roses and silver lettering. I could hardly believe it was happening. But there it was, in print: my name linked with David's.

We had known one another a comparatively short time; but it had been love at first sight — or so David said. I closed my eyes. I could see him as he'd appeared when we'd first met in spring of the previous year. I was playing tennis at Lymington Road, one of Torquay's

municipal parks, when David arrived at the courts. Fair
haired, attractive and of medium build, he'd looked well
in his white shorts, his limbs strong and brown. It had
been his partner, however, who had most attracted me.
I'd had problems concentrating on my own game.

'Hey, Susan! Got a hole in your racket?' my girlfriend,
Pat, had teased.

It was well known amongst my friends that I'd had
plenty of boyfriends and that a recent broken relationship
had left me on the rebound. Pat could hardly have failed
to notice my interest in the dark, handsome stranger on
the adjacent court. I'd always had a thing about tall, dark-
haired men.

When Pat and I had finished our game I'd left my
cardigan on a bench as the proverbial 'dropped hanky'.
It had been David, however, not his partner, who had
approached me with the errant garment when I'd run
back to retrieve it. David was quietly spoken and had a
boyish charm. He'd asked my name, whether I lived
locally, how often I played tennis. Tall dark strangers and
all previous boyfriends had rapidly faded into
insignificance.

'The trouble with you, my girl,' I said aloud to the
empty room as I lay in bed on my wedding morning, 'is
that you're a flirt. You just love men! But not any more.
There's only one David!'

David worked locally in Newton Abbot for a firm of
chartered accountants, and before long we were dating
regularly. Tennis, dancing and long coastal walks
featured high in our social lives together and, as the year
unfolded, romance blossomed naturally. Shyly, gently he
courted me, until that hot summer's afternoon, more than
a year ago, when we'd embarked on a mammoth walk
along the coast from Torquay to Dartmouth. There,
amidst the wild flowers and marsh birds, David had
declared his love for me and asked me to be his wife.

Now, here in my bedroom, the memory filled me with
pleasure. I pulled my left hand from under the blankets

and held it aloft to admire my engagement ring; diamond and rubies gleamed in the soft diffused light from the curtained window. In a few hours that engagement ring would be flanked by a narrow gold band.

'Are you awake, Susan?' A knock at the door heralded my father with the usual morning tea. 'It's a beautiful day for you, darling.' He set the cup down carefully, kissed my forehead, then turned to pull open the dainty lilac-flowered curtains.

Sun streamed through the dormer window and I blinked in the sudden brightness. I hauled myself up in bed and, propped against the pillows, sipped the hot liquid. The ritual of Dad doing the tea-round had gone on ever since his retirement had brought us from Ruislip to the semi-detached chalet bungalow in Kingskerswell. My marriage and imminent departure from my parents' home would spell an end to such little domestic ceremonies, for them as well as for me.

This will be the last time Daddy will spoil me in this way, I thought. *From now on, it'll be David* . . . I looked across the room to where my long white georgette dress, with flowing train and elegant pearl adornment, hung from the door of the wardrobe and tried to imagine life beyond The Wedding.

'The forecast's dry and sunny, but cool.' Dad loved recording the weather, with his curious, yet endearing daily ritual of tapping the little round barometer which hung in the hall downstairs. Year in and year out he carefully chronicled the details and made comparison with the previous day's readings. Another symbol of family life.

A sudden wave of love surged through me for this big, strong man who had always been my hero. 'I'll miss you, Daddy. And my lovely room.'

'Not as much as I'll miss you!' Perched on the end of my bed, he looked sad and wistful. I longed to throw my arms around him, to show him how much I cared. But, as usual, it seemed difficult, somehow, to express my feelings. Was he, too, thinking that soon another man would be replacing him in my life?

An image of David's blue eyes and gentle, boyish features came into my mind. I loved them both. He and my dad. But Daddy had Mummy. And now I had David.

'I can't believe the day is really here. There'll never be another day quite like this.' I hunched forward in bed and hugged my knees, shaking my head in disbelief. 'After all the planning! It's just amazing.'

Dad rose and walked to the door. 'Your mother will be up shortly. She's talked of nothing else for weeks.'

I nodded, understandingly, and with a brief smile of conspiracy he left the room.

It had taken months of planning on my parents' part – the wedding service, reception, dress, flowers, what to wear, whom to ask. With only their RAF pensions to live on, they'd had to watch the costs. But despite Dad's need to curb expenditure, he'd shared Mummy's desire for the wedding of his only living daughter to be as grand as possible. A list of guests had been drawn up, and carefully pored over. In addition to the usual friends and relatives, there was the canasta and bridge 'gang' – Mummy's and Daddy's old Ruislip friends. She missed them dreadfully, but they were so much more affluent than we were. This wedding was as important to Mummy as to me, a statement of sorts.

I swung my legs to the floor, slipped into my faded old dressing-gown, and crossed the landing to the bathroom. Tonight I'd wear the lovely new floaty negligee that was packed with the rest of my trousseau. Tonight I'd be Mrs James. Once again I held out my hand to admire the sparkling ruby and diamond cluster ring which David had placed on my finger on my twenty-second birthday ten months earlier. Then, like a ballerina, I twirled round the tiny room.

And twirled . . . and twirled . . . I gasped, caught sight of my ashen face in the mirror, clutched at the door. Still the room twirled on . . . Why *did* I get these dizzy spells?

They were so annoying. Whatever was the matter with me? I was young and fit. You had to be to cope with all the dancing I did.

I sat on the edge of the bath. There seemed to be no pattern to my continual giddiness; nothing that I could pinpoint, like alcohol, or dieting. Nor was a stuffy indoor atmosphere to blame. The balcony, outside the office in which I worked in Torquay, was an excellent place for sunbathing during summer lunch-breaks. However, I found that if I lay back quickly, I would experience alarming sensations, as if the sky and my surroundings were spinning around me. At other times my hands would shake uncontrollably, and cause me a good deal of embarrassment, especially when I was at a party and in danger of spilling my drink.

I put the plug in the bath and turned on the tap. Water spurted from the aperture and swirled in the base, dragging the chain from the plug in eddying currents. This morning's incident must simply be a result of excitement, I reflected, and added a generous measure of bubble oil to the water to help me relax. For a moment I watched as it frothed and foamed. Then, dismissing the whole episode as of no importance, I resumed my daydream of things more immediate and romantic.

'Darling, you look lovely.' Fondly, my mother smoothed the delicate fabric of my long white wedding dress and adjusted the short tulle veil around my shoulders.

'Oh, Mummy! I'm so excited. It's like a dream come true. I hope no one guesses I only paid fifteen shillings for these!' Carefully, I lifted the hem of my dress and thrust my feet into a pair of white satin shoes.

Hands on hips, I preened before the full length mirror in my mother's bedroom. My waist really did look incredibly tiny, I thought vainly. I smiled at my reflection. Beneath newly plucked eyebrows my dark eyes sparkled. I'd curled my thick brown hair the night before and it now framed my face in such a way as to accentuate its oval shape. I patted a stray lock into place and adjusted my veil yet again, feeling well pleased with my finery. Then I turned from the mirror and, with my mother holding my train aloft, left the room.

'David's a lucky man,' Dad said, looking up from the hall as I descended the stairs.

'Thank you,' I inclined my head.

The wedding car arrived to take my mother to church, leaving Dad and I alone in the house, each lost in our own thoughts. I watched him as he stood, hands thrust into pockets, staring through the lace curtains at the bay window to the street beyond.

Was there a hint of sadness in his posture? For a brief moment it occurred to me that his mind might be on that other daughter – my sister – though I found it strange to think of her as such as I had never seen her. And yet, in a way, I had her to thank for this day. For without her demise we might not have moved from London to Devon and I might never have met David.

Janet was no more to me than a face in a photograph; a pretty child with a mass of blonde hair. To my parents, however, she was a constant memory of anguish, a blight on the happiness they had once known, for her death had cast a long shadow down through the years.

Janet had been the victim of a tragedy that had taken place before I was born. On 30th May 1943, an off-course German bomber had discharged its load over Torquay in broad daylight. On the hill of St Marychurch, overlooking the South Devon coast and Babbacombe Downs, stood the twin towers of Anglican and Catholic churches. Inside the parish church the children of the town were gathered for Sunday school. One bomb from the German plane fell directly on the church, killing all twenty-nine children and teachers within.

My parents' house was situated close by, for Dad was, at that time, a Warrant Officer in charge of RAF airmen stationed at St Marychurch. The blast demolished the house, injured my mother and father and inflicted dreadful wounds on my sister Janet, who was only four years old. For weeks she'd struggled for survival in a hospital bed in Oxford but in the end she'd died and another tender young life had been snuffed out before its time.

Dad had been in Egypt when he'd heard news of my birth – only months after Janet's death. He'd bought a doll there and carried it around in a suitcase for two years until he was posted back to England and at last saw me, his 'new little girl'. But despite his love for me, nothing could quite erase the memory of Janet.

Janet: for eighteen years I'd hardly thought of her at all, except as a sort of fantasy figure, a friend in my imagination. Then, one afternoon in June 1961, my parents had told me they wanted to visit her grave in Torquay Cemetery and asked me to accompany them. I was suddenly afraid, not of the graveyard, but of seeing my mother cry. But Mummy didn't weep. Daddy did. Terribly.

The wedding car drew up outside our house and Daddy turned from the window. Wordlessly, he proferred his arm. For a moment I hesitated, the scene imprinting itself on my mind. Looking at him now, handsome in a pale grey tailcoat, his face beaming with pride and affection for me, his surviving daughter, it seemed hard to believe the extent of his grief four years ago. Then, I returned his smile, took his arm and together we went out to the waiting car and set off for the church.

Still apparently lost in thought, Dad gazed from the window at green meadows and open countryside that separated Kingskerswell from the outskirts of Torquay. I perched upright on the car seat so as not to crush my frock, and glanced across at him.

As a soldier in the First World War he'd witnessed all the horrors of the trenches and had seen brutality and sudden death again as a serving Warrant Officer in the Second. At eighteen I'd regarded Daddy only as a big, brave fellow who'd been awarded the MBE but whose

wartime stories were, nevertheless, a faint embarrassment and rather boring to my friends. Yet he'd wept at
Janet's grave, wept as if his heart would break. Until that
moment I'd never seen a man cry.

The decision to move after the pilgrimage to the
graveside had horrified me. The very idea of leaving
Ruislip with its proximity to London, my current
boyfriend, and a job in which I took a real pride had filled
me with rebellious dismay.

I'd been working as a very junior secretary in the Martin
Baker Aircraft company at Denham. The test rig for their
famous ejector seats and parachutes was just behind the
general office which I shared with a number of other girls.
Our desks shook as if in an earthquake each time a seat
was tested by one of the brave moustachioed squadron
leaders, every one of whom had volunteered, knowing
they risked permanent damage to their spines or perhaps
the sacrifice of their lives.

It was a fascinating and enjoyable job that instilled pride
in the humblest member of staff. Letters would arrive
from Air Forces all round the world telling us of pilots
who, by virtue of our equipment, had been saved from
disaster. Sometimes we would even hear news of a birth
some nine months later, as if in evidence of Man's
instinctive desire for immortality; a need to bring forth
life after so close an encounter with death.

In a similar way Janet's death had brought about new
life for me. Without the visit to her grave, this wedding
day would never have come about, I thought. A strange
twist of fate.

Life was rather like the jigsaw puzzles I loved as a child.
Piece by piece a picture grows, some parts dull, hazy,
even depressing, others bright, jazzy and sunny; none
of them making sense. Then, one day, the picture clears,
as if, like an open door, you can see beyond – a door
to Life itself. Though I had no concept that the Jesus of
whom I'd sung in school assemblies loved and died for
me, a time was to come, eventually, when I would look

back and see the picture clearly; see that he had loved
me all along, was waiting for me to call upon him,
acknowledge him, seek his Lordship in my life. One day,
he would become personal to me; and in that day I would
truly know New Beginnings.

David stood facing the front of the church as I processed
up the aisle on Dad's arm. To his right stood Ian, his
rapscallion brother, who for once looked quite debonair,
almost respectable in his smart tailcoat! His grey silk top
hat perched next to David's on the pew behind them.

David turned at my approach. 'You look lovely,' he
whispered.

I smiled from beneath my veil. I felt shining, special,
regal.

From the corner of my eye I could see my mother,
resplendent in a wonderful hat of peacock blue and green,
one of three she had bought to be sure of having just the
right one for this day of days. The organist struck up
familiar chords and the wedding guests rustled hymn
books:

> Lead us, heavenly Father, lead us
> O'er the world's tempestuous sea;
> Guard us, guide us, keep us, feed us,
> For we have no help but Thee;
> Yet possessing every blessing
> If our God our Father be.

The small congregation sang the well-known refrain.
Was there a prophetic significance in the words? Would
David and I, standing shyly together as we made our
vows, need guarding and guiding in the tempestuous sea
of life? If the thought occurred to me at all, it must have
been fleetingly, for in truth the religious side of the service
meant nothing to me.

'Oh do marry in church,' David's mother had pleaded,
and to humour her we'd agreed, since both she and

David attended regularly at the Belgrave Congregational Church in the centre of Torquay.

Apart from a strange and burning desire to have 'Jesu, Joy of Man's Desiring' as my wedding march, I wasn't too bothered about the Order of Service. I longed only for the pomp and ceremony to which a church wedding would entitle me.

The service was conducted by an elderly retired minister. Neither he, nor anyone else, had offered anything in the way of guidance about marriage. The entire focal point of my thinking rested upon this day – my beautiful long white gown and veil, and being the centre of attention. Isn't that where all the romantic tales from childhood finish: *And they all lived happily ever after*.

We sang hymns, spoke our vows, signed the register and, beaming at our assorted guests as we passed them, trod up the aisle and out into mellow sunshine.

'Oh David, wasn't it wonderful,' I clung to his arm as we posed for photographs. 'It's just like some beautiful fairy story actually happening to me. It's quite the most wonderful day ever.'

I laughed gaily into David's smiling eyes, and *knew* that we, too, would live happily ever after.

For the next half-hour the Big Event was recorded permanently on film, as alone, together, with parents, with friends we were snapped and photographed. A cool wind sprang up and, impatient to move on to the reception, I tugged at David's arm.

'Now, I'd like you to hold hands loosely in front of you so that the rings show.' The photographer posed in front of us, aping the stance he wanted us to adopt.

'Why on earth does he want photos of the rings?' I asked. 'Hasn't he taken enough now?'

'He's only doing his job, darling.' David took my left hand in his and followed the photographer's instructions. 'This'll be the last one, and then we'll be done,' he said.

'It won't take long. We'll soon be on our own. After all, we've got the rest of our lives in front of us.'

David's words caused me some discomfort. When the photographer finished and we walked from church to the Windsor Hotel on the other side of the road, they rang in my ears. I'd deliberately not allowed myself to dwell on what happened *after* the wedding – on *that* side of things. However, with the service now behind us, my mind began to conjure up images of what lay beyond this day. There'd be the honeymoon. And then there'd be the bedroom in our little flat in St Marychurch. Alone with David!

We walked through the hotel foyer to the ballroom which had been set aside for our Wedding Breakfast. Nervously, I threw myself into the party atmosphere of the reception. I smiled stiffly, forced myself to chatter – inconsequentials, trivia, anything to mask my apprehension. Around me, conversation flowed smoothly as wine – and probably in direct ratio! I took a second sherry, and gradually I relaxed and pushed the fear from my mind.

'What a gorgeous dress, Susan.'

'Its simplicity is quite stunning.'

'You make a beautiful bride, my dear.'

Flushed with pleasure, I basked in the limelight and soaked up compliments as a sleeping cat soaks up sun.

'It's a wonderful day. *The* most wonderful day.' Stiffness gave way to delighted laughter, but still I could eat nothing and marvelled at the way in which David tucked into the lavish buffet as if trying to hide his own nervousness. I felt mesmerised by the proceedings and the afternoon passed in a blur of unreality.

Eventually, it was time for speeches to be made. My wedding bouquet lay on the table before me. With one finger, I caressed velvet-petalled roses, and admired the rich contrast between the red blooms and dainty white stephanotis which surrounded them. Heady perfume assailed my senses, and I closed my eyes and inhaled deeply. Fragrance filled my being, drowning out the sense of touch and sight.

When I opened my eyes once more, I found David's mother, Mrs James, regarding me thoughtfully. Quickly, as if caught in some secret act, she glanced away.

'Was that your father at the church?' I whispered to David when applause for the best man's speech died down.

His face looked grave. 'Yes,' he replied. 'It's sad, really. He was in the back pew, and again in the background outside the church. Thankfully Mother didn't catch sight of him.'

David's parents had had a newsagent's shop. An affair between his father and one of the assistants had led to the birth of a child, and the resulting scandal to divorce. The consequences were stormy and sad. David's mother was the daughter of the mayor in a neighbouring town, and the stigma on the family's reputation was tremendous when Mr James left to live with the other woman. David had been about sixteen at the time and, though the episode had seemed not to affect his younger brother or older sister, it had had a profound effect on David.

Clearly, however, he wasn't the only one to have suffered. Once or twice Mr James had visited his ex-wife's home whilst I'd been visiting and his regret at losing his family had been quite apparent. It seemed a sad reflection on life, that a man whose actions had already cost him his home and family, should have to resort to stealth simply to see his own son married.

With my finger nail, I picked at a rose stem in my bouquet. Hidden amongst the red velvet petals, and obviously overlooked by the florist, was a single thorn.

The reception eventually drew to a close, and I had scarcely eaten. A restlessness amongst the guests indicated that it was time for the Bride and Groom to withdraw, to change out of our finery in readiness for our honeymoon. Quietly, David and I slipped out and made our way to the respective hotel rooms which had been set aside for our use.

'See you downstairs?' He kissed me, lightly.

My mother was waiting to help me, and once my veil had been removed, she unzipped my dress so that I could step out of it, then busied herself packing it carefully into a suitcase.

'Er, Susan, darling . . .' My heart lurched. Instinctively, I realised that my mother was about to brief me on the facts of life.

'Not now, Mummy!' I hissed.

Conscious of footsteps outside, I was stunned with embarrassment. I didn't want to hear of so unspeakable a subject from the lips of my own mother yet, paradoxically, I longed for her to continue, to put me out of the misery of my ignorance.

Acutely embarrassed herself, and perhaps believing that I knew more than she had given me credence for, my mother fussed over my going-away outfit. The opportunity was gone. I faced the night ahead knowing virtually nothing of the marriage bed. Nervously, I began to dress, fumbling with buttons that seemed suddenly too big for their buttonholes.

Soon a soft, brown, fur-trimmed suit replaced my bridal finery. I reapplied my lipstick and picked up my handbag. My mother fastened the suitcase and straightened up. 'Your father can carry this lot down later,' she said.

'Ready?' I held the door open and allowed her to go before me. David was waiting at the bottom of the stairs. 'I'm starving!' I said unromantically to my new husband.

He grinned. 'I thought you would be, so I've brought some goodies for supper.'

Together, we ran down the hotel steps amid a flurry of confetti, incongruously clutching two white carrier bags in which were deposited the remains of the wedding feast: the left-overs!

One of David's cousins had offered us hospitality in her

home for our first night before we took off from Luton
Airport next day, bound for Ibiza. We had a key for the
front door, and let ourselves into the empty house like
two naughty schoolchildren up to no good. Shyly, David
took me by the hand, led me up the stairs and pushed
open a door. The bedroom into which we stepped was
comfortably furnished and tastefully decorated,
embellished with little personal touches from the hand
of David's cousin. A vase of flowers stood on a table on
the far side of the room and, at the partially opened
window behind it, sheer net curtains billowed in the
breeze. A white candlewick counterpane covered the
double bed, except where she had turned down the top
to reveal two soft, plump pillows. Hastily, I averted my
eyes.

We were young and in love. This was our wedding
night; the night that every young woman dreams of,
yearns for. Romantic. Passionate. Adult.

I felt totally unprepared. Immature. The assurance
embodied in ceremony, so carefully preserved by
tradition and months of planning, now evaporated. I was
alone. Alone, yet not alone. No longer my own person.
Legally, morally, I was bound to another. And I found
the concept frightening.

Abruptly, I crossed the room and buried my face in the
flowers. 'How kind of Elizabeth to think of these.' I
straightened up, one long-stemmed chrysanthemum in
my hand.

David followed, stood before me, put his arms around
me and drew me close. 'I felt so proud of you, standing
at my side in the church.' His voice thickened. 'Your hair
shines as I've never known anyone's shine.' Softly,
gently, he stroked me.

Dear David. I longed to show him the love I felt, to
return his caress, the pressure of his arms around me,
the warmth of his mouth on mine. I yearned to be his,
to be one with him, subject to his desire. I wanted, with
all my heart, to be David's wife. Yet, with every touch

of his hand, each endearment that he whispered, I was miserably aware of the stiffening of my body in response.

A large moth fluttered at the window, withdrew a little, then hurled itself against the glass as if oblivious of the barrier. Again and again its wings beat softly on the pane in its desperate attempts to gain entry to the light in the bedroom.

Over David's shoulder I could see the road. Rain had begun to fall since our arrival at the house and the street glistened menacingly, black and wet, in the night air. A car drew up at the pavement, its metallic paintwork strangely distorted in the light shed from the street lamp. Doors opened, banged shut. The voices of Elizabeth and her husband could be heard, and the hard, clipped sound of high heels scurrying up the paved path, a fumbling, then a key being inserted into the lock. The front door opened, closed, with a heavy thud.

David and I drew apart. In one hand I still held the chrysanthemum I'd taken from the vase. But now, only the stalk remained. The flower head lay crushed and broken on the floor.

The minister had spoken, during the marriage ceremony, of the love between a husband and wife being a gift from God: pure and honourable. Confused and overwhelmed, I felt frozen into immobility. How did this 'honourable' love correlate with all I'd perceived in my parents' relationship?

Until today, and my mother's embarrassed attempt to 'educate' me, sex had been something 'one just did not talk about'! Both parents had, unwittingly, as well as by design, brought me up to believe that nakedness was something to be ashamed of. Overprotected and wrapped in cottonwool since my sister's death, I could not now, suddenly, shake free of the tremendous debt of gratitude and loyalty I felt I owed them.

As my frigidity conveyed itself to David through the long, first night of our lives together, he wept.

3

A Market Town Wife

Our first home was a rented one-bedroomed basement flat in a large house on Petitor Road, Torquay. With its dark oak beams and comfortable chintzy furnishings it had a cottage-style charm which delighted me. It boasted a grandmother clock in the tiny hall; and if you strained your neck, the lush grass of Petitor Golf Course was visible from the window of the minute kitchen. Beyond that, though out of sight, was Lyme Bay.

It was a long walk down the steep cliff path to the beach, but that didn't matter to me. Nothing fascinated me like the ocean: its omnipotence, its ever-changing face, its unfathomable depth. Almost every day of the week I walked the shore, imbibing the magical qualities of sand, sea and solitude.

With the move from our respective parental homes to our seaside cottage came new responsibilities. Whilst I balanced the task of homemaking alongside my job in Torquay, David continued his work at the accountants. Recently qualified, he began initiating me into the intricacies of book-keeping and insisted that I keep account of my weekly expenditure. I found the practice irksome and couldn't help feeling that this was a side of David I'd not seen before, quite unlike the boyish, romantic image of him I'd previously held.

'Do I have to keep a note of every little thing?' I complained one winter evening a few months after our wedding.

We had just finished our evening meal and David was still seated at the dining table. I laid my cashbook before him. He glanced at it briefly then caught hold of my hand and looked up at me. 'There's not much point in the exercise otherwise, is there, darling?'

'But I forget. It's all the silly little things, like the hairdressers, or a magazine. You surely don't expect me to remember everything?'

'If you kept a notebook in your handbag, you could jot things down as you get them.' David released my hand, took a pen from his pocket and began to check my arithmetic.

I seated myself beside him and leaned forward with my elbows on the table. 'But why is it necessary, David? I mean, we're quite well off, aren't we? The girls at the office certainly seem to think so.'

'It's not a question of affluence, Susan,' David explained, patiently. 'It would be irresponsible not to keep account of how the money's being spent. We have to budget for the future.'

I sighed, rose from the table and, picking up a copy of *Woman's Own*, crossed the room to the settee. Idly, I flicked through the pages. I was beginning to wish I knew more about life. Marriage was not proving as easy as I'd thought; there seemed to be so many new skills to be learned. For instance, I'd never before been called upon to cook a meal – let alone make love! The first could be gleaned from recipe books passed on to me by my mother; however, communication with David, on whatever level, seemed demonstrably more difficult.

Our cottage-style bedroom was warm and cosy. I was filled with a sense of pleasure when lying in the arms of this man to whom I was now mysteriously bound but continually found myself shy and tense when anything more intimate was suggested. I longed to be different, to be free and relaxed. I wondered how other women coped, but there was no one with whom I could share; certainly not with my mother when I rang her from the phone box on the corner of the road; nor with friends at work. Our landlady was disappointingly unfriendly and I felt isolated and alone in my inadequacy.

I laid the magazine aside, turned and glanced across the room. David had finished with my accounts and now had office papers spread across the surface of the table. He pored over them, utterly engrossed. The room was lit only by a standard lamp on my side and a desk lamp which David had placed on the dining table. We each seemed to be encircled in two separate spheres of light, with the shadow between us a vast, empty space. Across that divide, David appeared cut off from me, remote and unattainable.

I sighed and turned back. Soon it would be bedtime. I shivered. The fire I'd lit earlier in the evening had nearly burned itself out. One log, only, remained glowing amongst the ashes.

We had good friends in Richard and Mary Bell. Together, the four of us would spend many an evening playing canasta and drinking endless cups of tea in our tiny dining room. Richard and Mary had been married about the same length of time as David and me, yet already they were expecting a baby. I found myself feeling deficient – and a little jealous!

'Mary looks happy,' I remarked at the end of one evening as we stood in a pool of light at the door waving our farewells into the dark of the night.

'They certainly look well contented with life,' David agreed, putting his arm lightly on my shoulder.

'I suppose we do to them.' It was a half-statement, half-question, spoken barely audibly. I was sure that our friends were quite unaware of how fragile certain aspects of our relationship were. To others, all looked well. Only we knew otherwise. Only on our long walks together was the old carefree, boyish image apparent in my husband.

Still, as winter progressed, our natural affection for one another survived, a cohesive factor – even in the midst of difficulty. Our first Christmas was nearly a disaster. We'd wrapped the presents, decorated the tree, and put up the paper chains. All was ready. All, that was, but the Main Item.

'Mummy!' I cried in desperation from the draughty telephone box on the corner of the road. 'The turkey's off.'

'Calm down, darling. All you can do now is to soak it in vinegar and cold water overnight. Dry it well tomorrow, put butter and greaseproof paper over it and roast it as I told you.'

'Oh, thank you, Mummy.' I leaned back against the cold glass, oblivious of the condensation dampening my clothing.

'You should have taken it back really, dear.'

I gripped the handpiece defensively. 'I've only just discovered it,' I exclaimed. 'And it's not *too* bad.'

Friends at work had informed me that the butchers auctioned their turkeys last thing on Christmas Eve, I told my mother, and, with an eye for a bargain, I'd bought one. I'd puzzled all evening as to what could be causing the strange aroma which had filled our tiny home. Then, shortly before midnight I'd discovered the culprit.

I thanked my mother again, said goodbye and replaced the receiver. Returning to the flat, I dutifully carried out her instructions and, with some distaste, submerged the turkey in a vinegar solution. When I'd done, David joined me in the kitchen and together we surveyed the offensive bird.

'What a hopeless wife!' I said, despondently. 'First important meal I'll ever have cooked for your mother . . . what will she think?'

David lifted my chin with one finger. 'Stop worrying. No one will be any the wiser by the time you've roasted it, and any hint of vinegar will be disguised by all the different seasonings and trimmings.' He switched off the light. 'Come on, love, let's get to bed. It's nearly half past one.'

I was up early next morning and, following my

mother's directions to the letter, was well pleased with the result. By the time I lifted the turkey from the oven, shortly before lunch, it was golden and succulent.

David sniffed appreciatively. 'There you are, I told you it would be okay. It looks delicious.'

'If only it tastes as good as it looks,' I whispered, crossing my fingers for luck. In some trepidation, I carried the bird through to the gaily decorated dining room, where David's mother and brother were seated at the table.

'Been taking cookery lessons, Susan?' Ian jibed.

'Mmm,' I replied, non-committally.

'If it tastes as good as it looks we're in for a treat,' he continued, echoing my own sentiments exactly. David and I exchanged glances across the table.

My mother-in-law beamed. 'I'm sure it all looks very nice, dear.' Her eyes darted around, carefully scrutinising every dish.

I hope she doesn't ask too many questions, I thought, though with her sense of propriety that was unlikely. Motherly, homely, she seemed fond enough of me and was not in the habit of trying to catch me out. We had a good relationship, though by comparison with my own mother I found her flagrantly outspoken in conversation with Ian. Such broadmindedness was almost shocking, and seemed to me not to marry well with her refined manner.

David carved the drumstick and placed the meat on a plate. Ian eyed it, his mouth pulled down in mock solemnity. 'Right, that's for us to divide up between the three of us. Better put the rest of the bird on a plate, David, for Susan.'

'Don't tease the girl so.' Mother-in-law's remark went unheeded. It was a long-standing joke that, despite my tiny frame, I was well able to put away a vast quantity of food and frequently consumed more than either David or Ian.

Finally, we were all served and, with crackers pulled and paper hats donned, we began to eat. With relief I swallowed my first mouthful of turkey. There was no hint of its having been 'off'. David caught my eye and winked. I grinned back at him, relaxed and allowed myself to enjoy the rest of the meal.

'Thank goodness your mother never guessed,' I said to David when our guests had departed. We hugged each other and laughed at our closely guarded secret.

'I half-expected them to!' His face grew more serious. 'Mind you, it was a bit tough; a tough old bird, like you.' He ducked and pulled away as, wielding my shoe, I raised it to cuff him.

'Let's open our presents now we're alone,' I suggested, euphoric with the success of the day. I moved to the settee, seated myself at one end and tucked my feet beneath me. I looked at David expectantly. For days he'd been disappearing with mysterious packages and, with childish impatience, I could wait no longer to know their contents.

'Close your eyes,' he commanded and left the room, returning a moment later. 'Right, you can open them now. I love you very much, Susan.' The evidence was touching: on the table before me lay twelve beautifully wrapped gifts.

'One for every month of the year,' David said, diffidently, evidently trying hard to conceal the pride which lit his eyes. The sweater and car accessories I'd bought him seemed banal beside this generosity and forethought for me. I felt cherished and warmed with his love and, reaching out, touched his face lightly with one finger.

'Well, aren't you going to open them?' His voice was gruff.

I picked up the first gift and began to remove the paper; then another, and another. The depth of David's perception and affection was revealing: a cut-glass jam dish to satisfy my love of beautiful things; a lollipop embellished with a flower to appeal to my sense of fun.

Each gift was examined and exclaimed upon at length, until, finally, only one remained unopened; one which David had held back.

With trembling fingers I removed the paper and opened a small box. There, nestling on a bed of cotton wool, lay a fine gold chain from which hung a pearl pendant. David lifted it and fastened it about my neck. I felt suddenly shy, overcome with emotion. I fingered the smooth, creamy teardrop at my throat and smiled into David's eyes. 'I never dreamed I'd be loved like this. Thank you my darling.'

He reached out, pulled me to my feet and took me in his arms. 'Our first Christmas,' he said solemnly, looking down at my upturned face. For some moments we embraced in the centre of the room. In one corner stood the Christmas tree and in the coloured glass baubles hanging from its branches, I could see, reflected back a dozen times, a mirror image of our love for one another.

Then, ignoring the debris of torn and crumpled wrapping paper, we turned to go to bed.

New Year passed swiftly. January frosts, always light in this part of the world, melted one into another. The first crocuses and camellias appeared – promise of glories yet to come. A typical Devon spring, with its nodding, golden-trumpet heralds bathed in diffused gilded warmth was a pageant unequalled, and I longed for winter's chill to be gone.

It was due to the cold, I felt sure, that my giddy turns were exacerbated, likewise the tremor in my hands. I had always managed to conceal both from David but, one Saturday morning, could do so no longer. I was preparing lunch. Peeling vegetables had presented no great problem and a pan of potatoes was coming to the boil on the stove, alongside another containing cauliflower. I turned the chops under the grill then, glancing back at the hob, realised that the metal handle of one saucepan was protruding over the lighted gas ring. It would have to be

moved and I steadied one trembling hand with the other,
hoping to nudge it away from the heat.

'Ouch!'

I dropped the scorching handle, and with my hands
now shaking uncontrollably, grabbed foolishly at the side
of the pan. It tipped and boiling water shot out in all
directions.

I screamed. For a moment my hands felt numb, then
pain came in agonising waves of fiery heat. David came
running in from the garden, took one look and rushed
to telephone the doctor. When he returned he wrapped
my hands in bicarbonated bandages and led me, sobbing,
to the lounge.

It was evident, after seeking medical advice, that I was
going to be unable to fend for myself for some while.
David took charge, feeding me like a baby, cajoling me
out of my state of gloom and generally coping admirably
with the situation. Despite the pain from my burns, I
thoroughly enjoyed being petted and spoiled and told
him frequently how fortunate I considered myself to have
so supportive and caring a husband.

It was some weeks before my blisters healed and, by
the time I recovered full use of my hands, a much-longed-
for spring, vibrant with golden daffodils, was upon us.

A row with our landlady late in May precipitated a move
from the flat. We'd grown weary of paying rent, in any
case, and decided to purchase our next home. Armed
with Estate Agents' blurbs, we pored over details of
anything and everything with 3 Bed, 2 Recep. and All
Mod-Cons.

Camelot, so romantically named, came into that
category. The house was situated in a quiet well-to-do
residential area in the nearby market town of Newton
Abbot and was of a modern, open plan construction. It
was more expensive than anything else we'd seen but
we knew, as soon as the Estate Agent showed us around,
that we would not be able to resist it.

'Just look at that view, David! You can see the whole town!' I tugged at his arm.

'Wow! It really is magnificent,' he agreed, looking beyond the buildings. 'Fancy having Dartmoor in your lounge, so to speak! That outcrop over there, the nearest one you can see, is Haytor.' He pointed through the window.

'I never remember the names of the tors,' I replied, 'but isn't that the Teign Estuary beyond those houses?'

David nodded. 'It's quite a conservation area for all sorts of breeding wildfowl.'

Eventually, we dragged ourselves away to continue our inspection of the premises. The main bedroom captivated my attention. On one wall, prominently displayed, were several paintings of nudes. My cheeks burned and perspiration broke out on the palms of my hands. Try, as I would, to avert my eyes they would keep straying back to the graceful but shamelessly abandoned forms. *How can anyone live with those on the wall*, I wondered, passing swiftly to another room.

'Well, how do you like the house?' David asked in lowered tones when he caught me up. 'It's ideally placed for the office, and I know Wolborough Hill attracts folk of a similar ilk to ourselves.' He paused. 'Might be a bit far for you to travel, though. What do you think?'

I caught my breath. 'Do you mean we can buy it, David? Can we really afford it?'

David grinned. 'We can put in an offer, anyway. But are you quite sure about it?'

'Absolutely! The house is gorgeous, and I wouldn't mind the extra journey at all. Just to have our own home – and a garden too!'

It was settled. In no time, with a price agreed and conveyancing complete, we left the cottage at Petitor Road to take up residence in Camelot.

The move to Newton Abbot proved beneficial to David; less so to me. We now lived closer to his office, but further from mine. David was being given increasingly greater responsibility to the senior partner, and I was proud that they had such confidence in him. Nevertheless, the extra driving in and out of Torquay to the Insurance Broker, for whom I worked, was a strain. Shopping, cooking and housework were fatiguing at the end of each long day and, after a few weeks of living in Newton Abbot, I began to wish that I could find work locally.

Arriving home from work one evening, David hinted, with alacrity, that he had good news. Over supper he told me.

'I had a phone call from one of the directors of Watts, Blake, Bearne. They're looking for a good typist.'

David paused to wipe his mouth on his napkin, poured water into the tumbler before him and eyed me, as if to assess the effect of his words, before delivering the *coup de grâce*.

I waited, expectantly, while he drank from the glass and set it back on the table before continuing. 'He's heard about you. He's wondering if you're free to go for an interview.' Then, almost as an afterthought: 'I told him you were good.'

'Oh David!' I rushed round the table and flung my arms around his neck. 'You beast, keeping that news to yourself all evening! That means I can hand in my notice in Torquay.'

'Hang on. You haven't got the job yet.'

The pride in David's face and voice belied any doubts. So often I felt inadequate, a let-down as a wife. This news, and my husband's evident pleasure in being the bearer, did much to lift my flagging spirits. Convinced that the job was mine, I rang one of the partners next morning and set a date a few days hence for an interview. Within a fortnight, after a satisfactory conclusion, I'd handed in my notice in Torquay and was ensconced in the offices of Watts, Blake, Bearne.

Our social life in Newton Abbot was far more active than

it had been in Torquay. David's senior partner and his wife introduced us to their circle of friends and, gradually, my confidence began to grow. I discovered, in spite of my inadequacies in certain areas, that there was a pleasing status in being married to an accountant.

'Your wife's a real asset, you lucky man,' said David's boss, Ken Fairwell.

I flushed, delighted with the compliment.

Many of the married men in Courtenay Close, where we lived, were members of Round Table, and we were invited, occasionally, to take part in their functions.

'You really ought to join, you know, David,' Mr Fairwell urged, winking at me. 'Susan's presence brings a radiance into the lives of all we drab businessmen.'

'Yes, I'd like that,' David replied.

A good deal of heavy drinking and ribaldry went on at these events with which neither David nor I were completely at ease. Nonetheless, we found the social occasions diverting – and a means of getting to know our neighbours better. In this way we became frequent guests at the many parties which were offshoots of Round Table events and when we began to host our own we felt we were putting down enduring roots of stability and amity. Newton Abbot was Home!

I was growing to love this bustling market town. The mart itself was fascinating, and I frequently took the opportunity to linger and watch the sheep, calves and pigs in their pens, amidst the noise and cries of traders and auctioneers. Farmers, their wives and families, flocked from miles around and enthralled me with this glimpse of a life so different from anything I'd known before. In my own way, I was happy.

Certainly, I was increasingly contented with my new job. John Grey was marketing director, a stocky man, whose lack of stature was more than compensated for by his powerful personality. I started in the shipping office and found my world full of quotations for ball and china clay, and Bills of Lading to ship the material to over forty countries around the world. I was also telex operator, sending messages to agents and ports with strange-sounding names beyond my ken.

'It's fascinating; so interesting,' I said to David one evening soon after I'd started the job.

'Well I'm glad you enjoy it,' he smiled and pecked me on the cheek before going to change for dinner.

'John's only small,' I continued, when we were seated at the table, 'but he's like a human dynamo. You'd never believe it, David, his working pace is twice that of anyone else's. He goes through the office like a tornado, and he's still firing instructions when he leaves the room.'

David nodded and reached for the newspaper. 'What's on the TV tonight?' he asked, deftly changing the subject.

I stared at him, nonplussed.

Admiration for my boss grew with every passing week. When Cynthia, his secretary, left, I was delighted to accept John's offer to take her position. I couldn't wait to tell David the good news. 'It'll be super working closely with him. He's quite amazing: so fast and efficient.'

Often left to deal with foreign visitors in my boss's absence abroad, I immensely enjoyed the challenge and demands made upon me. John made me feel valuable and useful. By comparison, David's pride in me seemed to diminish. Where once he had praised my cooking and homemaking skills, he now began to denigrate me in company. Full of the excitement of work, I would recount the day's events in detail and wonder at David's lack of interest. Naturally, John always figured greatly.

'Sometimes I believe you think more of him than you do of me,' David rebuked me one day as we set out to walk across the headland.

'Oh, *darling*!' I said, reproachfully.

'Well . . .' He pursed his lips. '*Do* you find him attractive, Susan?' His gaze flickered over me.

'Well, yes . . . I suppose so,' I replied hesitantly, picking my way over a particularly rough bit of path. 'He is *different*. So exciting. And he puts such faith in me. He's away next week and wants me to meet the buyers from Greece at the railway station. It is a responsible job, darling. The ball clay is shipped all over the world, you know.' I raised my eyes, desperately wanting David's interest and respect for my secretarial achievements.

'I know,' he replied, turning from me to swipe at the tall grass which flanked the pathway. 'I have seen the ships leaving the port in Teignmouth, when I was there on audit.'

From time to time David's work took him away up country for several days in a row. One autumn evening, I set out, as I often did when alone, on one of my favourite walks around the Parish Church of Wolborough on the other side of the hill. I was curious, as always, to know what the church looked like on the inside, but was held back from entering the heavy oak doors by an irrational fear.

Memories of one of the few times my parents had taken me to church in Ruislip crowded upon me. They rarely thought of religion, but on one particular Sunday Mummy had dressed me in a detestable red suit with pleated skirt and matching hat and taken me to morning service. A meek and shy little girl, I'd felt far too conspicuous in the bright outfit. I'd had a coughing fit in the middle of the sermon, and had been unable to control the spasms. The vicar had stopped speaking and glared at me over the pulpit and I'd been filled with embarrassment and terror. Even now, standing beneath the thatched lych-gate of Wolborough Church, the memory caused a shiver to run through my body.

Storm clouds were gathering overhead, and I huddled deeper into my duffle coat and pulled up the hood. Turning homeward, I wished that David were with me, that I would not have to enter the house alone. I missed him whenever he was away and was nervous at night when the wind blew from across the moor and howled through the pine trees at the bottom of the garden.

Strange noises kept me on the brink of wakefulness, and I would long for the warmth and nearness of his body.

Even so, by the time I got home and undressed for bed, I knew, as I lay in the dark, that even if he was there I would not reach out as I should; that I felt as bashful and timid about entering into the physical aspects of love, as I did about entering a place of worship.

In all other respects, life was good.

During our first year at Camelot I was given ample opportunity to improve my cooking skills. My parents, other family members and friends dined with us frequently and their lavish praise was as eagerly devoured by me, as my culinary efforts were by them. One regular visitor to our new home was my grandmother, who had moved to Devon from Kingsbury, near London. Small, round – and deaf when it was expedient – she was not an easy person. She treated my mother like a scullery maid, yet seemed inordinately fond of me.

'It's a lovely house, Susan,' Nanny exclaimed, warmly, when we stood admiring the garden after her first guided tour. 'Mind you, the steep stairs frighten me, and this balcony isn't very suitable for children, is it? It's a long way down.' She peered over the railing and surveyed the steeply sloping lawn below, then turned back to the house.

We stepped through the French doors into the lounge and seated ourselves on the chintz settee which David and I had brought from Petitor Road. Despite the modern appearance of the house, old and new seemed to blend well together. A stone fireplace stretched the width of the lounge and, above it, the chimney breast had been painted black by the last owners. That black wall had horrified me to begin with but, with great insight, David had pronounced it the ideal spot to display a beautiful seascape painting he'd given me. It looked quite spectacular, I reflected, though Nanny's grimace had not escaped my notice.

She continued, now, with her gratuitous appraisal. 'Yes, I like the house and I like your David too. Tell me, when are you going to start having babies?'

The question was posed quite blatantly, in that almost impudent way which only the very old and the very young can get away with. David and I had been married for eighteen months and I knew that the answer was important to everyone, friends and family alike; it was just so much easier to field when referred to obliquely. Nanny's direct approach was not so easily deflected.

'I don't know, Nanny,' I replied light-heartedly, perching on the edge of the floral settee. 'It's difficult whilst I have such a good job at Watts, Blake, Bearne.'

It hurt to be so glib. I longed to have children; to know the joys of motherhood. At least, I thought I did. Memories of Mary Bell's baby flooded my mind. He'd been born with a harelip. I'd rushed up to the cot that first time, words of joyful praise on my lips, and recoiled in horror, unable to hide the shock.

Nanny patted my arm affectionately. 'Nonsense, dear. You can't put a job before babies.'

'We've only been married a short time, Nanny. And we have such a hectic social life.'

Nanny bristled visibly. I couldn't take much more of this and, jumping to my feet, retreated to the kitchen to make tea, swiftly countering her attack by asking over my shoulder, 'China or Indian? I've a lovely Sally Lunn cake. Or would you prefer plain bread and butter?'

Truth was, I reflected as I closed my eyes and leaned back for a moment against the kitchen door, my abounding energy was sublimated in as much physical work as I could find to do in my spare time.

Gardening, and all the most strenuous aspects of maintaining the house left me tired and ready for sleep at bedtime. I'd undress quickly each night in the locked bathroom so that I never had to appear naked, or even semi-clad, before David. Once in bed, genuine fatigue made it easy to draw away from the arms that reached out lovingly towards me. Deep within, however, an unfulfilled longing gnawed away at me.

We rarely spoke of the question. David was as uncommunicative as I and, if he found our relationship any problem, he kept it pretty much to himself.

I opened my eyes and pushed myself away from the kitchen door. Setting the tea tray with a daintily embroidered traycloth, best china and thin slices of bread and butter, I recalled a visit to the Family Planning Clinic. It had proved most unhelpful.

'Didn't you tell them we hardly ever make love?' David had challenged on my return.

I'd felt chastised, knowing I should have said something at the clinic. I'd wanted to, but had been tongue-tied. A pleasant, female doctor had been in attendance but, just as it had been on my lips to confide in her, another medic had entered the consulting room, effectively silencing me.

Remembering it now did not help. I filled the teapot and banged the kettle back down on the hob. It was ridiculous. I fumed inwardly at my stupidity. I loved the company of men; loved to flirt with them, to bask in their admiration. From that first wolf-whistle in my teens, I'd never looked back. I recalled it with pleasure. I was eighteen and wore the full skirts of the sixties, layers and layers of sugar-starched petticoats giving them the volume and swing which was *de rigueur* at the time. With a waspie clinching my waist and a carefully lacquered bouffant hairstyle, I'd cut quite a dash.

And then there was the time I'd been sent to deliver a letter at work and stopped the whole machine shop as every man had downed tools to look at me and whistle. Then, and now, I'd loved every moment of the *frisson* created between myself and men in general. Why, why could it not extend to *real* love for my husband?

It puzzled me. I loved David and wanted his affection. But once he drew me into his arms and began to fondle me, I froze.

'There's nothing to say. Nothing wrong,' I'd replied to his sad, anxious question after the visit to the Family Planning Clinic.

He'd turned away and never spoken of the matter again. But try as I might, in a frenzy of activity, I could never put the subject out of my mind, nor the image of David's forlorn face.

'Won't be a moment, Nanny,' I called through the kitchen door. 'Just cutting the cake and putting some biscuits out.'

I arranged a doyley on the plate and absent-mindedly selected the best of the confectionery from the tin, my thoughts still on the subject which Nanny had raised. What about the day Mummy had given me her one and only talk on the facts of life? I smiled ruefully at the recollection. It was whilst I was still quite young, during a walk to the shops in Ruislip High Street.

'One day, Susan,' she'd begun, her head held high and eyes fixed straight ahead, 'when you are older, you will be a little bit ill. You are not to worry.'

That was it. But it had not taken me long to realise, when I started menstruating, that this was the 'little bit ill'. It had made me vow that when I had a daughter I would be open in all aspects of communication. Yet oddly, it never struck me how incongruous that vow was in the light of my inability to communicate with David. With that sort of sex education, it was little wonder, I thought, that we'd had a few, minor problems.

Head down, the laden tray held before me like a battering ram, I pushed open the kitchen door and advanced upon Nanny.

Any sense of lingering guilt I might have had was quickly swallowed up in the lifestyle which David and I carved out for ourselves. Throughout the following year, my job, and our social and domestic life all served to minimise my sense of inadequacy. Gradually it seemed to matter less and less that my personal relationship with David included little sexual activity. I knew I could love him and care for him in every practical way and that seemed to be all that mattered. We were good friends and deeply protective and caring of one another. Both shy and retiring, we tended always to stick together and gave the illusion of an ideal couple. It was easy to believe it myself.

Golf was added to our sporting activities and we played in the early mornings before the more expert club members advanced upon the course. We enjoyed being together, particularly when sunbathing and walking. Trips to the moors, to Torquay, or round the Bay to Brixham – always a favourite haunt of mine – filled our evenings and weekends.

Beneath the seemingly happy façade, however, there lurked a restlessness. In some ways the two and a half years of our marriage seemed an empty sham. Life seemed to enclose us, trapping us by virtue of its lack of purpose. Where were we going? And what was the aim of our co-existence? Unformed questions arose in my mind, only to be pushed to one side in a further frenzy of activity.

One day, in the late spring of the following year, David returned home with news that was, ultimately, to change our lives.

'I've been offered a partnership with the firm,' he told me, throwing himself into a chair.

'David, that's great!' I exclaimed.

He looked glum. 'Well . . . I don't know,' he said. 'I was pleased to begin with. Now I'm not so sure.'

'But why ever not, darling?' His diffidence puzzled me; it wasn't like David to be downcast. I waited, expectantly.

He leaned back, one leg over the arm of the chair and said, 'It would mean putting in quite a lot of money.'

'Well, we've got it. That's no problem.' I leaned forward in my seat. Not given to great insight I was, nonetheless, sure that David was holding something back. I didn't have to wait long for my suspicions to be confirmed.

'Yes. But don't you see, Susan,' he blurted out, 'if we sink everything into a partnership here, we'll be stuck in Newton Abbot for the rest of our lives. We'd never know anything else!'

David jumped to his feet, walked over to the fireplace and leaned against the mantelpiece. 'I'm not convinced that I want that,' he said, the expression on his face imploring me to understand.

I wasn't at all sure that I did. Was he talking of leaving his job altogether; perhaps even a move, maybe somewhere like Exeter, so he could commute?

'There must be more to life,' I agreed, nodding slowly.

Relief flooded David's face. He crossed the room in two quick strides, flung himself down beside me and, taking my hands in his, eagerly began to confide what was on his mind.

The offer had unsettled David, that much was obvious. Aware of the need to make some sort of decision, he began applying for jobs in London, then abroad. Apprehension, tinged with excitement, filled my breast. What had I let us in for with my passive acquiescence?

Within the month, a position in Peru became vacant, but was then filled before David's application could be processed. Some weeks later he was invited to London, by the same firm, to attend an interview for a different posting. There, evidently impressed by his personality and qualifications, he was offered the position.

David accepted. His new employers: The Burmah Oilfield Company. His place of work: Ecuador.

4

En Route To Ecuador

I had never flown before and could hardly believe that
my maiden flight was to be to so far-flung a continent
as South America. My schoolgirl geography was vague
and sketchy; truth to tell, I wasn't entirely sure where
Ecuador was and, with a degree of embarrassment, I
admitted as much to David. 'What will it be like, darling?
I don't even know what sort of climate to expect, or what
countries we'll be near.'

David picked up a copy of *National Geographic* which
had been lying on the sideboard, together with an atlas
from the bookshelves. Opening the latter on the coffee
table, he adjusted a table lamp and, without hesitation,
traced an outline of the country with his finger. Evidently
he'd studied the map many times before.

'It's in the north-west corner of South America.' He
glanced at me sideways, excitement lighting his eyes.
Patiently, he explained. 'To the north is Panama; that's
the bit that links South America to North America. This
big patch here, sort of nor-nor-west,' he again outlined
the area, 'is Colombia. And then below that, stretching
down the coast, is Peru.'

I slipped from the settee and knelt on the floor; leaning
forward over the coffee table, I gazed at the map. 'So we'll
be right on the coast? Oh, David, how thrilling. You know
how I love the sea.'

'Hey, hang on.' David laughed at my naivety. 'It may
look small on paper, but it's quite a big area you know.

Ecuador covers some 106,000 square miles, and a lot of it's mountainous.' He pushed the *National Geographic* magazine across the table towards me. 'Here, you can read all about it in there.'

It was hard to tell much from the pictures: groups of people depicting the Aztec culture, palms, volcanoes and jungle. 'You mean we shan't be near the sea?' I was disappointed.

David grinned. 'As it happens,' he said, 'we *shall* be on the coast, for the simple reason that that's where most of the oilrigs are.'

David's job with the Anglo-Ecuadorian Oilfield Company, a subsidiary of Burmah Oil, was to involve the day-to-day recording of all financial transactions, and the periodic preparation of audited accounts. The fact that he knew nothing of the oil business seemed not to matter a jot. It was all quite beyond me, and I marvelled that his expertise in accountancy was the key to open doors with an international firm of repute.

He was scheduled to take up his new post at the beginning of July, 1968. That meant we had only three weeks before leaving the UK. We would both have to hand in notice to our respective employers; passports, visas, and health certificates would have to be applied for and inoculations attended to. David would make all necessary arrangements, of course, but even so there was plenty to occupy me during the short time still left to us.

Friends and family had to be visited. Nanny, as she kept reminding us, was 'filled with sorrow' at our imminent departure. When we broke the news to my mother, shock, initially, stunned her into silence. Later, groping to find the right words to express her sense of loss, she homed in on the insignificant. 'We shall miss your visits, Susan. And the lovely meals you produce.' And suddenly, in that one sentence, the reality of leaving home, of parting with loved ones, of travelling half way across the world to live, was summed up and seen for what it was. For the first time I was aware that there would be a cost.

For one thing, the house would have to be sold. It was going to be a wrench leaving our home, the very first we'd owned. Watching the post that would carry the For Sale sign being driven into the ground was a little like seeing a nail being hammered into a coffin. The end of an era.

Eventually, all the preparations were complete, a buyer found for Camelot, and our cases packed.

Early on the morning of our departure, I sneaked from the house alone. Heavy dew drenched the garden, weeping from the trees until the fingers of dawn arrived to wipe it away. Droplets, shed from overhanging branches, beaded the roses I had lovingly nurtured, and dripped from their leaves. Sparkling in the white light of morning, and running, slowly, merging, they hung on slender webs slung, precariously, between plants. Each web was an intricate and beautiful testimony of its creator's skill, yet I knew that, with one brush of my hand, the spider which clung to the centre of each small universe would be dashed to the ground. 'Home' was a fragile concept.

Leaving Camelot would be a little like handing over a part of myself. Into the bare earth of this garden I'd poured out the self-expression denied by virtue of my own inhibition. This small territory, fraction of a greater creation, was a statement of my personality; the affirmation of my own creativity.

I stooped to breathe in the fragrance of a large creamy tea-rose and as I straightened up a ladybird appeared from beneath its petals. For a moment, it hesitated, then flexed its wings, and took off.

'Ladybird, ladybird, fly away home; your house is on fire and your children all gone . . . '

With the words of the nursery rhyme ringing in my head, I turned back to the house, my bare feet and nightdress leaving a trail in the wet grass.

We'd been fortunate enough to make a quick sale on the house; had crated up our furnishings and ornaments, and with my mother's supervision had put the whole lot in storage pending their shipment out to our new home in Ancon.

David had planned a farewell dinner at the Ariel Hotel, near Heathrow, where we were to spend the night, *en famille*. It seemed appropriate to make a special event of our embarkation to foreign parts, and the festive atmosphere, as we gathered in the dining room, suppressed an excess of nostalgia. No one would admit to the underlying sadness of our parting, which was well hidden beneath a forced air of jollity.

However, when the family disbanded and David and I made our way to bed, I could no longer keep up the bright repartee. 'I wonder if there'll be green fields in South America?' I said, pensively.

David looked anxious. 'Not having second thoughts, are you, Susan?' he asked.

I shook my head and, as we approached the bedroom door, wished with all my heart that he would reach out to me; that in some inexplicable way, we could communicate openly. David unlocked the door. I smiled at him briefly and walked into the room. We'd get by. With a new start in life, in a new country, we might even become new people. Everything would work out fine. Just fine.

Early next morning we set off for the airport, a subdued little party, joining the queue before the TransWorld desk. Around me Terminal One throbbed with life: people of all colours and nations milled about; mothers chiding fretful children, fathers casting anxious eyes at the departure board, intrepid businessmen waiting nonchalantly for their flights to be called. Other families were there, like our own, to bid their loved ones farewell.

Soon we'd be parted. Soon there would be thousands of miles between my parents and me. I'd never before been separated from them for any length of time, and certainly never by so great a distance. I wondered how I'd fare without their support? After all, David and I had been married less than three years, a comparatively short time, and Ecuador was half a world away from home and family.

Even David looked a little grim as he turned from the desk. 'Okay Susan? Time to go.' He swung the flight bags over his shoulder. In one hand he held Boarding Passes and passports, symbols of our new life.

Daddy hugged me close. 'It's a long way, sweetheart. Take care of yourself.'

'We'll have to go, darling.' Awkwardly, David touched my arm.

'Now you be sure and write . . .'

Mummy's voice trailed after us as we stepped towards customs and immigration and, glancing back, I saw Daddy put an arm around her shoulder. A space had cleared around them and they looked lost and alone. Evidently taking a grip on their emotions, they stood with heads held high and waved us off. In a moment, we'd be lost to their sight, and they to ours. I raised my hand in a last farewell, turned my back on all I held dear and proceeded through the barrier.

Once on board the TransWorld jet, David and I were soon experimenting with the unfamiliar intricacies of reclining seats, pressurised air-jets, spotlights and 'piped' music. By the time the aircraft took off, spreading London at our feet, we were eagerly anticipating the pleasures of a late lunch thirty thousand feet up; and an inflight movie.

'You should see the Ladies Room,' I whispered, after a lengthy excursion. 'Talk about luxury. There's a full range of Elizabeth Arden Blue Grass products in there. This is what I call living.'

The long flight provided me with plenty of time for reflection and the image of my parents' sad faces rose periodically in my mind. I thought of the many ways in which they'd supported me, always there whenever I'd needed them. Would I cope, *could* I cope without their presence in the background? I glanced at David beside me.

As if sensing my gaze, he raised his head from his book and looked at me. 'Feeling nervous about what's ahead?'

He took my hand in his, and I was suddenly aware that he, too, might have reservations. I owed it to him to be cheerful. I smiled back brightly, banishing all negative thoughts from my mind.

'What do you think our new home will be like?' Deliberately, I turned my thoughts to the future. 'I wonder if we'll have a garden? I do hope so. I'd miss not being able to grow things. Do you think they have gardens in Ecuador, David?'

'I'm sure they do. I should think the company'll do us proud.' David grinned, tucking my hand through his arm and patting it as if to emphasise his point. 'After all, we're Very Important People, specially flown out to join a very prestigious firm. They'll roll out the red carpet for us. Not worried are you?'

'No, not really. I suppose it's just so far away. I can hardly phone Mummy every time there's a crisis like the turkey episode, can I?'

'There won't be any crises, darling. You've come a long way since then. From what I gather, there's quite a social life in Ecuador. You'll be the hostess with the mostest.'

In a happier frame of mind, I closed my eyes and allowed my thoughts to dwell on the dinner parties we'd hold. All my tried and tested recipes could make a second début with the new friends we'd have . . . Yes. It really was going to be all right.

Our two day stop-over *en route* was spent in New York. It was still light when we arrived and checked out of John F. Kennedy Airport. With our luggage safely stowed in the 'trunk' of a 'cab', we set off for the hotel into which the company had booked us – on Broadway, right in the heart of Manhattan.

'What an incredible city,' David exclaimed over and over as we gazed in awe at the speed and volume of traffic, and the proliferation of yellow cabs racing beneath the soaring skyline.

On arrival at our hotel, we followed the smartly waistcoated bell-boy who took our cases. 'This way, sir,' he said, as he led us from elevator to bedroom and ushered us in.

David selected a coin from his pocket and placed it in the outstretched hand. Without a word, the man held it up to the light, turning it first one way then another, his lip curled. David fumbled, hastily, in his pocket and, with much embarrassment, produced a note. He placed that too in the bell-boy's rapacious hand and, with a derisory nod, mercifully, he left us alone.

'He must have thought me a complete idiot.' David threw himself into a chair.

'Well . . .' I was beside myself. 'You wouldn't get that sort of rudeness at home in England. There'd be a bit more respect shown.'

Putting on his best American accent, David grinned. 'Darling, this is the US of A — land of opportunity. Obviously, we've got a lot to learn.'

That observation was later confirmed. During the next couple of days, we witnessed several unsavoury incidents and, by the second day, in spite of a wonderful itinerary of sightseeing, we were both disenchanted.

For our last trip, we'd planned a visit to the Statue of Liberty. We took the ferry from Battery Park and, turning our backs on the famous Manhattan skyline, gazed ahead to the even more famous statue — symbol of freedom and independence. One hundred and fifty-one feet tall, Miss Liberty stood atop a 142 foot high pedestal. Shaking free from her shackles, she bore, in her left hand, a tablet showing the Declaration of Independence and, in her right, the burning torch, of world renown.

When we'd disembarked, we climbed the spiral staircase from the statue's base to the viewing platform under Liberty's spiked crown. All around us was New York Bay, where the Hudson River and East River spilled out into the Atlantic Ocean. Within the bay were numerous islands and one in particular captured my imagination. Here we were looking out from Liberty Island, whilst a stone's throw away was Ellis Island, used to incarcerate New York's first malefactors. What a strange irony it must have been to them that not only must they endure the privation of their freedom, but that Liberty, herself, should fill the parameters of their vision. As the boat took us back to Manhattan, inexplicable depression took a hold of me; a depression that was only later translated to my own situation.

Not until I was alone in the hotel bathroom did I recognise its source. Whilst David watched TV in our room, I soaked in the bath, and contemplated the mysteries of life. Here I was, with what must have seemed to others, Everything Going For Me, but the truth was that I felt as those prisoners must have felt. The vision of marriage as a liberating experience had filled *my* horizons. Reality was another story. Fond though I was of David, I felt trapped and imprisoned, fearful of my capacity to sustain meaning and purpose in my life; unable to break free of the taboos which bound me.

I shivered, suddenly aware of the cooling water. At the foot of the bath a tap dripped, a monotonous, repetitive plop. Around me, the hard, uncompromising tiled surface took on a cell-like dimension.

The sightseeing had been wonderful, but the incidents we'd witnessed, along with the enervating heat, did nothing to endear New York City to us.

'I shan't be sorry to leave,' David said on the last morning, as we packed in readiness to continue our journey into Latin America.

David paid the hotel bill, arranged for a cab and we set off for the airport and the next lap of our travels. By nightfall we'd be in our new hometown, Ancon.

We boarded the plane on time, then spent two hours grounded whilst running repairs were effected. Sitting in stifling heat without benefit of air-conditioning left us irritable and exhausted, but we eventually took off and had an uneventful flight. Our next brief stop-over was Quito, seat of government for Ecuador. We couldn't wait to get off the aircraft and were eager to see whether the city lived up to its reputation. We were not disappointed. Our first sight of the world's second highest capital city, when we disembarked, was enough to lift even our downcast spirits.

'The hills in Newton Abbot hardly prepared us for this, did they, Susan?' David raised his eyebrows and surveyed the majesty and splendour of the Andes.

I laughed at his dry humour. The air had the effervescence of champagne, and the sweetness of honey. We breathed deeply of its heady fragrance and experienced an exquisite sense of intoxication which left us jubilant and breathless.

'Let's explore a little,' I pleaded, fatigue forgotten in the excitement of such novel experiences.

'Well,' David pursed his lips, 'it's only a short time before take-off. But – all right.'

We passed through the exit from the airport terminal and gazed in astonishment at the sight which greeted us. Countless, strangely garbed Indians congregated on a small roundabout between the Arrivals Hall and Departures. Stalls were set up in higgledy-piggledy profusion, each displaying quantities of vividly patterned shawls and ponchos for sale.

'They make quite a colourful sight, don't they?' An elderly gentleman, seated on a bench nearby, smiled a greeting. 'You in transit from Quito?'

'Yes,' we replied to both queries.

'This is their catchment area,' he continued, waving a hand in the direction of the Indians, 'a sort of mini-market. They hope to tempt foreign visitors to part with some of their *sucres* in return for Ecuadorian artefacts. Helps the locals eke out their meagre existence.'

'But they look so clean and well-dressed.' The words were out before I could stop them.

The old man nodded. 'They're the Otovalan Indians; the most fastidious of all the races in this country. But I think you'll find this is a land of contrasts. There's prosperity and poverty cheek by jowl, on a scale you couldn't begin to imagine. I believe something like 1 per cent of the population possesses more wealth than the other 99 per cent put together.'

We shook our heads in amazement.

We were to learn more, in time, of these social and economic contradictions. We were also to observe a disturbing disparity between the sexes. Peasant women would work as labourers on building sites and on road gangs, whilst their loutish husbands slept off the effects of alcohol. It was not uncommon, we were to discover, for whole families to camp out by the roadside on Sundays and Fiestas until the head of the household awoke and they could complete their journey home.

For the moment, though, we were enchanted. I fervently hoped that Ancon, which was to be our new hometown, would be as interesting and colourful as Quito. With a last look at the scene behind us, we took leave of the old man. That sense of adventure which had impelled us to leave the market town of Newton Abbot and embark on a new life in South America was now rekindled, and in high spirits we boarded the plane once more for the last leg of our journey.

Guayaquil was our destination. Tucked between mountain ranges and the most northerly tip of the great Gulf of Guayaquil, it seemed, from the map, to be idyllically placed. As the plane banked and turned into its descent, I craned forward in my seat, eager for a first glimpse of the area in which we'd be living for the next few years.

'See anything yet, Susan?'

I shook my head.

The plane touched down on the tarmac and airport buildings obliterated all else. It seemed an eternity before the 'fasten seatbelts' sign was extinguished. But, at last, with the customary surge of all airline passengers intent upon disembarking, our fellow travellers, festooned with personal property, started up the aisle. Swept along in the current we soon found ourselves in the terminal buildings.

Within the hour we'd collected our baggage and passed through customs. David gave instructions to the taxi driver and we set off for Ancon through the city of Guayaquil.

In great excitement, I peered through the taxi windows to be greeted with my first sight of the city. Round-eyed, I took it all in. In silent disbelief I sat and stared. All the exuberance I'd felt in Quito vanished. My spirits sank.

The heat was unbearable. It rose in steamy, stinking wraiths about the hovels that packed the waterfront. These shanties, perched above the water on wooden stilts, were home to the poorest of the poor. Lop-sided and precarious, the huts were linked by fragile, highly dangerous bamboo walkways. Without sanitation they were a breeding ground for disease, carried by the flies that swarmed over the reeking mounds of sewerage beneath.

This must surely be the most unpleasant city I shall ever have the misfortune to be in, I thought as, tight-lipped, we were driven through the port.

This was my first sight of the living conditions of people without a voice. Silently, unable to express the revulsion I felt, I wrinkled my nose; yet strangely, I was without any real compassion. Almost as a tourist gazes at some curiosity, I heard myself murmuring responses to David's observations.

'The mortality rate must be enormous.' He scanned the scene before him and wiped a damp palm on his trouser leg. 'If disease doesn't get 'em, then fire must surely do so. That lot would go up like tinder in this heat.'

I nodded. 'I wonder how many fall and break their necks from those walkways?'

'Thank goodness we're not going to be living anywhere near here!'

'Oh David! I couldn't bear it. Ancon will be better than this, won't it?'

''Course it will.' David patted my hand reassuringly, but I was not convinced and with every passing mile my spirits sank lower and lower.

We had left England in glorious summer sunshine, the countryside a medley of colour. Our brief glimpse of Quito had been exciting, a gleaming city surrounded by the Andes beneath an azure sky. By contrast, everything here was cheerless and grey, shrouded in what our driver informed us was the *garua*, a heavy, humid mist.

Our journey now took us along the Ancon Peninsula towards the oilfield community which was to be our home. The landscape was monotonously flat and unappealing and soon a steady drizzle cast a grey gauze-like curtain across what scenery there was. Oil lines, ugly and stark, gave the impression of lunar bleakness.

The driver manoeuvred through a sprawling muddle of wooden bungalows in the middle of what appeared to be some huge, grey desert.

'Thees is Ancon,' he told us.

Casting about frantically for some sign of warmth, of luminosity, and finding none, my heart lay like a great leaden weight on my stomach. *I'm so glad our parents can't see us now*, I thought, remembering the misgivings they'd shared when we'd announced our intention of living in South America.

I stole a glance at David who averted his gaze. But even in profile, in the gathering gloom, his countenance looked grim. I turned to stare through the opposite window, blinking rapidly to dispel my tears.

What had we come to? What had we done?

5

Ancon: Pacific Playground

We drew up before one of the bungalows, extricated ourselves from the taxi and walked through the swinging wooden gate and up the path. The garden, to either side, resembled little more than a barren area of dry twigs. I recalled, with irony, the words of the receptionist the day I'd accompanied David to his interview in London.

'Ecuador is one of our best postings. South America is such an exotic place of sun, and palm trees.'

I'd envisaged only warmth, excitement and happiness ahead of us. To think we had left the summer sunshine of England for this — what had the taxi driver called it? — this *garua*. The dank chill settled about us ever more insidiously.

David and I exchanged glances. 'Well, we're here,' he said, inanely.

Was he, too, fondly recalling our lovely home in Newton Abbot, with its panoramic views over Dartmoor? I gazed at the bungalow with distaste whilst David opened the door and crossed the threshold.

It was no better inside. We'd been told by the company that furniture was 'sparse but adequate'. *What an understatement*, I thought, as a series of stark rooms greeted our eyes.

The taxi driver dumped our cases on the floor and David paid him off. Dispiritedly, we prepared for bed. That, at least, had been made ready for us and, weary after our long journey, little time elapsed before we both slept.

Suddenly, the most fiendish sound filled the air. David leapt from the bed and switched on the light. Eyes round, mouths dropping open, we stared at one another, too frightened to speak. Then, intent upon discovering the source of the unearthly din, we rushed barefoot to the window and peered out into the darkness. There before us, picked out in the light from the bedroom, stood four skinny donkeys. Nostrils flaring, lips grinning to reveal yellowed teeth, they brayed and snorted. Then, ignoring us, they burrowed into the bare earth that was our garden.

For a moment we were stunned. Then, exploding with laughter, we collapsed into each other's arms.

'I . . . I thought . . . we were going to be murdered in our beds . . .' Great guffaws rendered David's words hard to hear.

'Oh, David . . . to think those scraggy looking creatures should have caused us such terror . . .' Wiping the tears from my eyes, I pointed at the startled, asinine faces we could see through the window.

David grinned. 'Welcome to Ancon. This must be the Official Reception Party. Which one do you think is Chairman of the Board? Oh, it has to be the one with the fat tummy — all those expense account lunches.'

I rolled on the bed, struggling to control my mirth. 'Do stop it, David. My face hurts. Now, come on, I'm going to be serious.'

Holding our aching sides we attempted to compose ourselves, only to be set off again in gales of laughter at the renewed cacophony from the garden. Eventually, however, we put off the light and climbed back into bed.

'Well, Susan, you can't say that living with me is boring. There can't be too many men would fly their wives half way round the world *and* lay on such lavish entertainment. 'Night, darling.'

'Goodnight, David.'

But it was to be some time before we both slept. Such hilarity caused giggles to erupt long into the night, and even in days to come. A balm to our flagging spirits, it did much to dispel the gloom that had threatened to engulf us.

The morning brought a visitor in the form of Joan. She was the wife of David's boss, Donald Jefferson, and was a plain and homespun sort of woman. Her unfashionable attire, plump figure and sun-wrinkled face epitomised all I imagined of women in the outback of Australia. My mother had used the term 'back of beyond' when referring to Ecuador and all we had seen so far seemed to confirm that opinion.

'Hope you're settling in all right,' Joan said kindly, taking not the slightest notice of the previous night's disorder. 'It takes a bit of getting used to, but you'll soon feel at home.'

I smiled diffidently, hoping to conceal my true feelings. 'Well, I've all day ahead of me to get this lot sorted out. David left for the office quite early this morning.'

'Yes, Donald picked him up. By the way, don't kill yourself, lovey; I've found you a *muchacha*,' the older woman confided, with evident delight.

'A what?' I asked.

'A servant, dear. Everyone has servants out here; you can't do without them. She'll soon get you straightened up.'

Before I could stammer out my doubts, Joan departed, waving expansively and leaving me to wonder how in the world I would cope with a servant of all things!

Such reflection was short-lived. Almost immediately, there was a knock at the door and in came a short, rotund woman. She gabbled away in something which I took to be Spanish, a further contribution to my growing sense of inadequacy. I rushed to find the Spanish phrasebook which I had, rather optimistically, brought with me. A rapid flick through the pages revealed the Spanish for 'please sit down', and I read out the phrase, flushing with pride when she recognised it and obeyed.

Not knowing what to say next, I made her a cup of tea. A certain smugness in her expression, as I handed her the steaming liquid, intimated that I was not exploiting my role of employer to best advantage. However, since there seemed to be no way of getting her on her feet again, the last vestige of my self-confidence vanished.

After this inauspicious start, Tejelia and I never got on to the right footing and, of all the servants I was to have, she was the one to cause most problems.

The following day, through a mixture of indecipherable hand wavings on Tejelia's part and great attention to the phrasebook on mine, I learned that she needed a boy for gardening and shopping. It was difficult to comprehend how a garden boy might be occupied in such a desert, but the boy duly arrived. He was called Julio, was exceedingly small and turned out to be a miniature nightmare.

'He's hardly been here two minutes, but he's already managed to break several things,' I complained to David as we sat on the verandah that evening, awaiting dinner.

'Have you tackled him about it?' he asked.

'Oh yes. But all he does is shrug with an expression of absolute astonishment, as if it had nothing to do with him. And then he says, "Eet fall off shelf, Señora." '

David laughed.

'It's all very well,' I grumbled, 'but there seems no end to the things that leap up and down this bungalow – according to Julio. You'd think they were endowed with a life-force of their own.'

'I know how you feel, darling,' David soothed, 'but if you saw the small boy outside my office, it would give you a different perspective. He's only about ten or twelve years old and he sits outside begging every day. He was born with his feet back to front and the only way he can get about is with the help of friends. They pull him along in a little cart.'

Instantly, Julio was forgotten. 'Oh David, how dreadful. How awful to have to be so dependent on others.'

Immobility and dependency seemed to me to be the worst kind of disaster that could be inflicted on any able-bodied person. I shuddered, wondering how I would cope were I to be denied the pleasures of sport, of dancing, of ordinary movement. Little did I know that one day I would discover just that, and in doing so would ultimately be brought into a new and different kind of Freedom.

For now, the present was as much as I could handle. I could not put the boy out of my mind and as soon as was practicable, I drove down to the district where David's office was situated. It was just as he had said.

This poor stunted boy was the only one in Ancon. In Guayaquil, however, I was to discover thousands and thousands across the city for whom life's meagre necessities had to be wrested from the harsh reality of penury and debility.

Such thoughts would occupy my mind as I sat, day after day, on the wooden steps of the verandah, contemplating the wisdom of our move. Whilst lizards scurried past, completely at home in this barren environment, I recalled, with regret, the beautiful house and garden we'd left behind. But to David, and to others, I said nothing. It was easier to keep smiling, pretending all was well.

During one such reflective period Gay Hammond came into my life. Young and attractive, mother of two pretty little girls, she was married to one of the other accountants. She and Mike had moved out to the oilfield only a short time before our arrival, yet, with great equanimity, she already seemed to have settled. With her affable, sparkling personality, she was just the sort of friend I'd hoped to make in my new life. Her openness delighted me.

'We sold a lovely house because we thought we'd be coming to something so much better, more sumptuous than what we'd given up,' she confided, taking the cup of coffee I'd offered her. 'The night we arrived and saw how bare and drab it all was, Mike and I sat down and cried.'

'I'm so thankful it's not just me,' I admitted. 'I daren't say anything to David, though I think he's just as disappointed. But I fancy he's got enough problems of his own in that great sprawling wooden office.'

'How's he coping with the language?' Gay asked.

I shrugged. 'He doesn't say, but I suspect not too well.'

'You'll have to come to our next party and meet a few folk.' Gay smiled warmly. 'You'll soon settle in.'

I rose to pour fresh coffee, feeling cheered by her kindness. The bleakness of the last few days was replaced by a hope for the future and I warmed to my new-found acquaintance.

The rapport was mutual, and Gay soon introduced me to her hairdresser. 'I go every week, and have a manicure and pedicure as well as a shampoo and set,' she told me. So we began meeting regularly to take our beauty treatments together, and in no time established a firm friendship.

'Gay says you have to look glamorous,' I told David. 'It's one long round of entertaining out here.'

True to her word, my new friend invited us to the first party of many. Over a delicious supper we met up with some of the expatriates working on the oilfield and began to make the acquaintance of a few of the Ecuadorian dignitaries. It was a time of learning about this new world and its people: of servants and parties, of quantifying crude oil, of the sunshine we could expect once the *garua* cleared.

Two new arrivals, with first-hand, up-to-date news of England, were guaranteed popularity amongst the expatriates. In no time we found ourselves in the social whirl, with dinner and buffet parties regular features on our calendar. It would have been difficult not to feel welcome.

It was at one such party, not many weeks after our arrival, that things took a turn for the better.

'Who's for a game of darts?' Mike asked of his noisy guests. 'Come on Susan. What's that you're drinking? Let me get you another.'

'It's my favourite: a Cubre Libre,' I giggled, downing the last of the rum and coke. 'And it's my fourth, Mike. You're just trying to get me tiddly.'

'That's right,' he grinned, slipping an arm around my waist and eyeing my husband. 'David's a lucky fellah. Scotch for you, old chap?'

David handed Mike his glass then steered me towards a dartboard on the far side of the room. 'Isn't this better than England?' he asked, passing me a set of darts.

'Oh much!' I agreed, holding one aloft and squinting to take aim. 'People make their own entertainment here instead of relying on an endless diet of television.' I hurled my missile at the bull's eye and pulled a face as it swerved, way off course, and stuck askew in the rubber surround.

'Whoops! Missed again. I used to be good at this game, believe it or not.'

'You're pretty hopeless now, darling.' David roared with laughter as I made another disastrous shot. I stooped to retrieve the dart which had failed to hit the mark and had fallen to the floor.

Just then, Gay approached with a dark, handsome man at her elbow. 'Husband and wife together?' she said in mock horror. 'We can't have that! Here Mike, drag David off to meet someone interesting while I introduce Susan to Greg.'

As David was whisked away I straightened and looked directly at the stranger, Greg. Tall and powerfully built, his hair gleamed, thick and black like a slick of oil, and his eyes were deep and unfathomable. I felt an instant and astonishing desire to win his approval and even as our gaze met and held, I was willing him to ask me to dance.

In the background someone had put a Frank Sinatra record on the gramophone – 'My Way' – and the lights in the room were simultaneously dimmed. Couples swayed to the strains of the ballad, clasping each other tightly, so that they seemed to move as one.

Inside my head a voice silently clamoured: *Let him smile at me. I want him to like me. I want to dance with him. I want him to hold me close.* And another voice, less demanding, warned: *No, Susan. No. He's not yours, and you have no right to him.*

'But what harm can come of it?' I murmured aloud.

'I beg your pardon?' Greg said.

I laughed and shook my head. 'Nothing important.'

He smiled broadly and made some remark or other and laughed again. It was as if we had known each other for ever.

He opened his arms. 'Shall we?'

Detaching myself from the inner conflict, I was like a child gatecrashing a party, faced with delicious treats that were not mine to taste. Only vaguely aware of David's presence, I moved forward into Greg's open arms. He held me close. We moved as one.

A week later I wrote, in one of my numerous letters home, to tell my parents of this new friend. As always, I sprawled on the floor at one of the low side tables.

'Dearest Mummy and Daddy, Today we had coffee with a very nice man called Greg Griffiths. He is great fun and a super dancer. His wife is in England with their children at the moment so he is generally my dancing partner at parties. (David dances with the Señoritas.)'

I closed my eyes remembering that first meeting at Mike and Gay's. For the duration of the evening Greg and I had danced together, oblivious of the party going on around us, enclosed in an aura of each other's presence. Finally, succumbing to exhaustion when the clock struck four, I'd allowed David to gather me up and take me home in the rising dawn. Against a dark, unfathomable sky, the last stars had trembled in fear of temporary obliteration and, as David drew the car into the drive, the pale horizon moved in.

Taking up my pen, I resumed my letter-writing.

'Then he came to us for lunch. A spur of the moment invitation, so nothing spectacular. I am lost without my cookery books, and it was the servants' day off so I couldn't ask the maid. After that he took us for a drive . . .'

A tremor ran through my body. 'He likes me,' I murmured, laying down my pen and gazing into space. 'I know he likes me.'

David and I spent most evenings either at the British Club or at private parties. In our first six weeks of living on the Ancon Peninsula, we'd rapidly acquired a wide circle of friends and if one of them was not holding a special function, then we were. I loved these opportunities to entertain: the planning, shopping, cooking; most of all the dancing . . .

We had brought records with us from England, and visits to the larger stores in Guayaquil helped us to keep our collection up-to-date. The strains of Frank Sinatra, Nat King Cole, Lulu and the Beatles rang out into the night air on a regular basis. Gradually, despite the inauspicious start to our new life, we felt increasingly at home.

Even so, I was aware that David was still struggling with his own shortcomings. Ecuadorian guests would ask him, 'Why do you not speak Spanish as well as the Señora?'

It was true that my command of the language had escalated far beyond David's. But any pleasure I might have derived from the back-handed compliments was diminished by his diffidence. Quickly I would leap to his defence.

'My husband is ensconced with other Europeans most of the time and has little opportunity to practise, whereas I have Spanish lessons and daily contact with the servants,' I'd explain.

David would shift uncomfortably from one foot to another and later he'd take me up on the matter.

'Thank you, Susan. I *can* defend myself.'

But David's linguistic inadequacy was to become an increasingly touchy subject. And one that was not easily dealt with.

As the sun swung downward from the Northern Hemisphere, the days lengthened imperceptibly. Here on the equator there were only two seasons, each very different from the other except in the length of days and nights. By Michaelmas, however, day and night were of equal duration, but there was little sense of springtime or early summer as I knew it. The seasons changed abruptly – and dramatically.

'Come and see,' I cried the moment David arrived home one evening. 'It seems I was wrong about Julio. It's really frustrated me to see the hours he's spent watering those barren, bare twigs in the garden. But he came rushing into the bungalow this morning and all but grabbed me by the hand.'

I had been leading David through to the back of the house whilst I'd been speaking and now proudly showed him what Julio had shown me. 'There! What do you think of that?'

Marvel of marvels, one of the dry bushes I had so despaired of now bore two beautiful red hibiscus flowers. David walked over to admire them.

'Poor Julio,' I said, 'I have rather maligned him. He's been really dedicated in attending to his duties out here, and had far more faith than I had. I never thought for one moment that anything living and beautiful could be made to blossom in this barren wasteland.'

'Well, the garden certainly seems to be his saving grace,' David agreed.

Together we admired the handiwork of our diminutive Percy Thrower.

But if Julio displayed the magic touch when it came to horticulture, he still left much to be desired in other respects. The following week, returning from a shopping expedition, I was furious to discover the extent of his stupidity. In high dudgeon, I rang David at the office.

'Do you know what he's done now?' I demanded. 'I asked him to clean the lounge windows, and he's taken the hose to the inside! It's ruined the carpet; that lovely one I bartered for from the travelling Indian trader.'

David was emphatic. 'You'll have to sack him, Susan. And Tejeila too since they seem to come as a pair.'

It took all my courage next day to confront my two servants with the fact that they were no longer employed. My knees shook to such an extent when I'd summoned them to the lounge that I was obliged to sit down. However, since this forced me to look up at them, I felt I was at a distinct disadvantage.

'I'm sorry,' I faltered, 'but you're going to have to go. You do understand, don't you? I just can't keep you on after all the recent blunders. My husband has told me to let you know that you have a week's notice.'

I was unable to meet Tejeila's eye, knowing that she had several mouths to feed at home and that she would have no letter of reference to show any prospective employer. By the end of the day, however, my own predicament took precedence. As the full import of the inconvenience these two servants had caused me hit home, I was filled with a sense of injustice.

'How on earth are we going to manage when they go, David? We've a dinner party arranged for next week.'

'I shouldn't worry, Susan. I'll keep my ear to the

ground at the office. Bound to be someone who can help.'

He was right. By the end of the week I was offered two new servants by Joan and Donald Jefferson, who were moving up to Quito. And I knew, from experience, that these two were superior to those I had sacked.

I rang David at work. 'You remember them? Edison's that good-looking black boy. He's an accomplished bartender; quite an asset, in fact.'

'That's right. And isn't Selina a pretty, dark-haired little thing? As I recall, they were both hard workers when we borrowed them to help at our first party.'

Subsequent parties, once Edison and Selina moved in, were to confirm David's recollection and, with the further endeavours of my two new servants, all the hard work was taken out of hostessing. After dancing far into the night, I'd awaken next morning to find every glass washed, every ashtray emptied. All would be set in order as if the night's revelry had never taken place.

By the time we'd completed our first trimester, David and I were well settled into our new life. Only the *garua* remained to plague us.

October brought the *temperada* – the summer season – and with it a lifting of my spirit. The mist dispersed and overnight, or so it seemed, the drab grey peninsula was transformed. From out of the dead earth new life erupted in a profusion of colourful plants.

Evening after evening the setting sun flared into a fiery furnace which shot flames into the darkening sky and licked along the surface of the sea like molten metal. Silhouetted against the glowing, red-hot Pacific Ocean, even the sight of an oil derrick became a stirring, almost beautiful experience and I marvelled at the wonder of nature. Never did it occur to me, however, to extend my thought to the how? or the Who? of creation.

As the gardens began to blossom, so did the people. We were invited, one evening, to a Moon-Flower Party.

'Whatever it is, it sounds lovely,' I murmured as David

and I set off for the home of our friends. A warm and balmy breeze blowing in across the peninsula from the Umboldt Current was dying with the evening light by the time we arrived at the house.

Douglas's garden was densely tropical and the air was heavy with the opulent perfume of cherished flowering plants and shrubs. Night fell in the twinkling of an eye so close to the equator. Backlit by a blaze of vermillion and yellow-ochre sunset, the many varieties of trees and palms took on exotic forms in silhouette.

We sat about sipping sangria and nibbling tasty morsels of sugar-dusted meat or tiny cheese pasties and waited curiously for the purpose of the party to be revealed. Before us the Moon-Flower bush bore one single, huge and heavy bud.

'It only flowers once a year,' Douglas explained. 'And then for only twenty-four hours.'

Suddenly, the moment arrived. Totally absorbed, we watched in fascination as layer upon layer of pink and oyster petals uncurled in slow motion, to reveal a bloom of exquisite perfection. Heady fragrance assailed our senses. We were spellbound. It seemed beyond belief that anything so enchanting should have so brief an existence.

With deep reverence Douglas cut the lovely flower from its host plant. Tenderly, he placed its fragile form in the refrigerator in the hope of prolonging its moments of crowning glory. Yet even as he did so, its magnificence was fading.

My recollections in later years were poignant. It seemed to me that here was a spiritual dimension denoting the frailty and brevity of human life when measured in the realms of eternity.

When we called next day to view the miracle once more, there in the fridge lay only an ugly, shrivelled stem.

Yet the theme of creation was in the air. At every party the Ecuadorians, to whom the absence of a family was a matter of great shame, posed the same queries.

'And how is your health, Señora? And that of your husband? Your children?' It was, naturally enough, assumed that after three years of marriage David and I would have at least one offspring.

The truth was that despite my yearning for a baby, we now rarely made love. Deep down, I was relieved that David made few demands of me, and seemed as happy as I with our near-abstinence.

However, my peace was disturbed by the arrival of a newly married couple on the oilfield. It was the custom for wives already established on the field to show hospitality to newcomers.

'I've been asked to get some food in for Sheila and Brian,' I told David over breakfast one morning. 'I think I'll take over some flowers too, to make them feel welcome.'

The day after their arrival, I went to see how they were getting on. Sheila was still in her nightgown when she greeted me.

'Come in,' she exclaimed, flinging the door wide open when I explained the purpose of my visit.

I stepped into the lounge. It was filled with packing cases, but that was as nothing compared to the chaos visible through the open bedroom door. Expecting any moment that my hostess would be overcome by embarrassment and rush to close it, I tried to avert my eyes. Not a bit of it. She seated me on the one and only chair, right opposite, and called to her husband. 'Brian, come and meet our visitor.'

A young man appeared at the bedroom door, and shambled into the room, clad only in jeans and slippers. Pushing back dark hair with one hand, he proffered the other, a broad beam of welcome on his face.

'I gather your husband is an accountant with the company?' He threw an arm around Sheila's shoulder, pulling her to him. Behind him, the door was even further ajar. And through it, only yards from where I sat, the room was clearly visible. It was like a battlefield!

For a few brief seconds, I just stared. All that I saw seemed to be evidence of a love that was beyond my ken. Regret seared my emotions. I thought of the barely disarranged bedclothes from which David and I arose each morning. We knew nothing of such passion and vitality in our relationship.

Pulling myself together, I wrenched my eyes from the scene and nodded.

'Yes . . . David's one of the accountants.'

Each day that I visited it was the same. I was acutely aware of this young couple's love for one another. There was no pleasure in the observation. It served only to highlight the extent of my inadequacies with David.

I felt guilty. The bond between Brian and Sheila was evident. Yet though I yearned to know that same oneness in my own marriage, the truth was that I was as embarrassed by their display of affection for one another, as I had been with David's attentions for me. And that embarrassment was a constant barrier; one which I was unable, or unwilling, to demolish. In my mind I saw myself as a failure, complete and utter.

I can interview servants in Spanish, and offer friendship to this young couple, I thought, *but I can't show my husband a love which is normal and natural*.

The sense of inadequacy which threatened to overwhelm me once more was paramount. For sanity's sake it had to be buried. And in this I was aided by two events: one was our move to the bungalow which Donald and Joan had vacated when they transferred to Head Office in Quito; the other was the arrival of Goliat.

David explained when he introduced me to the huge shaggy dog. 'Do you remember Patsy from back home in England?'

I nodded.

'Well by a huge quirk of coincidence she's living out here now. Goliat – Goliath in English, I suppose – belonged to her brother, who, I gather, adored him.

Trouble is they've only got a small indoor courtyard so the dog's outgrown them. They're looking for a new home for him and have asked if we'd like him. What do you think, Susan? He'd be a bit of company for you whilst I'm at the office, and specially when I'm away on business.'

What did I think? I was over the moon. Here, at last, was something on which I could pour out all my pent-up affection; something unthreatening in its demands upon me. In no time, the two of us became inseparable.

The collie was two years old, and had never been properly trained. I undertook his disciplining with gusto and, like a fond mother, took endless delight in recounting the details to friends.

'He's mighty class-conscious,' I told Gay whilst we sat under the hairdryer, 'with a great dislike of the poorer members of the community. Tradesmen are his speciality.'

'Well I'm glad he's getting to know me now and realises my standing in society,' she replied with dry humour.

He was a dog with hidden depths, I decided. With a display of great ferocity, which only I knew to be feigned, he would leap, snarl and bark at anyone approaching *his* domain. Yet at home, in the garden, his gentle and zany nature was very evident, as he raced the big lizards which lived beneath the house.

The new bungalow, which overlooked the sea, was built on stilts, to ensure adequate ventilation in the height of the summer season. Palms, gently swaying in the breeze, sheltered the wide verandah from a sweltering sun, whilst the garden was a brilliant and exotic display of frangipani, hibiscus, and bougainvilia. Love doves cooed in the eaves and humming birds were a constant source of fascination as they hovered, apparently motionless, before the flowers, seeking within each bright floret the deep cache of nectar. I was enchanted.

'Oh, David,' I twirled across the spacious lounge. 'This

is so much better than the last place, more as we imagined it would be.'

Pride lit David's eyes. He surveyed the profusion of flowers I'd arranged in vases, the Indian rugs scattered across the brightly polished parquet floor, the drapes at the windows.

'I must say you've worked wonders, Susan. Looks just like home, especially now our own furnishings have arrived.' His appreciation was very evident.

My mother had arranged transportation of our possessions, and I'd found unpacking them an exciting task. I laughed as I recalled a particular incident involving one of our servants.

'Do you remember how terrified Sirilio was of the artificial flames when we unpacked the electric fire and plugged it in for the first time?'

David grinned. 'And what about the "furniture removal team"?'

On arrival at the new bungalow we had found a queue of folk at the gate enquiring whether they could 'help'. Privately wondering what had prompted this offer, we were puzzled by the inordinate interest they displayed in our packing cases. However, in return for such unstinting labour from the local townspeople, the gift of so humble an item seemed a small price to pay.

A week or so later, while exploring the shanty town of Anconcito, a village on the outskirts of the oilfield, we'd discovered the reason. One tiny hovel housed a huge family, with mother cooking in the midst on a charcoal fire. Both walls and roof of this humble abode were liberally adorned with labels bearing the name: Mr and Mrs D. A. James, Anglo-Ecuadorian Oilfields. The entire place was built of 'our' packing cases!

The discovery had evoked in us no more than mild amusement and a degree of amazement. Only in hindsight was I to feel any real shame for the disparity between my affluent lifestyle and that of the poor of the world. And only in Jesus would I ultimately know for myself the depths of his compassion for families like this one.

'What with that and the way you've turned this place out, perhaps we ought to go into business as Architect and Interior Designer?' said David.

I laughed and straightened up the ornaments on the mantelpiece.

But the excitement of our move, and the way in which it served to mask my inadequacies, was short lived. All that I'd buried in the social whirl was resurrected in an incident later in the month.

It happened one day when Mike and Gay Hammond were away on holiday. Early one morning Clemencia, their maid, came knocking at my door. Dressed in a cheap, print dress, her usually smiling face was haggard and drawn and her gappy teeth hidden. In her arms she carried a baby. She clutched tightly at the small bundle and told me, with a sob, of his vomiting and diarrhoea.

'Eet ees the baby, Señora. He ees sick.'

Immediately, I ushered her into the kitchen. 'What are you giving him, Clemencia?'

'My milk, Señora.'

'Only milk?' I questioned her. 'No water or fresh oranges?'

Her face took on a pained expression. 'You cannot know, Señora. You have no children.' Sadly, she departed, her words ringing in my ears.

In a few hours she was back. The baby's appearance was frightening, his eyes huge and staring, his stomach terribly distended. Brooking no further argument, I bundled mother and child into the car and drove them to the clinic in Ancon. Here I was further to observe the disparities of life in Ecuador.

The doctor was a National. I watched, incredulously, as he puffed on a cigarette dangling from his lip whilst he examined the baby. When I challenged him he just shrugged; 'It's only from a poor family.'

It was so unfair, and I was incensed by the inequality between rich and poor. Life was cheap in South America; the infant death rate extremely high.

The next day, my own doctor rang. Clemencia's baby was dead.

The incident preyed on my mind; images of that tiny scrap of humanity and the failure of society to meet his needs surfaced with hideous clarity. How could life be so unjust? If there was a God, how could he allow this to happen?

When, within the month, I found my period to be late, a mingled thrill of pride and fear stabbed at the core of my being. Clemencia and her ilk might be dogged by ignorance and poverty, but I would allow nothing, nothing to blight the unborn life I carried within me.

Keeping my secret from David, I took to examining my body in the mirror, fancying that already it was swollen and rounded.

'What do you think of that, Goliat?' I asked my dog during one of our many excursions to the beach. 'Me. with a baby! Just think of it. I shall make sure I'm the best, the most loving mother ever.'

I leaped and danced the length of the long solitary stretch of white sand. Beside me, Goliat pranced on his hind legs and observed the dawning of his mistress's spiritual awakening.

6

El Temperada

One of the more unpleasant aspects of living in South America was the profusion of insects. At the height of the hot season, when the air hung heavy and humid, Nature seemed to surpass herself in inflicting upon us creepy crawlies of every description. We were dining with David's new boss one evening when we first learned what was yet in store for us.

'Wait till you see the *grillos*,' Andrew Walton warned us. 'They're huge! Great hard-backed beetles that dive-bomb you.'

My face must have registered horror, for his wife, Marcia, interposed quickly, 'Don't tease so, Andrew. You don't need to worry, Susan. They're not harmful in any way.'

I was soon to find out about *grillos* for myself, at the Ancon Library where I worked a couple of evenings a week. I'd been told that *grillos* liked paper. It had not occurred to me, however, that a library would, therefore, provide a veritable bean-feast for the little monsters.

One day, in search of a book that someone had requested, I reached up to an overhead shelf and – WHAM – something hard and leathery shot out and struck my forehead! Before I could draw breath another followed. Then another. And another, until I was covered with the creatures. I screamed. Panicked. In a frenzy I brushed at my hair, my face, my dress.

The air was thick with flying insects. I ran from the

building, blind terror propelling me. Up the road. Towards the bungalow. The door was black, a moving, living lacquer. Around its perimeter a crack of light showed. Thank goodness! David was home. Frantically, I wrenched at the knob.

Seeing my consternation, he rose to meet me, drew me into the lounge, sat me down and made hot, sweet tea. 'I came back from the office early so I could get on with some work,' he told me when I had calmed down. 'I put on the lamp and was bombarded. They're obviously attracted by light.'

I sipped my tea. 'I was so frightened at the library I ran out and left one poor man waiting for a book,' I confessed. 'But David, what ever have you done to yourself? You look so strange.'

He grinned, sheepishly. 'Had to tuck my trouser legs into my socks and put my shirt collar up to stop the little beasts eating me alive! They're all over the house.'

'Janet!' I exclaimed. 'Poor child. She must be terrified.' With a flush of remorse, I remembered suddenly that we had a guest in residence, the young daughter of a friend.

Together we rushed into her bedroom only to find young Janet calmly catching the *grillos* in her fist then squashing them on the floor. I shivered and grimaced.

'I suppose that having been born here she's used to them,' I said to David.

Grillos, however, were not the only insect life with which I had to contend, as I discovered the first time I gave a tea party. The trolley was set with best china, knives, cake forks, and tiny silver spoons. Cakes, pastries, and sandwiches were all delicately displayed on doyleyed plates. How my mother would have loved such elegance. I smiled at the sight before returning to the kitchen.

My smiles, however, were short-lived. Only moments before my guests were due, I went again to check on the trolley. How different it looked! Every carefully arranged dish, piled high with delicious morsels, was a heaving mass of blackish-red ants! Thousands of tiny ants were devouring my elegant tea.

I screamed and, as my maid came running in, wailed, 'Selina, Selina. My guests will be here any moment. What can I do?'

In a flash she crossed the polished floor, raised her hand and struck the trolley a firm blow. I blinked. It was staggering. In an instant not one ant remained to be seen. No time to check. The ladies were at the door.

Feigning calm, I spent the entire afternoon in a state of tension, certain that sooner or later the ants would creep out of sandwiches or cakes and disgrace me – yet not one appeared. They seemed to have vanished as suddenly as they'd come.

In time we grew used to the insects. In fact, they became a source of fascination and we often marvelled at the exploits of the tiny creatures. David would stand bemused at the sight of a line of cake crumbs moving, as of its own volition, across the floor.

'It hardly seems possible that they can carry something so huge. By comparison with their own body weight, it must be like you or I lifting an elephant,' he observed.

Years later I was to recall that simile; to understand, for myself, that God the Creator provides everything in perfection and according to need. He had given these ants the capacity to carry *their* needs, however cumbersome. And in time, I was to learn of his ability, not only to provide for me, but also to enlarge *my* capacity to bear the weight of my burdens.

In the meantime, such things were outside the scope of my understanding, and I found my own ways of coping, of fulfilling my needs.

I awoke early one morning, with a sensation of heaviness. Dull pain knotted the muscles of my lower back, dragging, achingly between my thighs. I groaned, and rolled on to my side, pulling my knees upward into a foetal position.

Fear flitted through my mind, paused, then gathered momentum. It couldn't be! There had to be some other explanation. With sickening familiarity I recognised the symptoms, so like the onset of a monthly period.

Dawn was sudden here on the Equator. Blossom scent, and sounds of movement drifted through the open window on the thin white light of morning. The servants would be tending their chores before the heat of day began. The drone of lorry engines indicated that the street cleaners had begun their task and, on the flat roofed carport at the rear of the house, vultures banged out an ominous message with their great curved beaks.

Quietly, so as not to disturb David, I rose and crossed the room to the bathroom, laughing a little hysterically on discovering that my fears were, as yet, unfounded. I ran some water into the washbasin, and splashed my face, its pallor a further indication that all was not well. For a few moments I stood before the mirror, smoothing my nightdress over my belly and turning first this way then that as I studied my reflection.

David was still asleep when I slipped back into bed, his face young and vulnerable in repose. Would our baby be like him, fair-haired and blue-eyed? Deliberately conjuring up images in my mind – a babe at my breast, a toddler clambering on my knee, a flaxen-haired boy trotting after David – I drifted, at last, into an uneasy sleep.

That sense of unease persisted throughout the day. Refusing to acknowledge the possibility of its source, I filled the hours with activity. By bedtime, reality could be ignored no longer. My monthly period was with me.

Slowly I undressed, reluctant to embrace the hours of darkness, when crowding thoughts and emotions could no longer be kept at bay. Scarcely able to contain myself, I said nothing to David as he switched off the light. Tears coursed down my cheeks, silent and salty as I waited for sleep to overcome him. Then, turning from his inert body, I buried my head in the pillow and wept. The shared bed and still form at my side further augmented my sense of isolation; that physical pain which was a sad reproach to my inner emptiness.

Once more I rose from the bed which seemed, suddenly, to epitomise so much of the futility of my life, padded across the floor and gazed from the window. In the blue luminosity of the night sky, the dark silhouette of a single oil derrick pierced the horizon, monument to the loneliness at the core of my being.

My eyes were puffy and red next day, but David seemed not to notice. He pecked me on the cheek then picked up his valise and briefcase. 'Bye, Susan. See you in a couple of days. Take care.'

I walked with him to the carport at the back of the house. 'Don't forget that we're due at the Walton's on Saturday, will you? What time do you think your flight will touch down?'

'Same as usual. There'll be plenty of time, don't worry.'

He loaded up the car, started the engine and reversed out on to the road, waving a final farewell as he reached the corner. I watched until he was out of sight. Trips to Head Office in Quito had become quite commonplace. All par for the course; a slight inconvenience when it came to arranging our social life, but nothing we couldn't handle, I told myself. I trailed slowly back indoors and turned my thoughts from David to that *other matter*.

The telephone stood, black and indomitable on the hall table. For a moment my resolve crumbled. Then I reached out.

My hand shook as I lifted the receiver. I'd traced his name in the company directory. Why shouldn't I call him? After all, I was only following up on his suggestion. And it was all so innocent. Hesitantly, I dialled the number.

'Greg Griffiths speaking . . . Yes, of course I remember you, Susan. Such a pretty girl with a beautiful speaking voice . . . A new fridge? I'll have one sent round.'

His voice sounded deep and mellifluous. 'Anything else you need?' he asked.

Greg had promised to procure anything I needed. I had only to say the word and – hey presto – delivery was effected. He had a finger in so many pies. It was all too easy, as the weeks went by, to give in to temptation; to keep ringing; to court and to foster this exciting new relationship.

We met frequently; at the club, at parties. I pursued him shamelessly and squandered a ridiculous amount of time on the telephone each day, feverishly trying to discover where he would be that evening.

As soon as I arrived at a party, I would search anxiously in the throng until I saw him. Then I would wait until he turned and saw me, and I would hold his glance until he beckoned me to him and, later, would take me into his arms to dance the night away.

Gay, by now my closest friend, passed comment next time we met at the hairdressers. 'You two certainly seem inseparable.'

I flushed. 'I'm so glad you introduced us. He's a superb dancer.'

'Don't forget he's also a married man,' my friend said dryly, flicking over the pages of her magazine.

'Oh, no. There's nothing like that.' Hastily I sought to change the subject, putting the innuendo from my mind.

But gradually, as I continued to meet with Greg, in thought, rather than in deed, I came to regard us as lovers. Lovers separated only by the existence of our spouses. And since social decorum prohibited my revealing to others, even to Gay, the intoxicating nature of this friendship, I found release elsewhere.

Goliat became my confidant, the non-judgemental, all accepting recipient of my fantasies and dreams. Dog and mistress: it seemed to me, as we walked and pranced together along the most isolated of the peninsula's white sandy beaches that, with canine intuition, he, alone, had

some inkling of comprehension. As I whispered my
secrets into the breeze, the sea took up a sibilant, mocking
echo.

'I know he's so much older than me and has a wife and
four children. And I have David. But you only have one
life, Goliat. You might as well seize happiness while you
can.'

I threw myself on the dry sand above high-water mark
and fondled my pet's long silky ears.

'You know how I felt in New York: the sudden
realisation that I should never have married David; that
we weren't right for each other.' I wrapped my arms
around the dog's neck, burying my face in his ruff. 'Oh,
Goliat! I have this great yearning to be happy, to be
cherished, to be loved for ever. Greg makes me feel so
good. And we're not harming anyone, after all.'

For a moment I remained hunched over the dog, then
raised my head to stare across the beach. Heat shimmered
over white sand, the images before me bent, distorted
and disturbing.

Yet it was true. My friendship with Greg *was* perfectly
innocuous. He was a popular figure with *everyone*.
Infinitely kind and amusing, he was considered the ideal
guest. And the fact that he spoke Spanish like a National
made him equally sought-after by Ecuadorians and
expatriates alike.

Down by the water's edge a group of pelicans and
cormorants took flight, galvanising Goliat into action. In
a flurry of sand he charged down the beach, leaping
upward in a futile effort to catch hold of them, to fly with
them. For a few moments I watched his antics then rolled
on to my front.

Palm trees fringed the top of the beach, similar to
those in our garden – a haven for butterflies such as
I had never seen before. Some were huge: the size of
birds. Thick, furry, striped bodies separated their
exotically marked wings, the long antennae wavering
curiously. Others were fragile and delicate, evoking

within me a tender caution. *They're like people*, I thought, *so easily hurt*.

I told myself that I needed this diversion with Greg; deserved the extra attention. David, of course, had never known of my 'pregnancy', nor the devastating discovery that it was no more than a phantom; mere wishful thinking on my part. How great had been my disppointment, how crashing my hopes when the truth had been made clear.

Perhaps if I'd shared with David my initial joy, we might, together, have borne the ultimate let-down. Perhaps, despite his natural reticence, David might have reached out to comfort me, to love me, to imbue me with renewed strength. As it was, there was nothing; only the usual implacable acceptance of fraternal affection where romance, desire and selfless love should have blossomed.

I scooped a handful of fine white sand and flung it into the face of the breeze. In an instant it was dispersed and the particles settled indistinguishably on the beach as if they had never been.

Our social life became more hectic still. As always, we were seen by our friends as the ideal couple, ever smiling and with never a cross word. On the outside all looked well. Inside was turmoil.

Thoughts of the pregnancy that never was loomed large. More irrational still was the feeling of having been let down by David. There was no *intention* of accusation on my part. Only a latent sense of betrayal; of martyrdom, which made it easier to rationalise my impetuosity and my all-consuming relationship with Greg. It began to seem to me that my marriage might have been flawed from the outset; now, insidiously, it was beginning to disintegrate.

By comparison with Greg's maturity, David appeared gauche. Constantly struggling with an inability to master Spanish, he seemed increasingly envious and resentful of Greg's linguistic skills – and the ease with which I understood and responded to him. Conversation with Ecuadorians, free and fluent to Greg and to me, left David excluded.

But if David's diffidence seemed to make him ever more remote, I barely noticed. I was too taken up with the thrills of flirtation to pay more than scant attention to its ramifications. Until, that was, the imminent return of Greg's wife . . .

'Everyone says how pretty and talented Clare is,' David remarked one evening as we set off for the Ancon Club.

'So I've heard.' I felt ridiculously jealous, resentful of what her appearance on the social scene would mean to my romance, yet anxious to see for myself if she was all that she was cracked up to be.

As with new arrivals, whenever expatriates were due to return from furlough, it was customary for one of the other wives to instruct their servants in making ready their home. Driven by my infatuation for Greg and my curiosity to meet his wife as soon as possible, I volunteered to oversee the cleaning of the bungalow and to ensure that a good stock of provisions was laid in.

Later that week, I told David: 'I've put a few flowers around the place for Clare's return home today.'

In reality, the 'few flowers' had been a lavish profusion and, somehow, in the midst of it all I'd lost Clare's scissors. Having heard from friends that she was a skilled craftswoman, I knew such tools would be of great importance to her. Even so, I had not expected, when we met later that day, that she would home in on that one incident and make a major issue of a simple accident.

'I think you've stolen my scissors,' she said, coldly.

The thought of meeting her had made me nervous enough, but now, faced with her beauty and vivacity, I felt like an awkward schoolgirl in the presence of a great lady.

'Oh no, Clare!' I gabbled. 'They must have been thrown out by mistake, along with the trimmings from the flowers. I'm so sorry. But they weren't your craft scissors; only an old garden pair.'

Secretly, I felt hurt that all my hard work had been
passed over for something so trivial. At the same time,
fear and guilt compounded the irony: Clare did not
suspect me of being a rival for her husband's affection,
but only of having stolen her scissors.

For a while I kept my distance, avoiding the painful
experience of seeing Greg with his wife on the beach,
Greg with his wife at parties, Greg with his wife on
expeditions to the jungle regions. Yet I was sure people
were talking.

Clare's arrival on the scene had suddenly put a whole
new complexion on things. For the first time I began to
be aware that my friendship with Greg might be subject
to the attention of others. In so closed a community as
the oilfield, servants gossiped, their speculation passing
swiftly from one household to another. Though in reality,
nothing improper had ever taken place between Greg and
me – only telephone calls, the excitement of meeting at
parties and dancing together, I knew that much could be
made of little.

Eventually, however, though I knew I was playing with
fire, I was unable to contain myself any longer. I rang
Greg at the office. 'I must see you. Can we meet?
Somewhere out of town?' I pleaded.

We drove out, separately, to a secluded place north of
the oilfield. There, on the road to Salinas, we sat together
in the car. Greg took my hand in his, placed in it a small
gift of jewellery – a keepsake – and urged me never to
forget him. As if I could!

Enthralled, I gazed across Punta Carnero beach, where
the surf pounded rhythmically against the shore. I had
no compunction in accepting this gift, no sense of doing
wrong yet, paradoxically, I shivered – as if someone,
somewhere, had walked over my grave.

Sport was one of the things David and I had continued
to enjoy ever since our arrival on the peninsula. The golf
courses were so different from those on which we'd

played at home, the verdant fairways and putting greens of Petitor and Stover now no more than a fond memory. Faced, in Ecuador, with a course which was nothing more than desert interspersed with a few scrubby bushes, it was a miracle, in those early months, that my game seemed not to have suffered. Even the 'greens' were sand, so that it was like playing on one enormous bunker.

'How on earth do you cope with this?' I'd enquired on the first occasion I'd played.

Joan Jefferson had enlightened me on several points. 'The Club employs boys to "sweep" the greens with a sacking-covered smoother every time anyone plays. Then there are other boys to caddy. You wouldn't be able to drag a trolley through the sand.'

'No more struggling round with David's clubs like I used to, then? I like that,' I'd said emphatically and, addressing the ball, had given it a mighty whack which had sent it soaring straight and true for the pin. I'd been well satisfied, at the end of the game, to find myself playing to handicap despite the adverse conditions.

Now, some seven or eight months later, that was anything but the case. My game was decidedly off and I was overcome by that most pernicious of diseases – Golfer's Gloom.

'My aim just doesn't seem to be very good these days,' I said to Gay in exasperation when I sliced a shot for the second time that afternoon.

'It's hardly surprising in this heat,' she said encouragingly as she set off for the distant flag. 'Everyone says the *temperada* has been particularly hot this year. Do you know we've had temperatures of 125°F in the shade?'

'Well I'm glad to know that it's not the norm,' I replied, trudging after her. 'But it still doesn't explain my ineptitude. Your game doesn't seem to have been affected.'

'I shouldn't worry too much, Susan. You're probably tensing up and making it worse.'

At the next tee, I deliberately relaxed my shoulders,

flexed my knees and took my alignment. Slowly, purposefully, I shaped my backswing, the club gathering momentum on the downward stroke as I uncocked my wrists. *Eyes down and follow through*, I thought, mentally rehearsing my strategy. Nothing.

Nothing! Meeting no resistance, the wood swung upward and forward.

'An air-shot! I feel so ashamed.' I whacked my driver on the ground in disgust. 'My handicap used to be quite low; now I can hardly hit a ball.'

'Come on!' Gay tucked her arm through mine. 'It's too hot anyway. Let's retire to the 19th and have a rum and coke to cool us down.'

That evening, over dinner, I recounted the story to David. 'Perhaps your swing's gone off,' he suggested. 'Why don't you arrange to have a few lessons with the Pro?'

'Yes,' I agreed gloomily. 'I might try that.'

'You haven't forgotten that we've a tennis match tomorrow, have you?' David sprinkled salt liberally over his meal.

'How could I after yesterday's success?'

We'd won a friendly semi-final at the Ancon Tennis Club the previous day, and the final was scheduled for lunchtime the following day.

I was still in bed next morning when David left for the office. 'I'll see you at the club, then?' he said, turning at the bedroom door.

'I'll be there,' I promised.

The soft purr of the car engine drifted through the open window as David reversed out. I threw back the cotton blanket, swung my legs to the floor and reached for my negligee from the chair. Instantly the whole room began swimming before me. I shook my head to clear my vision. For a moment the floor erupted in steep undulations before rising to meet me. I hit the bed. Bounced. Hit the floor.

I lay where I'd fallen. Nausea swept over me. Bed,

chair, walls spiralled, closed in, receded. I closed my eyes to shut them out, welcoming the hard, cold stability of the floor beneath me as I waited for the sickness and giddiness to abate. Weak tears squeezed from beneath my eyelids. Why did I get these dizzy turns? It was so stupid. I would *not* give in, would not even mention it to David.

As soon as I was able, I hauled myself back on to the bed. For a few moments I lay still. Once the dizzy sensation had passed, and with it the general alarm such an attack provoked, the tennis match was uppermost in my mind. With determination I resolved that I would not let the side down. All I needed was to rest for a while.

By mid-morning my recovery was sufficient for me to shower, dress and walk down to the club. Bright conversation and a beaming smile hid any residual fears from the scrutiny of the others, as we made our way on to the court beneath the hot, noonday sun.

The match began.

I saw the ball coming; felt, rather than saw my racquet swing into action. It hit nothing but air, empty and futile. With deep shame and embarrassment I turned to watch the ball bounce off the perimeter fence.

'Sorry,' I muttered.

'Fifteen, Love.'

Again, I missed.

'Thirty, Love.' 'Forty, Love . . .'

Throughout the afternoon, in mounting desperation, I lost every point that should have been ours.

'I don't know what's got into me.' Belligerence masked my misery.

'You're certainly not the same girl who played a couple of days ago,' David agreed. 'You sure you're okay? Nothing wrong is there?'

'Nothing,' I lied. 'I'm just having an off day.'

Over the next few weeks, determined to prove my own lie, I took myself off for tennis lessons, as well as a golf clinic. But, as bouts of giddiness increased in frequency I could ignore them no longer. Quietly I arranged to see my doctor.

'Nothing to worry about,' he said when he had examined me. 'It's just dehydration because of the heat. I'm going to prescribe some salt tablets for you, and I want you to increase your fluid intake.'

Promising to down several pints of water a day and as much orange juice as I could stomach, I left the surgery feeling vaguely reassured.

'Have you told David?' Gay enquired when I relayed the diagnosis to her.

I nodded. 'He only got back from Head Office yesterday. He agrees it's best if I take it easy for a bit.'

I didn't mention that David had seemed to shrug off my news as if his mind was elsewhere, nor that after each of his trips to Quito he appeared increasingly remote.

'Why don't we make up a foursome and go to the beach this weekend?' Gay urged. 'We could make a day of it.'

There was nothing new in this; we frequently went to the beach, but it was good to know, when we set off that Saturday, that my friends were concerned and sympathetic when it came to my health. As always, the sky was unclouded, the sun a great white ball of heat and light which sparkled with diamond brilliance on the surface of the Pacific. Whipped up by an unseen force, the ocean waves coiled, reared and struck, expending their energy in thunderous splendour upon the soft, mobile sands.

'Race you in,' David said to no one in particular.

'You two go on,' Gay urged. 'We'll put up the picnic in a cool spot.'

'Ready?' David glanced at me.

Goliat barked and leaped in the air with excitement as we set off down the beach. He loved to ride the surf and had no fear of being submerged. No more did I. Sometimes it was expedient to duck beneath the waves as they rolled in. What was more significant was the shifting floor of the ocean that was so much a feature of this coast.

'The undertow seems particularly strong today,' I remarked as we waded out.

'Once you get beyond the surf it'll be okay. Look, Goliat's heading out there even now.' David threw himself at an oncoming wave, sliced through it and reappeared a few yards further out.

For a moment I turned back towards the shore to see if Gay and Mike were ready to join us. Next moment I gasped. The sand, shelving steeply, was suddenly sucked from beneath my feet whilst, at the same time, a wave knocked me off balance. Instantly, I was tossed into the churning, foaming deep.

Fighting the instinct to draw breath I felt myself being dragged under. A bubbling, boiling fomentation of gritty sand whirled over my face. I closed my eyes, squeezing the lids tight against the all pervasive force so that I sensed rather than saw the forward thrust of water. Faster and faster, knees grating against abrasive sea bed, I was hurled shoreward. Then – just as the pain in my chest reached a point where I knew I could take no more, I was impelled upward.

Spluttering, struggling weakly, with a great shuddering sob I filled my lungs with air. The beach was only yards away. With a cry of relief I staggered to my feet. For a moment everything around me hung suspended – motionless. Then, with a sickening force the undertow tugged at my feet, my ankles.

'David! David!'

I lurched, lost my balance and fell, but not before a brief glimpse had shown me that my husband was wading for the shore with his arms wrapped around my dog.

He's rescued Goliat and left me to my fate, I thought, as the current tore at my body, and coarse, pulverised fossil shell scraped agonisingly on my battered flesh.

7

Quito: City of Eternal Spring

'Susan, what happened?'

'Are you alright? Now take your time. Just sit quietly for a moment while you get your breath back.'

Gay and Mike hovered protectively over me as I sat shuddering on the sands, out of reach of the waves which crashed on the shore. Mike had plucked me, only moments earlier, from the undercurrent which had snaked around my ankles, toppling me, and threatening to drag me back out to the deep. Of David, there was no sign.

I turned, shakily, to my friends. 'Thank you, Mike. You saved my life.'

'Well I wouldn't go so far as to say that, m'dear. But it's a good thing Gay spotted you when she did. I fairly raced down the beach and just reached you in time to save you from another ducking.'

'What's going on? Are you okay, Susan?' David came into sight just as Mike was helping me to my feet. Silently, I bit my lip and left it to Gay to explain. Resentment simmered inside me. It was obvious to me that David had had no thought for my safety and, from what I could hear of his conversation with my friend, it was very evident that Goliat had come first.

Slowly we moved up the beach. David continued to fill Gay in with details of Goliat's rescue, whilst Mike still supported me with an arm around my waist. Gratefully, I leaned against him, adjusting the strap of my swimsuit with my free hand.

'My pendant,' I gasped. 'It's gone.'

All eyes turned on me enquiringly. 'The little gold chain I always wear, with the pearl drop . . . I'll have to go back to look for it.' I turned to retrace my steps.

David caught my arm. 'Don't be ridiculous, Susan. you'll never find it now.' His voice was redolent with long-suffering. *Like that of an adult with a recalcitrant child*, I thought.

For a moment I hesitated.

'I'm afraid he's right, you know, Susan.' Gay's face puckered in sympathy, as tears welled up in my eyes.

'I suppose so.' Reluctantly, I acknowledged the futility of a search. I stared out to sea — a vast emptiness which all but engulfed me. The little pearl teardrop, symbol of David's love for me five Christmases ago, lay for ever submerged beneath the might of the ocean, its slender chain torn and broken. There seemed a certain significance in the loss — as if the last modicum of affection which David and I held for one another had been wrested from us and swallowed up. In its place, a great ache inhabited my heart.

February, 1970, and we were on the move again. David had been offered promotion, which meant that he would be permanently based in Head Office in Quito. Because of its temperate climate, the capital was known as the City of Eternal Spring and was considered an idyllic place in which to live but, in spite of this, I was ambivalent about the posting.

'Looking forward to the move?' Gay asked during one of our visits to the hairdresser.

'I shall be glad to escape the next *garua*,' I admitted, 'but I'll miss the social life and all our friends.' My thoughts centred on one particular friendship.

'Nonsense. The social life in the capital is every bit as good as here on the peninsula. You'll love it there,' Gay said, encouragingly.

I wasn't convinced. 'But what about the beaches? All

the miles and miles of white sand and palm trees . . . City life will be quite different, full of traffic noise, crowded . . .'

'Susan! How many times have I heard you rave about the beauty of the mountains in Quito?' Gay held her hands before her to admire her newly painted nails. 'I know how you feel,' she continued, 'but you'll soon settle in. Besides, you won't have time to worry about what you're leaving behind.'

She was right, of course. At least ostensibly. There was precious little opportunity for reflection during the next few weeks, as we made our farewells in a flurry of parties and supervised the crating-up and storage of our possessions pending the time when we found a house to rent.

I assumed a brave face on the day of our departure for the capital. Hiding a heavy heart, I waved gaily and blew kisses to our friends whilst David manoeuvred the car, for the last time, from the bungalow's driveway. And then − we were off.

As soon as we had left Ancon behind, gloom settled upon us. David had little to say. When he did speak, his tone was like the desert around us, arid and barren.

Suddenly, he could contain himself no longer and burst out, 'How long do you imagine you can go on making a fool out of me with your flirting?'

Outside, dry scrubland, recumbent as bleached bones beneath a white-hot sun, stretched into the distance, and the grey dust lay heavy − like ashes on a grave.

For a moment I was stunned; then buried resentment surfaced. Indignantly, I defended myself. 'I don't know what you mean!'

David's face was set. 'Oh, yes you do. You laugh with all these other men, but your attitude to me is careless and callous.'

My heart beat faster. I hated rows; wanted only that this one should not develop. Deliberately, I lowered the pitch of my voice. 'I shall miss the sea and our friends, that's all.'

Quietly, cuttingly, David said, 'You'll be sorry some day.'

What was that supposed to mean? A prickle of fear ran through me. Despite my defensiveness, I knew he was right. In his usual taciturn manner, David had revealed the truth. Miserably, I wondered what it was that made me think I could go my own way, and make my own rules?

'Oh, you just don't understand,' I cried and turned from him to stare through the car window at the parched soil. For the rest of the long journey north we were like strangers, the silence between us desolate and bleak.

Night had fallen by the time we arrived in Quito. Since we had no home in the city, we had booked accommodation in a hotel. It was my task, in the coming days, to find a new house for us to rent, a tacit acknowledgement, on David's part, of my superior command of the language.

Early next morning I began my search. Reconnoitring in the company's chauffeur-driven limousine, I was able to appreciate to the full the beauties of this wooded, mountain city and, armed with Estate Agents' blurb, to view numerous 'desirable residences'.

By the end of a week, I had found an ideal place. I wrote to tell Gay: *'It's perfect; a large house, graciously proportioned, in a lovely setting among eucalyptus trees. Their heady fragrance and the awe-inspiring view of snowcapped mountains make it a natural beauty-spot, well known to courting couples. We move in next week.'*

The excitement and enthusiasm I conveyed to Gay and other friends was real enough but did nothing to heal the rift that had opened between David and me. From the outset, our life together in Quito was destined to be tense and superficial. Stung by David's caustic remarks and lengthy brooding silences, I turned my thoughts elsewhere.

Greg. What was he doing at this moment, I wondered as I walked my dog, or rested on a bench in the lovers' trysting place? Did he miss me, as I did him? I longed for his company, his wit, his gentle care. I longed to hear his laughter and feel his arms around me as we danced. While Goliat prowled amongst the trees, snuffling, and wagging his tail in canine ecstasy, I gazed blindly into space. My romance, heady as the scent of pine and eucalyptus, now seemed as unattainable as the distant mountain peaks of Chimborozo and Cotopaxi. And I mourned its passing.

Parties in Quito were as frequent — and as alcoholic — as they had been on the peninsula. Drunkenness, however, was not the only hazard — as we were to discover. We were invited, one day, to the home of a colleague and his wife, a young couple whom we had met once when they were visiting friends in Ancon. After searching for the house for some time, we eventually drew up in one of the well-to-do, tree-lined streets of Quito's suburbs and were instantly surrounded by grubby, runny-nosed children — each with outstretched hand.

'*Guarda su carro, Señor, Señora?*' Pushing and jostling, they besieged us with offers to keep vigil over the car.

David was not at all sure of the best policy to adopt, and when our host and hostess appeared at the door, asked, 'What do you think, Steve? Should I pay them?'

Steve spoke from experience: 'Certainly! I'd advise you to take them up on the offer, David, otherwise, you're quite likely to return after a night's revelry to find your vehicle stripped down.'

'Stripped down?' That seemed a puzzling term to me.

Steve explained. 'They'll take everything that's removable. So if you want to keep your car intact — cough up. Marie and I came out from a party soon after we arrived in the city to find our car minus lights, mirrors, bumpers . . . they'd taken the lot. Had to make a special trip down to Thieves Alley to buy everything back again. Cost me a fortune!'

Blanching visibly, David extracted a large handful of coins from his pocket. Then, not without difficulty because of the press of eager brown bodies around him, he paid the tallest and, he hoped, most responsible boy and urged him to guard our car with his life.

Steve made a face. 'You can say what you like to them but it's a risk whatever you do. Sometimes they see we *gringos* coming and take us for a ride.'

'How do you mean?' I asked, in all innocence.

Steve ushered the three of us through the door before replying. 'Sometimes,' he paused cryptically, 'sometimes they accept your money, pop round the corner and alert another gang of thieves to a good haul.'

It was a sobering thought. However, in all our time in Quito, David and I were to lose only one set of lights and hubcaps.

But 'car guardians' were not the only hazard the City had to offer. El Quiteno Libre, the up-market residential area in which we lived, boasted a Watchman, a self-appointed, brown-bodied, sinewy little man, armed with a shotgun and — a whistle! This he blew loudly and continuously. It was tempting to ask, when we paid the weekly charge for this dubious 'service', whether the whistle was intended as a deterrent to would-be robbers or a homing device to guide them to the spoils! And was the gun loaded, we wondered? We never did discover the answer to that question, which was perhaps just as well.

Despite the sinister implications of such events, and the contrasting freedom I had enjoyed in Ancon, I was not without a certain independence in Quito too. When it came to lengthy excursions, Goliat and I merely exchanged the isolated beaches of the peninsula for the equally solitary lower slopes of the Andes. On a more daily basis, we took to the pavements, admiring the colonial elegance of nearby suburbs where large houses were set in spacious, landscaped grounds. The only problem was that we had to run the gauntlet of the fierce, snarling bulldogs and alsatians which guarded them!

'Goliat and I are regarded as something of an oddity, I think,' I confided to Marie.

'I'm not surprised!' she laughed. 'You are rather an unlikely pair — huge shaggy dog and petite mistress. This is a city of contrasts, of extremes in terms of wealth and poverty. Dogs are kept solely for the protection of property. You don't actually *walk* them!'

It became easier to understand the native derision towards the *Eengleesh Promenade* when I was bitten, one day, by one of the alsatians. The attack drew blood and thoroughly frightened me. David, too, was most concerned and phoned the doctor. 'Nothing to worry about,' he was told, 'ring again when the Señora starts foaming at the mouth.' My husband's astonishment rendered him speechless!

Later, he urged caution. 'Do be careful, Susan. It's just not safe to walk everywhere. You know the company's limo is always available for the use of executives' wives.'

I was too shocked to do anything but concur. 'Yes, I'll ask Marie to go with me when I visit the Indian markets downtown.'

After our first trip together, Marie and I met frequently to explore, and to shop. The markets and backstreets, so different from anything to be seen in England, soon became favourite haunts. A cacophony of street trading reverberated in the confined spaces, packed with vivid displays of fruit, flowers and vegetables, meat stalls and fish barrows. Indians, garbed in paintbox colours, flat brown faces smiling yet impassioned, pleaded with us to buy, buy, buy. And weaving their way through the throng like the brightly hued threads of the mats on display, came the children. Bare footed, sticky-nosed, always grimy, they nevertheless captivated us with their shining eyes and impish humour, so that we were easily persuaded to deposit our money into their ever-outstretched hands.

With my new friend as my guide, I soon settled into city life.

David had seemed a little offhand when we'd first renewed our acquaintance with Marie and Steve, and I was anxious to remedy what I saw as his indifference towards her.

'I like Marie,' I told him. 'She's really good company. Besides, she has her own transport so I don't have to ring for the limo every time I want to go anywhere.'

David grunted and disappeared behind his newspaper. 'She's okay, I suppose. Did I tell you I'd be late back from the office tonight?'

I shrugged and picked up a magazine.

Marie introduced me to the shoemakers who plied their craft in the narrow backstreets of Quito. Their tiny premises were packed tight with a huge range of many-hued leathers, some of which were soft as a baby's skin. After selecting just the right shade to match an outfit, we would then have to decide upon the shape of the heel, and finally, we might add a buckle or bow as embellishment.

The shoemaker would then make a newspaper template by drawing around our feet with a charcoal pencil. Within the week he would have fashioned a perfectly fitting pair of shoes such as would not disgrace any house of *haute couture*. It was no wonder that my friend and I were enchanted with the whole process and novelty of owning custom-made shoes, nor that we made frequent trips downtown to make our purchases.

One day, in need of new footwear to match a party outfit, I rang Marie as usual. Her number was engaged. I sat at the telephone table and waited a few moments before trying again. Still it was engaged. Idly, I thumbed through a magazine to pass the time.

When some moments had elapsed, I tried the number again. Once more I was thwarted. Steve, I knew, would be at the office so it had to be Marie on the line. Whoever could she be talking to all this time? I turned again to the phone.

'Come on! Ring!' I willed under my breath as I redialled. The mechanism whirred and clicked in typically South American fashion. A moment's silence followed, then the familiar busy tone echoed in my ear.

'Bother!' Peevishly, I banged the receiver back into place and stared into space. Then I picked up the magazine again and, with a complete disregard for its contents, flicked the pages rapidly past my fingers, whilst I tried to recall if Marie had mentioned, when we'd spoken the previous day, whether she was expecting any important telephone call? Nothing came to mind.

There was always the possibility, of course, that a fault could have developed on the switchboard. I rang to check with the operator. No. There was no trouble. It was, as the signal indicated, a busy line. Exercising great self-control, I thanked her for her services and hung up.

My friend was obviously tied up for the morning! 'Blow you, Marie!' I said aloud and, lifting the receiver once more dialled David's office to ask for the company limo to be sent round for me. His number, too, was engaged. Impatiently, I drummed my fingers on the table, then tried again. After five or six fruitless attempts, I was tense with frustration. Finally, when I was almost at the point of giving up, I was connected to David's office.

'What is it, Susan? I'm awfully busy.'

'Busy?' Irritation spilled into my voice in a great pool of frustration. 'You've been busy, alright. I've been ringing for ages.' I twisted the line from the receiver into a great loop, laced it through my fingers and pulled it tight like a tourniquet. 'I don't know what it is, but every time I need transport these days, first Marie seems to be nattering away to someone, then your office number is engaged. All I can say is, you must both spend an awful lot of time on the phone.'

David merely laughed. 'I'll have the limo sent round,' he said.

There were many diversions in Quito for oilmen's wives. DAMAS, an organisation for American and British women, for instance, met in the luxury Hotel Quito, overlooking the Valley of Santo Domingo. This was a most attractive venue, and provided a welcome opportunity to dress up in a 'posh frock'. No sandals for me that day!

Marie had initiated me into the association and, over sandwiches and coffee, we met, with dozens of other women, to plan fund-raising events – a supper, a lunch, perhaps a dinner-dance – in order to help the 'shoeshine boys'.

'They're the street urchins of Quito,' Marie whispered during the proceedings.

Later, she told me more: 'We raise money for schools, too. Some of those high in the Andean Sierra region have no books, no pencils, no paper. At that altitude, the schoolrooms are always cold and comfortless, yet the Indian children go barefoot. They're too poor to have even the essentials of life.'

I was shocked. But it was good to know we could help in some way. DAMAS meetings obviously made the women feel involved in something worthwhile and, to judge by the conversations which buzzed around me, Quito's elegant 'leading ladies' considered them good fun too.

Marie continued to take me for some weeks but, once the novelty wore off, I began to consider how incongruous these meetings were. I wrote to Gay: '*Here we are, doing "good works" for the impoverished Indians, all from the security and comfort of our own marbled opulence.*'

Gradually, the gratification of being included in Quito's

high society began to pall. Secretly, I was on the verge of boredom; and though everyone seemed friendly, I frequently felt myself to be a misfit, standing outside the sophisticated, brittle clique of self-confident wives. Yet, always anxious to impress, I was filled with a sense of my own shortcomings. The hub-bub around me no longer seemed warm and inclusive, but oppressive and isolating. I saw myself as a lonely figure in the crowd.

One day, at the end of a meeting which had been presided over by a visiting dignitary, the secretary turned to me. 'Will you give the vote of thanks?' she asked, casually, as if asking nothing more than the time of day.

'Me?' I stuttered. 'Well . . . I . . . what do I have to do; what should I say?'

As the ladies applauded, I was urged to my feet. With knees shaking, and tongue sticking to the roof of my mouth, I looked out at a collage of expectant faces. What had I of worth to contribute to all these Beautiful People? How could I stand before them and say anything of merit? They were all so self-assured.

Or were they? Did they, looking at me, think likewise? Taking some small courage from the thought, I stammered a few words, then sat down. If anyone had told me, at that moment, that I would one day speak regularly and fluently to groups of women I would, undoubtedly, have viewed their sanity with suspicion. Me? A Speaker? Oh, no, no, no.

For weeks I dwelled on my inadequacy: an unsophisticated nobody; a childless woman; a hopeless wife. Alone in the evenings with David, depression set in. I could not even make conversation, witty or otherwise, with my own husband. I was useless.

If only I'd known then what I now know: that in God's eyes I *am* a person of worth, loved and cared for, a woman for whom he gave up his very life.

'All my life I will dance!' I announced to one and all and, kicking off my shoes, threw myself into the Twist.

We were at one of the numerous parties that formed the basis of our life together and I was determined to do all I could to shrug off my feelings of inadequacy. At least I knew myself to be good at dancing. And dancing led to other things . . . Wasn't this how I'd met Greg? I missed his easy companionship, his ready admiration and in consequence flirted openly with any attractive man.

'My! But you're a beautiful mover.' The army Captain made no effort to hide his admiration as he partnered me on to the floor. 'In fact, you're a pert little miss altogether.'

I dimpled, flashed him a flirtatious glance and exaggerated my body movements. For some minutes we twisted in silence, too breathless to converse, then, when the number came to an end and the band launched into a Beatles song, the tall, uniformed stranger took my arm and steered me towards the bar.

'You're an exceptionally pretty girl, Susan.' Again blatant admiration showed in his face as he handed me a Cubre Libre.

I raised the drink to my lips. 'Oh, thank you, kind sir,' I replied archly, opening my eyes wide above the rim of the glass.

'Ever thought that your looks might be your downfall?' he asked, huskily.

I was both shocked and amused. 'I'm a happily married woman,' I replied, mockingly.

'So I see.' He pursed his lips, aping regret.

This man, like all our friends, saw only what David and I chose to reveal: the image of a perfect couple. The aching silences, those silences which were filled with the clamour of unspoken thought, were known to us alone and, like a guest at a masked ball, the face of truth was hidden.

The whole of life is a masquerade, I thought, with a sudden flash of insight. *We all make gods of our reputations, our standing in the eyes of family, friends – even ourselves.*

I knew nothing of the Father-heart of God, he who sees beyond the masks to the hearts of stone; he who longs to take those hearts of stone and melt them into hearts of flesh, of life, of love.

The music started once again, a slow, smoochy rhythm. I glanced beyond the figure of the uniformed stranger to where my husband was moving towards the dance floor. Taking Marie in his arms, David began to dance. Softly, almost oblivious of those around me, I began to sing the words of the ballad, about the days that we thought would never come to an end.

8

The Road To Nowhere

I had so much in that city on the Equator, *la mitad del mundo*, and believed, in my materialistic way, that it would last for ever. The Bible says: 'Fix your thoughts not on what is seen, but on what is unseen. What is seen is temporary, yet what is unseen is eternal' (2 Cor. 4:18). Little did I dream that everything would soon tumble down and collapse around me. How could I know that ahead lay a bewildering time of misunderstanding and darkness?

It seems strange, in hindsight. There was beauty all around me in the mountains, in the sweetly scented woodlands of eucalyptus trees beside our house. Yet I never thought of the Creator of all this splendour. Never thought of God. God? Who needs God? Nevertheless, little by little, despite my indifference, the Almighty was beginning to awaken within me a spiritual dimension.

'How about exploring?' David asked as we lazed around after lunch one Sunday. The sun was hot, with a brilliance we were becoming accustomed to since our move to the mountains. It would be good to get out and about. I nodded.

We set off in the car, winding downhill to pick up the main route out of town. Small groups of men in familiar dark ponchos and wide, white trousers, straggled tipsily across the road before us. I leaned back in my seat, resigned to the fact that we'd be going nowhere fast.

'Sunday's always a popular day for *paco*,' I remarked.

The locally brewed alcoholic beverage was quite potent, having, so we were told, been made from leaves which were first eaten then regurgitated! So far I'd resisted all attempts to persuade me to try it.

David sighed. 'Mmm . . . not the best day for travelling, I must admit. It's rather like a game of pin-ball. We're the ball and the peasants are the pins. Only difference is that they're moving targets!' Carefully, he manoeuvred the car past the staggering drunks.

I smiled wryly, then turned my attention to the scenery. Pot-holed roads hedged with cacti and sisal took us past an ever-changing vista which was enchanting and, for once, the old companionable bond drew David and me together.

'Just look at that!' He pointed out a lone Indian woman with both a pig and a dog on a piece of rope, a baby on her back, and handfuls of flax, which she spun as she walked. So absorbed was she in her task that she nearly careered headlong into an overloaded Mixto, whose passengers waved gaily from inside and outside the cabin. We laughed, delighted with the entertainment.

As the car climbed higher into the mountains, the road hung precipitously above deep ravines. I almost dared not look, but the sights were too wonderful to be missed. Waterfalls slashed the green and purple foothills and the mountains were like cassocks, over which surplices of snowy white had been flung haphazardously. At intervals along the roadside crosses and wreath-bedecked stones marked accident spots, grim reminders to drivers of the need for vigilance.

Suddenly, less than a third of the way up the mountain, we came across a sign which read: PAN AMERICAN HIGHWAY. We'd heard tell of this major undertaking, a roadway driven straight across Latin America.

'Steve says the government initiated construction because it's anxious to keep up with Big Sister,' David explained.

'You mean the United States of America?' I asked. He nodded.

When the motorway came into view, I gasped. It was huge, multi-laned, and channelled through the core of a mountain. As smooth and even as a length of polished black satin, it stretched before us invitingly.

In terms of motoring, an open road was an unaccustomed sight in South America. Pot-holes, slow-moving livestock and puttering old vehicles denied any opportunity for speed. Faced now with this great, wide, empty road, David surrendered to temptation and pushed his foot to the floor.

'This is great!' he cried in exhilaration. Some of his old, boyish charm was apparent in his enthusiasm as the car bounded forward. Tarmac streaked away beneath us and the miles rocketed by.

For some time we motored in silence, both caught up in an ecstasy of power and motion. Adrenalin coursed through my veins and thrust aside the despondency of recent weeks. I glanced at David. He gripped the wheel, his torso inclined forward, arms, neck and shoulders tense with concentration, like that of a jockey urging his steed to greater things.

The speedometer registered 90 mph. Still the red metal needle advanced around the clock face; pushed ninety-five, ninety-seven, a hundred. The roadside was a rushing linear blur. My heart raced, and I laughed aloud.

Suddenly – around a bend – and a screech of brakes. The car slewed wildly in an arc before shuddering to a halt. Ahead of us was a solid wall of rock. As suddenly as it had begun, the road now ended, blanked off by a vertical cliff-face.

'Well, I'll be damned! What do you make of that, Susan?'

I shrugged, too stunned to pass comment.

Dry, scorching heat shimmered off the tarmac and a faint acrid odour of overheated rubber hung in the still air. Silence, so deep as to be almost tangible, filled the man-made ravine that cut deep into the mountain. Coming so soon after the breathtaking roar, this sudden stillness was eerie.

David hunched over the wheel and stared ahead dejectedly. 'I suppose they just ran out of money? You'd think they'd put up a sign to tell you you're on a road going nowhere wouldn't you? What a futile excursion.' He started up the engine, turned and headed home. The balloon had burst; our spirits were deflated.

I said little on the journey back. A strange depression took hold of me, a wistful certainty that my life was like this road. Lovely. Broad. And smooth. But going nowhere. Somehow, there was this sinister feeling that I, too, would soon reach a dead end, that in days to come there would be sheer rock blanking off the way ahead. Nothing more. Just – darkness.

'My life is meaningless. Empty, and meaningless.'

It was some weeks later, and I shouted the words out loud as I surveyed the wealth which surrounded us.

David looked long and hard at me, offering no response.

For once we were home; one of those rare evenings when there was no party to tempt us out, no social whirl to mask the bankruptcy of our relationship, our lives.

'Just look at today.' My voice rose in frustration. 'A thief steals my wallet in the supermarket. One phone call to your office, and along comes my knight in shining armour – you – to bale me out. It's all so easy. And yet there are people out there starving. Literally starving to death.'

I leaped from the chair and began to pace the floor. 'And another thing,' angrily I turned on my heel to confront my husband, 'what was Marie doing with you when you arrived with the money? The two of you seem to be around each other rather a lot these days.'

Abruptly, David jumped to his feet. 'Oh for goodness'

sake, Susan! You're just imagining things. I'm going out till you cool down.'

The door slammed behind him and I was left with my thoughts. Marie, with her long fair hair and wide, laughing eyes. She and Steve were such good fun. We were constantly in their company: a happy foursome. I didn't seriously think there was anything between her and David, did I?

Once, quite recently, in fact, David had caught me watching Marie with her children. 'Wouldn't you have liked a baby?' he'd asked me. Memories had come flooding back of that time in Ancon when I'd thought . . . really believed . . . But it had all come to nothing. There was no point in dragging it up. 'Yes,' I'd replied matter-of-factly, 'very much so.'

What had gone wrong? Where were the bright hopes we'd shared less than five years ago? Had they been dulled down through the years? Had we, with our inherited embargoes on honest dialogue, stifled the dreams, so that they now lay at our feet, lifeless.

Outside, an unknown bird warbled softly, a hushed, restrained sound, as if its disturbed utterance were a thing to be ashamed of in the midst of its sleeping world. In the distance, a lone dog bayed an uneasy message to the twin peaks of Cotopaxi and Chimborozo and, nearer to hand, backlit by a rising moon, a bat swooped noiselessly upon its prey.

I readjusted my focus and gazed, unseeingly, across the wide expanse of our lounge to the black night beyond.

Here, on the Equator, we were in a seismic zone. Our home was built to earthquake specifications, a fine, large house, with bar, lounge and, since it was occasionally chilly at that altitude, a wide-breasted log-burning fireplace. A raised dining room, reception area, study, four bedrooms with en-suite bathrooms and servants' quarters completed the accommodation.

We were entertaining one afternoon in May when we

had our first experience of a tremor. David and I had just stepped into the garden with our friends when a loud cracking sound arrested us. Simultaneously, the lawn beneath our feet moved in a strange way. A tiny, involuntary scream was torn from me and I quickly clapped a hand to my mouth.

A strong smell of sulphur hung in the air and an extraordinary stillness settled around us. Nothing moved. Birds, usually bustling and rackety, were suddenly silent, frozen into immobility. The dogs ceased their customary barking. All was hushed and suspended.

Eyes wide with fear, hardly daring to breathe, we glanced nervously at each other and stood uncertainly, poised for flight. Goliat was very perplexed and I hung grimly on to his collar to keep him from running away.

Eventually, after a few moments, our guests gave us the benefit of their wisdom and experience. 'It should be safe to return to the house now.'

Released from my restraining hand, Goliat rushed from room to room, sniffing and snuffling to ensure that all was well. And amazingly, as we made our own inspection, there seemed to be no damage whatever, though every picture and mirror in the house hung at a crazy angle.

'Wow,' David exclaimed, and sighed, explosively, as if he had been holding his breath since the tremor began. 'I wouldn't want to go through that too often. What a terrifying experience. Makes you realise how tenuous your hold on life is, doesn't it, when even the very ground on which you stand lacks stability.'

Later that evening, as if in response to that observation, David referred obliquely to our rows. 'I've been thinking, Susan. Perhaps we need a holiday?'

It seemed an excellent idea. David had a period of leave due to him and we discussed the best way to use it. We were torn between visiting the Galapagos Islands and the Amazon jungle; the latter involved a demanding journey, but one we both agreed would be fascinating.

And so it was arranged.

Everything started well enough. We left Quito for one of the other larger cities, Cuenca – City of Flowers – and from there we travelled to Loja, a town renowned for the longevity of its inhabitants, some of whom were reputed to be 115 years old.

'It's the therapeutic effect of the mud,' we were told whilst we gazed in astonishment at Methuselahs buried up to the neck in a thick, viscous, grey sludge.

But if either of us had nurtured a secret belief in the therapeutic effect of our holiday together and hopes that it would bring us closer, those illusions were soon to be shattered. Bereft of the routines of work and our social life, we were cast exclusively upon each other for entertainment and conversation. And it didn't take long to realise the impoverishment of our own relationship.

Perhaps it will be different when we reach the jungle, I thought. Wistfully, I yearned for the romance that had been so evident when we'd been sweethearts in England.

A military plane took us on the final stage of our journey. We travelled with two soldiers and several huge drums of gasoline, the contents of which swished about so alarmingly that I expected an explosion at any moment. I was tense with apprehension. And after we disembarked in the steamy atmosphere of the South American jungle that tension mounted and became, suddenly, horribly real.

The soldiers followed us from the plane.

'*Adelante! Adelante!*' With abrupt, stabbing movements they gesticulated with the barrels of their rifles. At gunpoint, we were marched down to the edge of the River Napo and forced into a canoe. Then, without a word, their faces grim and uncompromising, the two khaki-clad men commenced to paddle us down river.

Even as fear seized me I was filled, too, with a sense of excitement. I gripped my hands together, so that the knuckles stood out hard and white.

'Here we are,' I whispered to David, under the watchful gaze of the soldiers, 'at gunpoint, going goodness knows where down a tributary of the mighty Amazon, while my parents are safe at home in their tiny bungalow, thousands of miles away. I wonder what they'd think if they could see us now!'

David shook his head, gravely.

Only recently, we'd learned of a band of missionaries murdered by Aucu Indians way back in 1955. The widow of one, Elizabeth Elliot, had later returned to live and teach the very tribe who had murdered her husband. Recalling the story now, I marvelled anew at such forgiveness and wondered if we were now to be shot and lost for ever just like those poor missionaries? The brown, muddy waters of the Napo swirled ominously beneath the fragile vessel in which we travelled.

Finally, we reached a landing stage. '*Mi Coronel,*' barked one of our guards and, still at the point of a gun, we were hustled through the jungle to a group of huts which evidently constituted an army base.

All around us and high above, the raucous cacophony of tropical birds and chattering shrieks of wild animals echoed menacingly through the rain forest. The sounds closed in around us and seemed to intensify our isolation and clamour for our impending doom! With dry mouth and trembling knees I followed David and, obedient to the dictates of our guards, we stepped into the wooden office of the unknown *Coronel*.

He was red-faced and beefy, quite unlike any officer I had seen. He lounged back in a chair behind a desk and we stood before him whilst he questioned us. Who were we? Where were we going? Who knew we were here?

Eventually, he arrived at the truth. We were not spies, we were English *extranjeros*, with *cedulas* which entitled us to live in Ecuador and to carry out work for an oil company. This last piece of information seemed to carry some clout. It certainly galvanised the *Coronel* into action.

'Bring chairs,' he roared.

It was hard not to laugh as two guards staggered in with two huge armchairs.

'A photo – me with you.' He jabbed a fat finger at David and me, indicated that we should seat ourselves, then took up a position behind us, his face now wreathed in smiles.

David put on a fixed grin.

'Wonder if this'll make the *News Of The World*?' he said between his teeth.

When we returned home, it was depressingly clear that the holiday had done nothing to draw us closer together. Within a short time we were behaving as if we had not been away. We never spoke of the tedium which had been so evident in our relationship during the last few days of our trip, nor of the relief, which we were both so intent upon hiding, that it was now over. Easier by far, simply to immerse ourselves once more in the usual social intercourse and to pretend that nothing was amiss.

The first party, after our arrival home, was to be rather a special event. Paul and Anne Anderson were renowned for their social gatherings: the sumptuous fare, their elegant home, a guest list which included the cream of Quito's high society, and an inimitable creativity which made each function a pinnacle of success. On this occasion they had conceived of a Schnapps Party. I wasn't at all sure what a Schnapps Party might be, but it sounded fun, especially as Steve and Marie were to be fellow guests.

I dressed carefully, that evening, in a brand new outfit with matching, handmade shoes. 'Ready?' David asked. I threw a wrap around my shoulders, picked up my clutch bag, and together we set off for the Andersons' graciously appointed home.

The party began in delightful fashion. Drinks and titbits were served outdoors, and a hilarious game of croquet on the lawn was enhanced by warm, mellow sunshine that flickered through the trees of the large walled garden. Quito's soft night air was filled with laughter and music.

Suddenly, in the midst of the gaiety, I felt alone. David

had been scoring well in this silly game of croquet. Now, with the others, he began to tease me. 'Missed again!' A chorus of laughter rang out as I attempted a second and third shot.

I never seemed to hit anything these days. It was *their* fault, I thought, crossly. They shouldn't keep watching me. My ineptitude was humiliating – especially in front of Marie. It seemed that whenever I made a fool of myself *she* was there, with David. In fact, they seemed to spend an inordinate amount of time together. A quick stab of jealousy ran through me.

'Come on everybody. Time to eat,' called our host.

It was over, and relieved at having to aim no more balls through hoops, my spirits rose as we went in to dinner.

The table was elegantly laid, the food dainty and delicious. As the first of several courses was brought in, Paul, our host, made an announcement.

'This is a Schnapps Party,' he said solemnly, his eyes crinkling with barely disguised humour. 'You down the Schnapps in one go, gazing into the eyes of the person sitting opposite.'

A servant poured clear liquor into the small glasses adjacent to each guest. Paul watched me as, along with others, I proceeded to toss the potent drink down my throat, then he continued, 'Ah! Did I mention this?' He held aloft a small handbell. 'Well, every time I ring this, you drink the Schnapps. And don't forget the beer, the chaser!'

I was seated opposite Jeremy Browne, the General Manager, a handsome, intelligent man who'd always filled me with apprehension since I never knew what to talk about. The bell rang. Dutifully, I gazed into Jeremy's eyes, and downed the Schnapps. 'It's quite pleasant!' I murmured with some surprise. 'I've never tasted it before.'

The beer was untouched. That I had had before, and loathed.

As the meal progressed my diffidence lessened. I talked

of the Beatles. Surprisingly, Jeremy had a large collection
of their records.

The bell rang again; down went the Schnapps.

I really felt quite animated. Scintillating, in fact. Why
had I ever worried about conversing with this kindly
man? General Manager or no, it was evident from his
laughter that I was quite up to entertaining him. A fit of
giggles overcame me.

The bell rang once more: I poured more Schnapps
down my throat.

On the far side of the table, David seemed very taken
with Marie. And she with him!

Suddenly, idiotically, I was engulfed in tears. Jeremy
Browne's laughing face blurred, distorted, changed to
annoyance. Watery images of other guests showed them
to be clearly embarrassed. My tears flowed on and I
sobbed hysterically.

'What ever is wrong with you?' David appeared
suddenly at my side.

I pushed him away, resentment and nausea rising in
me, and ran from the room.

For days after, hot shame flooded through me at the
memory of my behaviour at the Schnapps Party. What
a fool I had made of myself! A drunken fool. The party
had fizzled out. My outburst had had the effect of sending
other guests in search of coats. With hushed voices, they
had made their departure.

I hardly dared venture from home. And when I did,
a single chance encounter with a member of Quito's high
society was enough to send me hot-foot in the opposite
direction. I had become a laughing stock, a figure of
ridicule. In a moment of extreme provocation, I took it
out on poor old Goliat, beating him relentlessly for some
minor misdemeanour. More shame and remorse
followed.

Relieved, to begin with, that David had made no
reference to the party, my feelings gradually changed.

Did his silence indicate more than mere circumspection? Was he shocked? Angry? Ashamed to own me as his wife? Did he consider me beneath contempt? Why, oh why, was he so . . . so inadequate, so unable to communicate, so unwilling to reach out to me.

'You don't care about me at all,' I rebuked him. 'It wouldn't matter to you whether I was here or not.'

We were in the lounge, waiting for Rosita to bring in the coffee. I was seated in my favourite position, on the floor before the blazing log fire. Dinner had been a largely silent and stilted affair and my bruised ego needed the balm of a spoken forgiveness. David offered none.

Exasperated by his continuing quiescence, I started up again, 'In fact, I expect you'd rather I wasn't here. Then you'd have a clear field.'

'And what's that supposed to mean?'

For a moment I hesitated. His eyes seemed haunted, filled with a terrible despair. Did he dislike me so much? Hastily, I dashed the thought from my mind and continued. 'You know very well what I mean. You and Marie . . .'

David leaped to his feet. 'For goodness' sake, Susan. Leave Marie out of it.'

Heat surged through my body. 'That's right. Protect her. I might as well go home to England,' I shouted vengefully, 'and get a divorce.'

A log settled on the fire, sending a blaze of sparks up the chimney and, in response to the flowing sap in the unburned portion of wood, the flames leaped upward, hot and red.

At that moment Rosita entered with the coffee-tray. David said nothing, watched her set it on the table then withdraw. Inwardly, I winced, aware that my voice had sounded childish and petulant. Why ever had I said that? Surely David would realise I hadn't meant it? Surely he wouldn't take me seriously?

David lifted the coffeepot and began to pour as if nothing had happened. Relief flooded through me.

Thank goodness! He obviously hadn't registered what I'd said.

My voice returned to normal. 'Perhaps it *would* be better if I went home on leave ahead of you, David.'

He nodded gravely, and passed me my coffee.

Sleep was a long time coming that night. Minutely dissecting each nuance of argument, I lay open-eyed in the darkened room. The incident was reminiscent of certain teenage events. My mother's voice echoed down through the years: *'That's right, Susan, cut off your nose to spite your face.'*

In my mind's eye, I saw myself as a teenager standing in the narrow hallway of our Ruislip home, deliberately whipping myself up into a tantrum in front of my parents, my tearstained face swollen and ugly. I'd returned home very late, with a boyfriend of whom my parents disapproved. A terrible row had ensued. Thwarted in having my own way, I'd shrieked at my parents: nasty, spiteful words, that had been torn from my lips without thought or expectation. It wasn't even as if I'd really liked the boy.

Then, and now with David, I seemed to be driven by some perverse desire to flout the wishes of those who were closest to me, even if it meant making a spectacle of myself.

It was just as well I had brought forward my departure from Quito. My absence would allow for the Schnapps Party scandal to die down. People had short memories. In no time there would be some other juicy morsel of gossip to chew over. It would give David breathing space too. We'd talked it through. David had pointed out that I could spend a month touring North America at the company's expense before I returned to England. By that time, I reflected, David's leave would have begun, and he would be free to join me.

In a happier frame of mind, I slept, at last.

'Señor! Señora!' It seemed only moments later that Rosita burst in upon us, her excitement causing her almost to drop the tea-tray she held before her.

We shot up in bed. 'What is it?' I cried in alarm.

She set down the tray, then turned to survey us, evidently well-pleased with our rapt attention. With hands clasped before her, she looked from one to the other.

'There's been a revolution, Señores.'

PART
THREE

9

Did No One Care For Me?

The train clattered over a junction then picked up speed.
The last lap of my journey home, from London to
Kingskerswell in Devon, was quite a come-down after the
frantic activity that had gone before it. Two weeks had
elapsed since I'd left Quito: two weeks of touring and
sightseeing in Mexico, Miami, Georgia and Montreal.
Even without David's company it had been an exciting
end to two years in Ecuador.

End? That seemed so final! Yet, even as the thought
occurred to me, I had an uncomfortable premonition that
nothing would ever be the same again.

I gazed from the train window and, as the first glimpses
of Devon's red soil came into view, my thoughts strayed
to my parents. I'd missed them more than I'd expected.
Dear Dad. Always so generous, though life had been less
than kind to him.

Childhood memories flooded my mind: days at Ruislip
when Dad was in the RAF. He had always been the one
to take up collections for retiring colleagues and organised
their farewell parties. On his own retirement, however,
there had been no party, no formal presentation of
retirement gifts. I could not forget how he'd arrived home
from his last days at work and held out a cheap cigarette
lighter for our inspection, a look of bewildered hurt on
his face, and how I'd longed to reach out, to touch him,
to erase the pain.

Since then, how often had I wanted to reach out in a

similar way to David? But, as in those early days of childhood, all traces of affection, of deep, enduring love, had been submerged under a sea of embarrassment.

The train drew into Newton Abbot station and, even as I searched the crowded platform for a first glimpse of my parents, my thoughts were drawn back to Quito and I was already impatient for David's return, for in him, I now realised, lay my security. And my happiness.

'Your hair's so short, Susan! How are you, darling? You look a little lost.'

My mother's voice, though fond, carried a note of disquiet; almost, though surely not, of accusation? I was aware, too, of a guarded quality in the welcome both she and Dad gave me. Although they could not possibly have any precise idea as to why I had come home ahead of David, it was obvious that they had their suspicions. Equally obvious was the fact that they were none too happy! An old, familiar, childlike guilt welled within me as we gathered up my luggage and made our way towards the ticket collector's booth.

Outside the station Dad hailed a taxi and, once the baggage was safe on board, we set off for Boundary Close.

'How was Montreal? And Miami? And what of Cousin Enid?' My mother's barrage of questions scarcely allowed me time to reply. She paused only to explain to the taxi-driver. 'My daughter's been jet-setting round Canada, America and Mexico, you know. And . . . where else was it, darling?'

Embarrassment flared inside me, only to be smothered by guilt. Why was she always so anxious to impress? I glanced at Dad who sat quietly in the corner. He looked older and seemed, somehow, more withdrawn.

My mother chattered on. 'The garden's looking especially lovely, Susan. You remember the family of ducks I wrote of to you? The ones that adopted us? Well, there was this one lone female that joined them. She was so tame! Came right up to the door to be fed. Then last week she took off with a cry of farewell, and disappeared into the evening sky.'

Much hand-waving and energetic gesticulation accompanied the story; a family trait for which both Mummy and I were often teased.

The taxi pulled up outside the bungalow. Leaving Daddy to sort out the luggage, Mummy drew me towards the gate, still talking. 'Your bedroom is exactly as you left it. Oh, it's so lovely to have you home again . . .'

By the end of the week I was beginning to doubt if it really was so 'lovely' to be home again. Two or three days later I well and truly regretted my impulsive decision to return early. In a word I was – bored. Time passed so slowly. Conversation was limited to the garden, television, the price of bacon. It was all so . . . dull. Whatever had possessed me to leave the pleasures of Quito – the parties, the dancing . . .

Keeping up the pretence with my parents that all was well between David and me was also proving to be a strain. I would have liked to be more open with them, and with my mother-in-law, but couldn't bring myself to worry them. Fielding awkward questions was a tiring business and I looked forward to David's return if only to bring to an end this sojourn at Kingskerswell. Much as I loved my parents, I couldn't help feeling that, as far as they were concerned, I'd reverted to being their 'little girl'. Reluctantly, I seemed to be conforming to that image.

One afternoon, they suggested a walk in the nearby village of Coffinswell, which was much admired by tourists for its quaint thatched cottages and well-tended gardens. Mummy particularly enjoyed spotting unusual flowers and plants.

'Just look at that splendid ceanothus. Did you ever see such a vivid blue.'

I nodded, vaguely, my mind elsewhere. There was The Linney where David and I had enjoyed our first dinner date together. Later, he and Dad had often come here with one another for a beer and a game of darts. As if reading my thoughts, my father glanced at me and asked, 'Remember the game of darts we played for old times' sake just before you and David set off for South America?'

I nodded, and smiled wryly. Little did Daddy know that that was the last time I'd played a decent game. Once in Ancon, it seemed I could hardly even aim straight.

'You had a natural eye for the board,' Dad continued. 'Do you and David still play?'

'Sometimes,' I replied briefly, recalling recent embarrassing occasions when my darts had missed the board completely. It had been worse still in Quito. But then that was probably the altitude.

'Did I tell you I had to get special recipe books when we moved?' I asked, anxious to change the subject. 'The mountain air was so thin you couldn't even boil an egg.' Dad dropped back as my mother caught me up, frowning uncomprehendingly. 'The more rarefied the atmosphere,' I explained, 'the higher the temperature needed to boil water.'

'Oh! I see,' she said, obviously trying to conceal the fact that she did not.

'Keep in! Car coming,' Dad called.

A Ford Zephyr swept around the corner. For a brief moment it was alongside us, as we pressed into the high banks of the narrow country lane. Then it was gone.

My heart jolted against my ribs as I stared after it. It could only have been in my line of vision for a few seconds, just long enough for me to register the occupants. A pretty, blonde-haired woman sat in the passenger seat, and behind her a little girl – obviously her daughter. The car was driven by a man – handsome and dark-haired.

'George!' I breathed.

'Someone you know?' Mummy asked, startling me.

'No! No, not really.' Evidently, neither she nor Daddy had recognised the motorist as my old boyfriend, George.

The hum of bees replaced the growl of the car's engine. In the hedgerow, a wren sounded a shrill note of territorial warning to a blackbird which landed nearby. The interloper seemed oblivious to the din erupting from the wren's tiny throat.

I swallowed as painful memories flooded my mind. Before I'd met David, I'd had a romance with George which I'd believed would lead to marriage. George, however, was a tremendous tease. 'If we got married, Susan, I suppose you'd be like all women and want to change me for the better, wouldn't you?' he'd say one day. My hopes would be raised, only to be dashed next day. 'Of course,' he'd counter, 'I couldn't ask *you* to be my wife because I'm only going to marry for money.'

When Janice moved into the area, my dreams were shattered. She was pretty, blonde and full of bright repartee, whereas I'd always been lacking in conversation, to the despair of my mother. Throughout my teenage years, her 'I hope you'll grow out of this my girl' had rung constantly in my ears. But the badinage which was so freely exchanged between Janice and George was out of my league and I'd known instinctively that I'd lose him.

Even so, foreknowledge had done nothing to negate the hurt of being jilted. Nor, whilst on the rebound, had dating with David been instant compensation. Later, the two of us had been invited to George and Janice's wedding, and I'd sat at the back of the church overwhelmed by a desire to be married also.

Now, although it had happened so long ago, there was an immediacy in the relation of my thought process. *That little girl in the back of the car could have been my daughter if I'd married George.*

An unwarranted sense of loss washed over me.

'Phone. It's for you. A *man*.' My mother's mouth pursed so tightly it resembled a poke-bag with knotted drawstrings.

I raised my eyebrows and hurried from the room, my heartbeat inexplicably erratic as I lifted the receiver to my ear.

'Hello?'

'Susan? It's Greg.'

'Greg!' The name was torn from my lips in an involuntary cry of amazement and delight. I glanced quickly at the lounge door, still partially open, and lowered my voice. 'Where are you?' I demanded urgently.

'Surprise, surprise! I'm in London. Alone. Any chance of your coming up?'

My heart raced. 'When?'

A time and date was arranged. It was difficult to appear unruffled when I returned to the company of my parents, and I was conscious of a strained atmosphere when I casually tried to invent an excuse for a jaunt to the capital later in the week.

I dressed carefully on the chosen day, my stomach knotted with nervous excitement. The journey seemed endless and the imminent reunion was rehearsed in my mind a thousand times.

Greg met me at Paddington Station. He hugged me long and hard before leading me, chattering excitedly, to a taxi. He'd reserved a table for lunch in the small, discreet hotel in which he was staying. It lent itself admirably to the romance of the occasion. His dear face was unaltered; his voice as melodious as ever. He, for his part, seemed delighted to see me. He held my hand across the table and gazed into my eyes as if we'd never been parted.

And later, as the afternoon unfolded, we shared the illusions of love.

There was plenty of time to cry on the journey home; to weep bitter tears of frustration and gentle tears of mourning. Greg had a wife. A family.

And I had – David: a husband with whom I'd lost

touch, a lover whose advances I'd spurned but, nevertheless, a friend whose companionship I missed.

Later, back at my parents' home, I lay in the pretty chintzy bedroom of my girlhood and acknowledged, perhaps for the first time, the reality of the situation. I thought back to the time in Ancon when my period had been late. I'd never told David of the false alarm. Never admitted to my yearning for a baby. There had been so little in the way of communication between us. I knew, too, that the shame I felt for my naked body – and his – had further separated us.

Now, with the moon shining brightly between the lilac curtains at my little dormer window, I was full of hopeful anticipation. I felt sure that my romantic interlude with Greg in London, brief though it was, had liberated me of inhibition. In consequence, I now felt I had something of worth to offer David and, armed with this assurance, I was resolved that, on his return, a new level of communication, love and tenderness would exist between us. We would talk as never before; exchange confidences; hear each other's points of view.

I was no longer the shy young bride whom David had wooed and cosseted. Nor was I the strident, disenchanted malcontent I'd been in Quito, when I'd walked out on all that mattered in my life. In a few, brief hours with Greg I'd grown up. I knew what it was to love, to give of one's all. Selflessly. Unstintingly. Or so I thought. Only later, in God's grace, would I see that adultery could never be a part of his will, nor of his selfless love.

But I knew none of this. Was David missing me, I wondered – if for no other reason, than for my culinary skills, and acknowledged prowess as a hostess? I was lonely for an arm around me and longed to know if he cared. What news would there be of Goliat? My dear dog . . . he was the child I had never had . . . My thoughts whirled, steadied, settled. I drifted, at last, into sleep; deep, peaceful sleep, where, bright lit by mellow sunshine, and fanned with balmy, sweet-scented breezes, a path lay clearly before me. Unerringly, I set my foot upon it . . .

'There's a letter for you, Susan. Looks as if it's from David.' Mummy passed the blue envelope and poured my breakfast tea.

I scanned the brief note, written in David's small, neat hand. 'He'll be back on Thursday.'

Greatly excited, I began to outline plans.

I would hire a car, drive Mrs James to Heathrow to collect David, then the three of us would spend a few days with his brother and sister-in-law.

Mrs James was a motherly woman, refined, but broadminded – the result of having had two lively sons and a daughter. We had always had a good relationship, and chatted merrily together during the journey up to London.

There was great excitement when we met up with Ian and Sandra in Arrivals. David had been expected to come in on the flight from Ecuador, so we were thrown into confusion when, for some unknown reason, he appeared at a different gate – that of the SAS (Scandinavian Airline System) flight from Denmark. My heart pounded when he came in sight. I anticipated a fond reunion. Next moment my spirits plummeted. David looked so serious as he approached the concourse where we waited. Tanned and healthy as he strode towards us, he seemed, nevertheless, to be tired and withdrawn – almost distant.

'Hi, David!' Ian raised a hand in salute to the luggage-laden figure. With much back slapping and jocularity the two brothers greeted one another.

'Here, this is for you.' David produced a huge sombrero and clapped it on Ian's head. 'And this.' He unrolled a large, skin rug and offered it to Sandra. 'For the two of you.'

I couldn't help wondering what on earth they would do with it and, from the look on their faces, it would seem that the same thought had also occurred to Ian and

Sandra. So far David had barely looked in my direction but since it had been two years since the brothers had met, I felt I must be patient. There would be time enough for us to talk later. Even so, it was hard to restrain myself.

At last we were out from the Terminal building and Mrs James headed off with Ian and Sandra to their car. For the first time in a month David and I were alone. I felt suddenly shy.

David loaded the luggage into the boot of the car, while I looked on, searching surreptitiously for his gift to me. There seemed to be none. I lowered my eyelids to hide my disappointment and, embarrassed by my juvenile reaction, rummaged in my handbag for nothing in particular.

'Why did you have to change your flight?' I asked.

He slammed down the lid of the boot. 'Oh . . . tell you later. Are you driving?'

In deference to David's jet-lag, I took the wheel and in no time we had left the airport behind and were on the M4 heading for London. He seemed quietly bemused by the volume of traffic in contrast to that of Ecuador, and spent a good deal of time staring through the side window.

I seemed to be doing all the talking. 'How are Rosita and Rosario and dear Goliat? Oh, David! I'm longing to see them all again, especially Goliat. I've missed him terribly.'

David did not respond. I glanced quickly at him before turning my attention back to the road. Was it my imagination or was there a guarded look about him? Almost a haunted appearance? From the corner of my eye I could see his face averted as he continued to gaze out of the window. His hands twisted together. Then he raised a fist to his mouth and coughed, a habitual nervous trait. Abruptly he broke the silence.

'Susan. It's over. I'm going to marry Marie. I don't want you to return to Ecuador.'

The car swerved as I gripped the steering wheel. From

behind, a car horn blared and, moments later, a Jaguar appeared, its passenger glaring angrily as it shot past. Perspiration broke out on the palms of my hands, and, involuntarily, I braked.

Over to the right I could see the red aviation-warning lights flashing from the roof of Brent Towers. That meant we must be approaching the outskirts of London already. On our way to Ian and Sandra's. Ian and Sandra! Oh, goodness! How could we face them? What would they think? This was unreal.

'But I *have* to come back.' My voice sounded unnaturally high. I cleared my throat. 'I have to see Goliat. All my belongings. It's my home, David.'

'I'm sorry, Susan,' he said again. 'It's over.'

Somehow we arrived at the home of my brother-in-law and, once in the comparative sanctuary of the bedroom, I hoped we might resolve this nightmarish situation.

'David. Please . . .' I reached out and put my arms around the husband whom I had so recently resolved to cherish. Wordlessly he pushed me away.

'You can't do this . . .' A note of fear, of hysteria, rose in my voice.

'I'm sorry, Susan. What's done is done.'

'How long? How long has it been going on?'

David spread his hands in the air, a graphic gesture of the futility of my question. 'What does it matter now?' he said.

I gasped. 'I've just realised – the two of you met when Marie and Steve were down in Ancon on holiday. That means you were probably seeing her every time you went to Head Office in Quito? It must have been lovely for both of you when we moved up there – so much more opportunity . . .'

David busied himself with unzipping his suitcase.

'And what about the times when I tried to ring Marie, then your office . . . All I got was the engaged tone. I suppose the two of you were engrossed in cosy little chats?' A telltale flush began above David's collar. Relentlessly, I pressed on. 'And I suppose the reason you came in on a different flight is because you and Marie had been off on holiday together?'

David hunched on the edge of the bed, his hands covering his face.

'Oh, you may well look sorry for yourself. But what of me?' I demanded.

Slowly he raised his head. For a long moment he stared, his eyes narrowed. 'Yes. Marie and I were in Denmark together. But what of you and Greg? All the years you've flaunted him.' His voice was cold. 'I told you you'd be sorry some day.'

I crumpled. Tears ran unchecked down my cheeks. The stiffness went from my body, and my hands, which had been clenched, now hung limp and heavy by my side.

'David, I'm a different person now. Being with Greg has helped me to see how . . .' I searched for the right words.

David shook his head. 'Look. I've told you I'm sorry, Susan. What more can I say?'

There *was* nothing to be said, nothing of substance, nothing that could appease. All that was spoken in that upstairs bedroom, the bitter words, the tears, the subdued shouting . . . They made no difference. David's face was hard and resigned.

'We'd better go down. They'll be wondering . . .' He moved to the door.

He was right. How were we going to face everyone, to pretend that all was well? I squared my shoulders, dabbed at my reddened eyes, and prepared to act out the lie. All around me, my world was disintegrating. Yet perhaps, even now, there was hope? Perhaps even at this stage David would change his mind? Together, yet apart, we went downstairs.

Over the next few days, it was hard to keep my emotions hidden, to conceal tears, to prevent others hearing our raised voices when we were alone in our room. Yet somehow, we succeeded. Since it was expected, we still shared the double bed. The formality of our discussions seemed incongruous in the light of such enforced intimacy.

'I feel we should tell our parents simultaneously, Susan. Do you agree?'

Like partners in business, we debated the principles and strategies before us. Divorce was not mentioned at this juncture, and as long as the matter was kept between the two of us I felt that there was hope. I still believed that David would change his mind, though it was becoming increasingly obvious that we had nothing of value to say to one another. By the time we left Ian and Sandra's, nothing had been resolved.

After our arrival in Torquay, we went straight to Mrs James' home, where, once again, we were expected to share a double bed.

'This is becoming intolerable,' David said. 'We must tell our families.'

And so, one afternoon, he took his mother to one side, whilst I drove over to Kingskerswell to break the news to my parents.

'I'm not going back to Ecuador with David,' I said simply. 'Our marriage is over.'

For a moment my mother stared, too shocked to speak. Then she burst out, 'I knew there was something wrong. You should never have left him on his own, Susan.' She sniffed her disapproval. 'Gallivanting all over America, indeed!'

Dad rose, laboriously, to his feet and leaned against the mantelpiece. 'Your mother's right, Susan. A woman belongs with her husband.'

'Have you thought of what your wedding cost us? Your father's not a wealthy man. There's only his pension. We had to make considerable sacrifices . . .'

My mother tailed off as I stared in disbelief. Then taking my hand in hers, she softened her tone to one of camaraderie. 'Now no more of this nonsense, dear. You just see that you patch things up between you. Buy yourself a new frock, and put on some perfume. A man likes his wife to look nice.'

'I can't patch things up, Mummy. He wants to marry someone else. A friend, actually.'

Mummy withdrew her hand. 'And there's someone else in your life, isn't there?' Blatant accusation filled her voice.

'No.' I lied.

'What about that man who rang the other day. I'm no fool, Susan. What's his name?'

'Greg? No. There's nothing in that. He's a married man.'

'And you're a married woman. Just see that you behave like one.' She rose from the settee, and marched to the door. 'I'm going to attend to supper now.' The subject was dismissed.

'I suppose I'd better take the hire-car back to the garage.' I, too, rose to leave the room, fumbling in my handbag for the keys.

Dad walked with me to the garden gate, past the cherry tree, like so many times of old.

'We thought there was something wrong when you arrived back ahead of David,' he said stiffly. 'What you have done to your mother and me, Susan, is worse than our first daughter dying.'

I ignored the hurt in my Dad's face and climbed into the Hillman Hunter hire-car, slammed the door behind me and started the engine. I raced up the road with tears smarting in my eyes and Dad's words ringing in my ears. Terrible words. Wounding words. Did no one care for *me?*

'*I'll make them care.*' I shouted aloud, and the tears spilled over, blinding my vision.

I could hardly see but I wrenched the wheel to one side and pushed the accelerator to the floor. The engine note climbed. The car leaped forward. I guided it as best I could. Straight for the stone parapet of Scotts Bridge. Closer and closer it loomed. Faster and faster. Larger and larger.

'I'll show them!' I cried. 'I'll make them care.'

10

A Frankfurt Affair

Traffic was persistently heavy on the Newton Road. Sole route in and out of Torquay, it was a potential death trap as frustrated motorists vied for position on the single carriageway. The sense of impotence increased in direct proportion to commuter density so that, during the Season, when carloads of holidaymakers streamed into the popular English Riviera resort, blood pressure soared and tempers frayed.

On that particular August day I knew a more peculiar impuissance. *En route* to return the hire-car to Quay Garage, I'd been filled with an urge to bring an end to my pain. But it seemed that no matter what I attempted to do, I was confronted with my own inadequacy. The tears I'd shed earlier had dried in stiff, salty rills on my cheeks and, conscious only of having failed again, I was numbed by my sense of defeat. Miserably, I voiced my disappointment aloud.

'Can't even make a good job of killing yourself!'

Scotts Bridge spanned the railway line and twisted the road into a sharp S bend. Though I'd ploughed straight at the wall of the bridge, foot to the floor, my hands gripping the steering wheel with steely determination, the car had merely glanced off the barrier and continued round the corner virtually unscathed. Shaking with fright, I'd pulled in to the side of the road and, for a few minutes, had been unable to move. When I'd calmed down, I'd walked round to the nearside to see what

damage had been done; but even close scrutiny revealed
no more than a slight dent – barely worth mentioning
to the hire-garage.

My vain attempt at suicide had made me feel decidedly
foolish and I resolved to say nothing to David or the rest
of the family. Once at the garage, I paid the bill, handed
in the car keys, and set off to walk the half mile or so
back to my mother-in-law's secluded semi, mentally
rehearsing my strategy to her reaction, and wondering
how she had responded to the news of our impending
divorce. Would she be shocked, I wondered; fearful of
scandal; disappointed? Would she, like my parents, turn
hurt into venom?

In some trepidation I opened the gate, walked up the
path, and let myself into the house. Closing the front door
quietly behind me, I stood, for a moment, in the hall,
straining to pick up any hint of an altercation. I need not
have worried. There was none.

David was not in evidence, but Mrs James was seated
at a small desk in the corner of the room when I came
into the lounge. She raised her head, though she did not
meet my eye, but fixed her gaze instead at some point
beyond my left shoulder.

'Did you get the car back alright?' She didn't wait for
a reply, but continued, 'There's tea in the pot, if you'd
like some.'

In one swift movement she rose from her chair,
indicated the tray and, brushing past me, stepped across
the hall to the kitchen. I stared after her, then, with
shaking hands, turned to pour myself tea.

The silence was unnerving. No mention was made,
throughout the evening, of the news which David had
broken to his mother. To a casual observer the whole
ghastly nightmare might never have happened, but my
sensitive eye picked up what even David missed. In one
respect only had Mrs James manifested her feelings.

Framed family photographs stood on every surface of
the large, chintzy lounge – on side-tables, mantelpiece,

inglenook and dresser, in carefully arranged disorder. Of every shape and size they jostled for attention: a declaration of comfortable kinship and memorabilia. But no longer for me.

Each and every photograph which contained an image of myself had been removed. It was as if I had never existed.

'I don't understand,' I cried when David and I were alone in the bedroom we were still expected to share. 'Does she hate me? Why can't anyone see my side? You're the one who wants this divorce, not me.'

David said nothing.

His parents had divorced when he was in his teens. Could his mother be reliving the past? Had old wounds been re-opened in her? And was she now driven by an unreasoning need to deny *my* pain, and thence her own? If so, it was equally beyond *me* to bind up the rejection and isolation which were gaping sores in my side. A great dragging weight of misery bore down on me.

'She's hurt,' David said, at last. 'It's just her way of coping.' He sat on the side of the bed, his body stooped and his shoulders sagging.

It seemed that everyone was hurting and that divorce was a shameful business all round. The family might choose to ignore reality but I could not go on with the charade.

'I'm going to have to get away.' I searched David's face for some inkling of comprehension. 'Perhaps London? I could get a job up there. I can't stay here.'

Even as I spoke the words, a glimmer of hope lit within me. Suddenly, the anonymity of life in the capital appealed to me. I could make a new start there, though I found the prospect both alarming and exciting. *Perhaps David will change his mind?* I thought. *Or I might meet somebody new.*

I turned away, lifted the curtain at the window and gazed out to the road. Small halos of light radiated from each street lamp, holding at bay the black night which pressed upon them. I'd told David, in Quito, that my life was meaningless, though I had no idea how; nor why I had said it. I had thought, at the time, that I had all I needed – and that it would last for ever.

The words of Jim Elliot, one of the five missionaries murdered by the Aucu Indians, returned to me. '*He is no fool who gives what he cannot keep, to save what he'll never lose.*' I had no real understanding of their meaning. Nor could I comprehend that as long as I was engrossed in the pursuit of all I could see, the unseen would mean nothing to me. So conformed was I to the world that, unbeknown to me, I was hiding from reality and was, therefore, unable to appreciate that I was totally absorbed in myself – though the absorption gave me no joy.

David roused himself. 'London? Sounds like a good idea, Susan.' He hesitated. 'I could drive you up; see you settled somewhere. That is – if you'd like me to?'

I nodded, dropped the curtain and turned back to the bedroom. It seemed suddenly ill-lit and cold.

The hotel was small and shabby.

'It's only for the first night, Susan. You'll find something more suitable later.' Shame-faced, David took the key from the male clerk at reception, whose bored expression seemed dismissive of there ever being anything 'more suitable' for someone like myself.

David and I mounted the gloomy staircase and, three floors up, he inserted a key in one of the doors, throwing it wide to reveal a small sparsely furnished room. A dressing table, brown varnish dulled with age and misuse, stood before the window. A scratched wardrobe, of mean proportions, a straight-backed chair and a bed were the only other items of furniture.

The bed looked hard and uninviting, its white cotton counterpane holed and dingy. I perched on its edge and absent-mindedly pulled at the frayed threads, still unable to piece together with any degree of reality the events which had brought me here. As if in a dream I stared at the wall; hideous brown wallpaper, once heavily embossed though now faded and worn, pressed in upon my tired senses.

David deposited my luggage on the linoleum-covered floor where it stood forlornly on a cotton rug of indiscriminate hue. The solitary, brown leather valise and red vanity case looked too small and insignificant to be the sum total of my possessions. With a flash of recall I contrasted all that I'd left behind in Quito – the clean, sweet, mountain air, sunshine and laughter, wealth, servants and friends with this – dump.

A rush of tears started to my eyes, and in an instant I was overwhelmed, my body heaving in a great expulsion of loss and grief. On and on I cried, desperate in my attempt to expunge the spectre of a future alone; a future in which the support of all whom I had held most dear had been wrested, violently, from beneath my feet as surely as the shelving sands of Ancon's beach.

David turned to go. 'Don't cry, darling.'

The words were sweet to my ears – the kindest remark he had made to me in a long time. Then he was gone, effectively pre-empting any protracted farewells.

Traffic noise rose from the street below, a dull, muted roar, distant, and isolating. The brown walls converged upon me and I shuddered, involuntarily.

Secretarial employment, fortunately, was not difficult to obtain and soon I found myself a job with a firm of architects in Knightsbridge: Michael Lyall Associates. Accommodation was another matter! For a week I scoured the city in search of a flat, returning fatigued and depressed at the end of each long, weary day, to the cramped and ugly little hotel room.

Every evening, jostled in the crowded confines of a commuter tube, I studied the newspapers. One evening, a particular advertisement seemed to stand out from the rest. The King's Court Hotel, Bayswater, offered a double

room with bathroom, plus breakfast. It seemed too good
an opportunity to be missed.

As soon as was feasible I inspected the premises,
packed up my meagre luggage and checked out of my
hotel room. But if I was hopeful of The King's Court being
my Utopia, I was soon disillusioned. That same sense of
rejection and pain which had been my bed-fellow
throughout my sojourn in London followed me into what
I soon came to think of as Heartbreak Hotel.

The Manager was a dark and greasy character who
leered at me as he handed me the key of my room.
Definitely someone to be avoided, I decided, but, a few days
later, lonely and in need of company, I foolishly accepted
his invitation to attend one of his oft-mentioned cocktail
parties. It didn't take me long to discover that I was the
only guest and, making a rapid exit, I renewed my resolve
to avoid him at all cost.

The days stretched before me, a great yawning abyss
of social celibacy. Sorrowfully, I reflected on my changed
circumstances. I, who had regularly danced till dawn,
now dreaded the prospect of a desolate weekend alone.
The hours between leaving the office on a Friday evening
and resuming work on Monday morning accentuated,
like nothing else, the utter emptiness of my life.

It was in just such a frame of mind that I entered the
breakfast room one Saturday morning. A great crowd of
people seemed to have converged upon the hotel, and
there wasn't one vacant table. Suddenly, one of two
American Airmen, who were seated at a small table by
the window, stepped forward and, pulling out a chair,
indicated that I was welcome to join them. Murmuring
some expression of gratitude I seated myself.

'Hi! My name's Brill; Sergeant Tom Brill, and this is
Bud.' My knight errant smiled disarmingly as he lowered
his lanky frame on to the seat beside me.

They were, he told me during the course of breakfast,
stationed at Wiesbaden, headquarters for the entire
United States Air Force in Europe. Tom's conversation

continued at an easy pace and, lifted from the despondency which had dogged me, I responded in kind.

And so began a friendship which was to plunge me briefly into a happiness as fleeting and transient as the lifespan of the Ancon butterflies which I had once so loved and admired. Tom was to introduce me to an entirely new world. Or was it? Though indiscernible to me at the time, it was, at its foundation, as unstable as any I had ever known. Once more – despite, or perhaps because of, pain and rejection in the past – I mistakenly believed that romance would bring me the elusive satisfaction that I craved.

'Care to visit Madame Tussaud's with me?' Tom asked on the first Sunday morning after breakfast. 'I guess there's not a lot else to do on a day like this.' He indicated the steady downpour which rendered the view outside a uniform grey. 'At least we'd be dry.'

'I'd love to,' I said with heartfelt relief. 'To be perfectly honest, I was dreading another day alone in my room.'

Tom was an amusing and attentive escort, empathetic of my hurt, since his marriage too, he told me, had broken down. By the time we arrived at Baker Street and had run through the rain to Madame Tussaud's, we had shared confidences more reminiscent of old friends than new acquaintances, and a warm rapport had grown between us. Determined to make the most of our day together, we saw everything. Even the most gruesome scene in the Chamber of Horrors failed to put a damper on the general air of high-spirits which prevailed between us. It was good to laugh. I felt, when I looked back over the past few weeks since my arrival in London, that I'd almost forgotten how.

'Here, give me your umbrella,' Tom said when we emerged from the building later in the day and walked up the road to stand beneath the canopy of The Planetarium in the hopes of hailing a taxi.

Prancing on the pavement's edge, Tom twirled the umbrella and sang Gene Kelly's famous song. Tears of

laughter ran from my eyes as I watched his antics. It was
the best medicine I could have received!

Tom had served in Vietnam, and shocked me with
stories of that terrible war. He told me of the drug-abuse
of ordinary young men who had been called to fight in
the cause of idealism but whose experiences were of terror
and revulsion. 'The use of hallucinogens and sometimes
amphetamines gives them a false sense of reality which
helps them cope with the horrors of jungle warfare,' Tom
explained, soberly.

'But aren't they just running away and ruining their
own lives?' I asked.

'Oh, yeah. But most forms of escapism tend to do that,
don't they?'

I was to recall those words in weeks to come.

Through Tom, Bud, and another friend, Carl, I became
reacquainted with the area of my childhood. Frequent
trips to the lively clubhouse at the US Air Force Base in
Ruislip became an established part of our social routine.
I was proud of my handsome escorts, resplendent in their
uniforms. Constant male attention brought out in me a
tremendous flair for comedy which restored my self-
confidence in a way that I would not have believed
possible.

As his days of leave in London became ever more
frequent, Tom and I grew increasingly fond of one
another. It seemed natural that our relationship should
blossom into physical fulfilment. If I had any pangs of
conscience they were quickly appeased by the thought
that I was mistress of my own destiny, and could make
my own rules.

Or so it seemed at the time. Now, I realise that
following the perfect Law of Christ and his Truth sets men
free – free to make choices – whether to serve Christ
with the help of the Holy Spirit, or to go their own way.
As I did in London.

One evening, I was sitting alone in the hotel bar when

an attractive, well-spoken girl on the next bar stool leaned towards me.

'May I buy you a drink?'

Gratefully, I accepted. Introductions were effected, and we moved across the room to a small table. There, Sheila explained that she worked for Shell USA, and was in London for only a short stay. 'It's a bit lonely on your own, and I was wondering if you'd keep me company?' she asked. 'Perhaps we could share a meal together in my hotel, then go on to the cinema?'

I was impressed with her forthright manner and warm friendliness, even more impressed when I discovered that the hotel in question was no less that The Inn On The Park, Park Lane.

'I'd be delighted,' I said, flattered that she should have singled me out.

We arranged to meet later when we had showered and changed and, in due course, a chauffeur-driven car arrived to convey me to her hotel.

Sheila's kindness was overwhelming; she would allow me to pay for nothing. Shell was a most generous employer, she told me, allowing her to put everything on her company expense account. For some days we enjoyed trips to the theatre and the cinema, took sumptuous meals in her suite at the hotel, and generally lived at a level of elegance and ease which I had taken for granted in South America, but which had been so lacking since my return to the UK.

Each morning, the chauffeur-driven car arrived to take me to and from work, and each evening I was transported to meet my new-found friend. Sometimes Sheila, herself, would be *en route* to Shell Headquarters when I was picked up from work. 'I have to drop off some files,' she'd explain, 'so it's no problem to collect you.'

'*It's so wonderful to have found this truly nice friend,*' I wrote happily to my parents. '*We get on so well, and Tom has met her and likes her too.*'

I was working in Piccadilly as a temp. when the bubble

burst. It only took a phone call. Sheila's voice came evenly down the line. 'There's a Shell Executive Jet going to Wiesbaden this weekend. Would you like to take advantage of a cheap trip? The fare would only be seventy-five pounds, and you could spend some time with Tom.'

I could hardly believe such a marvellous offer. Naturally, they needed my passport for insurance purposes. And since, for some strange reason, I had taken to carrying the document around in my handbag, it was arranged that Sheila would call first at my office to collect it.

Conscious of the proximity of my superiors, I held the receiver close to my mouth and spoke softly, 'Look, I can't leave the premises myself, would it be too much to ask you to collect the money direct from my bank? I'm sure there'd be no problem. I could telephone to endorse you as my agent.'

Within the hour, all was arranged and Sheila breezed into the office, collected the passport and left, with a comment inviting me to a New Year's Eve party at her hotel.

That evening I got myself ready in good time so that I could ring Tom. He was as thrilled as I at the prospect of a few days together and promptly made plans for our mini-vacation. My excitement mounted as he outlined our itinerary.

After some moments I glanced at my wristwatch. 'Tom, I'll have to go. Sheila's chauffeur will be here any moment.' Reluctantly, I rang off and went downstairs to wait in the bar.

The limo had always been punctual. This evening was an exception. Repeatedly I consulted my watch. Eight o'clock came and went; then nine. I became increasingly anxious. Had I made some mistake?

Suddenly, I felt quite ill as everything began to fall into place. This 'very nice' girl was not all I had taken her to be. There could be no other explanation . . . the huge expense account, my money and passport, her non-appearance this evening. Unwillingly, I began to wonder if I'd been duped.

At nine-thirty I rang The Inn On The Park. Contrary to the usual courteous response to my request to be connected to Sheila's room, I was immediately put through to the Manager. The angry suspicion in his voice further confirmed my growing sense of hurt and rejection. If there'd been any lingering doubt in my mind of my friend's duplicity, it was surely confounded.

Bit by bit, I learned of the deception. Sheila's room, he told me, had been found empty except for a small, broken vanity case. Furthermore, she had left the hotel without settling her account. As he went on to tell me of the unpaid bills for theatre, meals, cinema, and, of course, the hotel chauffeur service, my heart pounded with fear as well as hurt. I began to cry hysterically, realising that I would be seen as an accomplice to the fraud.

Eventually, when I'd heard all there was to hear, I put the phone down and fell upon my bed. I wanted to die. Was there no end to the hurt I was expected to endure? Could I believe in no one? With that thought came the notion that Tom, too, must be involved. I felt full of hate for this world. Nobody cared for me. No one was trustworthy. Not even Tom.

Later, at the Police Station, I searched through endless books of photographs of suspects and the CID man explained to me kindly: 'She was a professional criminal. It's easy to be fooled by such people.'

Yes, I thought, mistrust of Tom growing by the minute. There could be no doubt. He was Sheila's accomplice; or she his; it made little difference. Between the two of them they had set me up. How Tom must have laughed at my naivety. I was sickened with the memory of how easily I'd fallen into bed with him. Poor little rich girl, he must have thought, knowing of my propensity for the trappings of wealth and pleasure. And how eagerly I'd responded to all that he'd offered – he and Sheila together. Together? Were they together in more than the con? Could they be lovers? With the thought came pain of a new intensity.

As soon as I returned from the Police Station, I flew up the stairs of the hotel, threw myself on the bed and gave in to a prolonged bout of weeping.

The sudden shrill of the telephone startled me. Composing myself as well as I could, I lifted the receiver to my ear.

'Hello?' It was Tom. 'Susan! What's happened? I've checked out every flight into Frankfurt, and I've been calling you for hours. I've been real worried. You haven't gotten into any trouble, have you?'

With some hesitation, I filled him in on events. He was clearly not a party to the crime, and my relief was great. His exclamations of horror in response to the details I unfolded, further confirmed his innocence. 'So there's no flight, no money and no passport,' I finished.

'No problem.' Firmly, Tom took control. 'Susan, you get yourself down to Petty France for a duplicate passport. I'm gonna wire you the money for your fare, and you get yourself out here as fast as you can. What you're in need of, my girl, is a little TLC.'

'Why don't you stay on in Germany?' Tom reached across the table in the small, warm, restaurant, took my hand in his and traced the creases on my palm with his forefinger.

I smiled, then looked out across the Rhine, thinking of the pleasures these few days had brought my way: the excellence of German food and wine; the grandeur of scenery. We'd been sightseeing, heard of history and legend – of Lorelei, a rock with a remarkable echo, where, it's said, a maiden, who drowned herself because of an inconstant lover, became a siren luring sailors to their doom with her song.

Tom had been caring and considerate, showing in every

way possible his fondness for me. Now our holiday was drawing to a close I dreaded my return to London. 'I feel so safe here, with you,' I'd told him.

As if reading my thoughts Tom continued, persuasively: 'You could find work here. No problem. What d'you say?'

Could his suggestion become a reality? Was it feasible?

His confidence was infectious. Next day, as soon as we returned to Frankfurt, we began to explore the possibilities.

'There's an opening in the Personnel Department at US Headquarters,' Tom told me over the telephone. 'Can you get down here at the double to interview?'

The prospect excited me. So many handsome men in their handsome uniforms! I duly presented myself at the Base.

'We'd like you to take a little typing test, if you please ma'am.'

No problem, I thought, borrowing Tom's favourite phrase.

I seated myself before the typewriter. It was bang up to date; the most modern and advanced piece of technology I'd ever encountered in my years as a secretary. Confidently, I began.

Half an hour later, my confidence had evaporated. The wastepaper basket was evidence of my mounting sense of frustration. My fingers were utterly uncoordinated and I'd torn sheet after sheet of mumbo-jumbo from the platen of the machine, scrumpled them vigorously in my hand and ejected them into the bin.

'I'm so sorry,' I apologised. 'I don't know what's the matter with me. I don't seem to be able to hit any of the keys correctly.'

'Don't worry.' The head of Department smiled warmly. 'You're probably a little nervous. Sure, you'll be OK when you're not pressurised.'

With utter amazement, it dawned upon me that this kindly assurance constituted an offer. The job was mine!

Back in Tom's office, I rapidly communicated my excitement. 'Tom! I've got the job. I can stay on in Germany. We'll be together.'

'Yippee!' With typical Yankee abandon, he grabbed me in his arms, lifted me from the floor and twirled me around and around.

Tom had asked a young corporal to take me back to my overnight hotel. 'This is Davis. He'll look after you, and I'll call you later.'

Tom handed me into the car, and we set off down the autobahn, Davis casually pointing out the sights with just a touch of insolence that hinted that, perhaps, he did not quite approve of me, for some reason. At the approach of the city, we passed an ugly apartment block, incongruously situated in what was obviously a reasonably affluent district. Uncompromisingly functional, it stood gaunt and darkened by age, like a lone tooth in the gums of a hag. No attempt had been made to soften the severe building lines by even so much as a tree or window box and I marvelled at the difference in culture between this place and home, recalling the profusion of potted plants on my own window-sill.

'Oh, I'm sorry? You were saying?' Davis was pointing towards the apartments and, engrossed in my own thoughts, I'd missed his last sentence.

Traffic had slowed down considerably now that we were nearing the metropolis. Nevertheless, we were still proceeding at a steady pace and the apartment block was no longer in sight. Davis jabbed a thumb over his shoulder to indicate the subject matter of his latest 'tour guide info'. Expectantly, I awaited his explanation. It came at precisely the moment we stopped for the lights.

'I was jes' pointin' out the condominium where Serg'n Brill and his wife live, ma'am.'

As if in a dream I heard the Deep Southern twang; saw Davis' grinning face. Red . . . Green . . . In slow motion the lights changed. Ahead of us and to one side, a souped-up French Citroen reared gracefully on its hindquarters, tyres silently smoking on the tarmac and, still with a ponderous, languid movement, leaped forward like a jaguar intent on devouring its prey. I could almost see the rippling muscles . . .

I felt the blood drain from my cheeks. My heartbeat seemed unnaturally loud, a rising volume of sound that boomed in my head. Something lay heavy and bilious on my stomach. Davis seemed not to notice and, grinning, chattered on and on . . . and on . . .

'I just can't believe it,' I told Tom when he telephoned. 'You always led me to believe you were divorced. How could you make such a fool of me?' My voice was stiff with the effort of holding my tears in check.

'Honey, I never meant to hurt you. Let me come see you. I can explain.'

But I'd wanted none of his explanation. I was through with men. Cheated and lied to, deceived and deluded, I would no longer be a pawn to every advancing knight. Would I never learn?

I took the first available flight out of Frankfurt and was back in London before midnight.

11

Heartbreak Hotel

And then there was Gerry!

Gerry Wyndham was a fellow-resident of King's Court Hotel, with whom I had frequently passed the time of day whenever we'd met on the stairs. Sandy haired, with fair complexion and of only average height and build, he was quite unlike my vision of the Ideal Man. Nevertheless, he was good company, and after we discovered a mutual interest in cinema we soon became firm friends.

But, I told myself, *I'm not about to step into any further foolish relationships.*

Gerry gave the King's Court its nickname. 'Just look around you,' he urged me. 'I reckon every resident in this hotel is nursing some sort of secret heartache. Why else would they be here? They're all loners, and it's pretty obvious that there's some background of broken relationships. This place should be renamed after Elvis Presley's song: Heartbreak Hotel.'

As if to confirm that concept, my next blow came shortly afterwards. The month was April; London parks were taking on their spring beauty and, as I strolled beside the Serpentine in Hyde Park and admired the dazzling display of daffodils, I realised that I had grown to love the capital. It was a shock, therefore, to return home to the hotel, one afternoon, to find a letter from the management requesting me to vacate my room. The rental was to be tripled in expectation of an influx of spring visitors and I was required to move out by the end of the week.

My immediate response was to share the news with Gerry, and I flew up the stairs to his room, fluttering the letter before him. 'Have you seen this?' I demanded in consternation.

'I've had one too,' he said, ushering me in.

'I just don't know what to do.' I sank on to a chair while Gerry perched on the edge of the bed. 'I've looked at flats from time to time, though only half-heartedly, and there really doesn't seem to be anything suitable within my budget.'

'I know what you mean. London's not easy on a single person. But I'm sure something will turn up. Try not to worry, Susan.'

But worry I did! No wonder I lost sleep during the next few nights. Inwardly, I still hankered after the elegance and affluence of Quito's suburbs, a lovely house and servants, space, harmony and tranquillity. The ideals embodied in those memories influenced the way in which I viewed London properties, and I was eventually forced to the conclusion that reality fell far short of my standards! As the day approached on which I was to vacate I despaired of ever finding a new home.

Then one evening on my return from work, Gerry came up with an idea.

'Here, take this. You look as if you're in need of a drink.' He pushed a Dubonnet and soda across the bar table to me and watched silently whilst I drank. I leaned back and closed my eyes, struggling to shake off an overwhelming fatigue – the culmination of a full day's work followed by hours of flat-hunting.

'Now don't shout me down, Susan,' Gerry began tentatively. 'What I'm about to suggest may sound rather forward but no ulterior motive is intended.' He paused long enough to take a quick drink from his own glass, then continued in a rush, 'It's just that I feel it would make sense to pool our resources and look for a place that we could share rather than trying to find separate pads. Two-roomed flats are much easier to come by than singles, and you know what they say about two living as cheaply as one.' He studied my face anxiously then, as my enthusiasm became apparent, he gradually relaxed.

'Oh, Gerry, you are brilliant. That sounds absolutely wonderful. I've seen some awful dumps for one. We could find something really nice for the two of us.'

The following day Gerry indicated a tiny advertisement in the evening paper.

'Chelsea!' I exclaimed.

Not only was the little basement flat in that most desirable of suburbs, it was actually just off the lively and fashionable Kings Road. We couldn't sign the Tenancy Agreement fast enough! Occupation also entitled us to a key to a neat little park, set aside for the exclusive use of residents. It was easy to kid myself that I was Someone again.

The Kings Road was a colourful and trendy environment with numerous restaurants and bistros, buskers playing on every street corner and easy access to the West End. On the far side of the road was Chelsea Hospital within whose grounds could be seen the red-uniformed veterans of the First World War. I would often pass the time of day with them, telling them of my father's exploits, and thinking, wistfully, how much he would enjoy their company. However, I couldn't imagine Daddy approving of my current domestic arrangement, despite the contentment it brought me.

'Gerry, this flat – moving in with you – it's the best thing that's happened to me for ages.' Fondly, I regarded the man who was becoming increasingly important to me.

Gerry nodded. 'That goes for me too. You know what you mean to me, Susan; and we certainly couldn't have found a better place to live.'

Gerry was employed as a Sales Representative by a firm dealing in insurance. At my request he invested most of the few thousand pounds I'd smuggled out from Ecuador

in a Property Bond in my name. With the balance I bought
a second-hand car, a small green Singer Chamois. Built
like a Mini, it was ideal for nipping about London's
complicated street system and, once used to the traffic
speed, I found the experience exhilarating. I wish I could
say the same for Gerry.

'I do sometimes wonder at the wisdom of your having
a car, my sweet,' Gerry admitted on more than one
occasion, as he clutched at the dashboard and stamped
on an imaginary foot brake.

Once or twice, he even confessed to being terrified by
my driving skills – or lack of them. 'Susan! Watch
out . . . Watch out . . . Didn't you see that bus? You'll
have us both killed.'

Over a period of weeks, I, too, had to admit to a
deterioration in my ability to judge distances. A couple
of 'near-misses' left me thoroughly frightened and,
though I wouldn't admit it to Gerry, I was beginning to
have second thoughts about London traffic in general,
and my driving capabilities in particular. Eventually, with
our money exhausted, and after an uncomfortable row
with the landlord, it seemed expedient to sell the little
green car.

'I shall miss it,' I admitted, 'but at least I can hang on
to my Property Bond.'

'Yep! That was a good investment,' Gerry said, 'though
I still think you should have taken up the permanent
health clause. For the princely sum of one pound a year
extra the company would have continued to pay all future
premiums in the event of your illness.'

'Oh, Gerry, we've been through all that. I'm never ill.
Remember I told you I've only ever had one operation
and that was for nothing more serious than appendicitis
when I was in Ecuador. Nothing will ever happen to me.'

'You never know,' Gerry said with typical insurance
salesman's pessimism. 'However, back to the car. I think
we'd get a better price for it out of London. P'raps if we
advertised it in the Provinces somewhere . . .?'

A scheme was beginning to formulate in my mind which I felt sure would solve all our problems. 'Why don't we move down to Devon and advertise it there,' I suggested. 'We could probably get work there too; and accommodation would be far cheaper.'

A move to Devon would also resolve the ongoing problem with Tom, who'd telephoned on several occasions. Once, we'd even met, and it had been obvious that he was extremely upset by my refusal to live in Germany as his mistress. Though I'd never told Gerry, I was still fond of my American friend in spite of the way he'd hurt me, and had not found it easy to resist his constant rhetoric. Leaving London would be advantageous all round, I reasoned. I hoped Gerry would agree to my proposal. He did.

'What a fabulous idea!' he said, with a grin.

We went first to Kingskerswell, where Gerry met Mum and Dad. I was amazed at how generous-spirited they were. Dad gave me a big bear hug. 'We thought we'd lost you when you went off to London,' he admitted.

Later, Mummy took me on one side. 'I can't say your father and I really approve of you and Gerry living together, but it's so lovely to have you home again that we'll turn a blind eye to it. I've made up the bed for you in your own room.'

I wondered what she would think if she'd known the extent of my relationship with Tom – a married man! But then, I hadn't known myself that he was still living with his wife. I was hardly to blame in that respect.

Shyly, I escorted Gerry to the little room under the eaves, with its pretty, feminine wallpaper and matching curtains. 'It must have been really hard for Mummy to do this for us,' I said when we were lying in one another's arms. 'Not only for her, but for Dad too. It was from this room that he escorted me in my long white gown and train, so radiant and happy on my wedding day. They were really hurt when it all ended in failure and I stormed off to London.'

Memories of David flooded my mind. *We could have made a go of it*, I thought with sadness. Then, aware of Gerry at my side, I continued, 'Still, that's all in the past now. I've returned – the Prodigal Daughter, and I think my parents are terrified of losing me again.'

It was obvious, however, that this arrangement could not go on indefinitely. And when I found secretarial work in Exeter, Gerry and I made arrangements, with my parents' blessing, to move out. We found a delightful chalet in the grounds of a big house in Pinhoe, where, after the hustle and bustle of London, I felt as if I was permanently on holiday. However, within a short time we were on the move again. In fact, throughout the summer, we rarely stayed anywhere longer than a few weeks. We were a little like refugees, constantly on the move, but our homelessness came about through our own lack of purpose, like the Israelites wandering in the wilderness.

By autumn we'd moved to Exmouth where we rented a most elegant apartment in Rolle Villas. From there we were able to enjoy invigorating walks along the miles of sandy beaches and red sandstone clifftops or gentle strolls around the town's tiny port. The sheer size of the apartment and its expensive and well-appointed furnishings and fittings further augmented my self-esteem and social standing and we took to entertaining my parents and friends in the graciously proportioned dining room.

This was important to me and were it not for the fact that I was again suffering severe headaches, I would have been reasonably content.

Our landlady lived with her husband on the top floor for six months of the year when they were not resident in America. In motherly fashion, she took me under her wing. I was grateful for her kindness and concern for, sometimes, my headaches seemed too great to be borne.

'Mrs Scott says it's probably migraine and keeps coming up with remedies for me to try,' I told Gerry. 'She suggests I stop drinking tea and coffee, in case caffeine's to blame.'

Still the agonising pain kept recurring, like a great ball pressing against my scalp.

I worked for an American engineering firm on Sowton Trading Estate, where I shared a cream-painted General Office in a small prefabricated building with two or three other women. As secretary to the boss, part of my job was to deal with his filing and, each morning, I would find a pile of papers awaiting my attention. Every time I stooped to open the bottom drawer of the filing cabinet I experienced the sensation of a ball of fire dropping in the back of my head. No matter how slowly and carefully I moved, I was unable to avoid the terrible pain it induced.

Gerry's suggested cures and Mrs Scott's remedies brought no relief. Eventually, I decided that the pains were psychosomatic. 'I'm just going to ignore them,' I said, 'and I bet the symptoms will disappear!'

Though some mornings it was all I could do to lift my head from the pillow, I doggedly persevered with my self-imposed treatment. Gerry had been a mental nurse in a psychiatric hospital and had a good practical experience of caring for people, but even he found my condition hard to cope with. Inevitably, my persistent malaise put a strain on our relationship.

Devon was an area of high unemployment for men, and for the first six months of our stay there Gerry was unable to obtain work. Secretarial posts, however, were plentiful, and I had never been without a position. Although the tremor in my hands grew worse, I put it down to fatigue caused by my headaches, and managed well enough. But the fact that I had a job and he had not was salt in the wound to Gerry.

Increasingly, we quarrelled. I began to see his unemployment as self-imposed, a reflection of his general lack of purpose. My dwindling savings had to be used to augment our only income – my salary, and I was resentful. I longed for David's financial acumen. Gerry, by contrast, seemed not only inept, but unstable. My distrust for him grew daily.

I'd been conned once too often. Determined to take no further risks, I waited until Gerry was out one morning, then wrapped all my jewellery in the little soft, blue bags in which each piece had been purchased in Ecuador and placed them in a cosmetic hold-all. After careful consideration, I jammed them behind a chest of drawers in the bedroom.

Despite my deep scepticism as to Gerry's integrity and the flaws in our relationship, God knew that soon I would need the encouragement and practical nursing skills of this man who had, subtly, come to mean so much to me. And so we stayed together.

Apple blossom came late in the spring of 1972. Like strawberry milkshake it frothed upon the trees in the large neglected garden of our Exmouth bungalow. On the sand reefs and mudflats of the Exe estuary, families of cygnets straggled untidily behind their ungainly parents until, taking to the water, they sailed off like a tiny flotilla behind majestic white galleons.

More than a year had elapsed since Gerry and I had left London, and in that time we'd drifted, aimlessly, from one apartment to another. At last, Gerry was back in his old line of work, selling insurance door-to-door, whilst I was still with the American company, based at Sowton. My headaches persisted, though, and my typing was becoming increasingly erratic.

We had just moved yet again, and the old bungalow we were renting offered enormous potential. Given my penchant for cooking, the large kitchen particularly pleased me, though its wall were covered with the grease and grime of years. Enthusiastically, I contemplated a transformation.

'I shall have to tackle some spring cleaning,' I said to Gerry. 'Then we'll really be able to go to town with entertaining.'

We were reclining on the settee in the lounge, half-heartedly watching television whilst I outlined my plans for improvement. Secretly, because I knew it would incur disapproval from Gerry, I determined to move a wardrobe from landing to bedroom, since its present position caused me some irritation.

'Just don't go at it hell for leather,' Gerry warned. 'It's no good making yourself ill.'

I'd been unable to hide the sickness which now accompanied my headaches and which was becoming increasingly debilitating. I shrugged and adopted my usual policy of refusing to acknowledge that a problem existed at all.

'Oh, I'll be all right. I'm as strong as an ox really, Gerry. It won't take long to lick it all into shape.'

Suddenly, a terrifying explosion rent the air. Gerry and I shot upright, grabbing each other in alarm.

'What on earth . . .?'

The report was immediately followed by a crashing sound and, before our eyes, the huge, uncurtained plate-glass patio doors shattered into a heap of lethal, jagged shards. Glass lay everywhere. The cataclysm had even propelled it across the room, and we marvelled at our escape from injury.

No plausible reason for the disintegration of the window could be offered by the glaziers who effected repairs the following day. And only with hindsight were Gerry and I to see the incident as an omen of foreboding; a portent of catastrophe to come.

Nothing daunted, I began the very next day to shift the wardrobe on the landing, bending low to push it along the floor. Frequent bouts of pain slowed me down but, determinedly, I persevered. Then, armed with cleaning cloths and buckets of soapy water I attacked the grimy kitchen with as much gusto as I could muster. But the chore was to prove more irksome and protracted than I'd envisaged and by the end of the day, when Gerry returned from work, I was utterly exhausted and had nothing prepared for our evening meal.

'I'm sorry, Gerry. I feel so ill. And I'm terribly worried; my hair's coming out in great handfuls.'

Always proud of the abundance of dark curly hair which framed my face, the loss of my 'crowning glory' filled me with dismay. Tearfully, I took to examining my head in the mirror, certain that I was fast going bald. Sickness and blinding pain now tormented me daily, setting back not only my plans for our home, but also affecting my job.

One day in mid-June, almost fourteen months to the day after we'd left London, the state of my health reached a climax. I was in the office, at the time. A wire tray stood on my desk, full of papers to be filed. I sighed with exasperation; filing was my least favourite job! I set the tray on top of the smaller of two grey metal filing cabinets, and stooped to pull open the bottom drawer. Again, I sighed. Why was it always the bottom drawer?

I grasped the handle and yanked hard on the laden filing system, then gasped and reeled backwards in the throes of a sudden intense attack. In an instant, a burning, moving ball of red hot pain seared through my brain. Nausea rose within. Dizzy and dazed, I reached weakly for support. Office walls whirled around me – faster and faster – a kaleidoscope of cream-turning-red; everything red; Red; RED.

'Susan! Are you okay?' One of my colleagues caught me and helped me to a chair.

For a few moments I was unable to speak. Tortuous waves of pain rolled over me, excruciatingly intense. I closed my eyes. Hot tears squeezed from beneath the lids; slid over hotter cheeks. Sweat broke out on the back of my neck; prickled my face. Hands clenched tight in my lap; nails dug deep into soft flesh. Wordlessly, screaming . . . Then — beyond the pain barrier; over the threshold of reality; into soft, diffused, white, light; weightless, drifting, soundless . . .

'Susan. Susan. Shall we call a doctor?'

'I'm . . . I'm all right.' Giddy, light-headed, but — miraculously — all right.

'Are you sure?' Concern; kindness.

'You really ought to go home . . .'

'Take tomorrow off. See your doctor.'

Gingerly, I nodded.

As soon as I got home Gerry took one look at me and rang to make a doctor's appointment.

'. . . And so, my boss felt I should come to see you.' Diffidently, I explained to the GP, a kindly, white-haired man of indeterminate age, whom I had never met before, but whose name Gerry had found in the telephone directory.

'Have you been taking anything for the headaches?' Dr Dearing asked when I had seated myself.

'Aspirin. Quite a few. But they don't seem to do anything.'

'And you say you've been vomiting? Any double vision?' Sympathetically, the doctor continued his questioning.

'Just going to do one or two little tests, Mrs James.' He rose from his seat and placed another chair close beside me, then drew down a blind at the window. He picked up an ophthalmoscope and when he had seated himself next to me, leaned forward, held my right eye open and peered through the small, cylindrical instrument.

'Now I want you to look straight ahead. You'll see a little white light, like a star. Try and focus on that . . . Right, now look up . . . And towards your nose . . . Now over to me.'

Obediently, I followed his instructions, and the whole procedure was repeated with the left eye.

When he had finished and raised the blind, the doctor sat in front of me. 'I want you to follow my finger,' he said, raising his forefinger in front of my eyes and moving it first to the right, then to the left. My head ached and my eyes hurt; but at least something was being done to discover the reason why. I did as I was bid.

'Good. You can relax now, Mrs James.' His hand brushed my shoulder, and he smiled briefly.

Dr Dearing returned to his desk, lifted the telephone and, twisting the swivel chair so that his back was to me, spoke in rapid and subdued tones. I glanced around the surgery, at steel instruments, enamelled kidney dishes and, on the far wall, an optical chart – which seemed oddly blurred. When the doctor finished his call, he swung back to me, wrote swiftly on a small pad, tore off the sheet and addressed an envelope.

'I'm arranging for you to have further tests in hospital,' he explained, handing me the envelope, and smiling kindly. 'Nothing to worry about, Mrs James. Just give this to the receptionist at Casualty. An ambulance will be here shortly to take you in. In the meantime you can relax in the Waiting Room.' He escorted me to the surgery door.

Hospital! I'd only ever been to hospital once before, when I was rushed in with a severely ruptured appendix in Ecuador. When I'd come round after the operation, I found they'd left the offending organ in a tiny glass bottle at my bedside. It was a gift, the surgeon had told me proudly, as if he thought I should thank him. Instead, I'd been violently sick. I smiled wryly at the memory and sat down to wait for the ambulance.

I was taken to Exeter hospital where I duly handed the letter in at reception, then seated myself in the Waiting Area. After what seemed an interminable delay, I was shown to the duty doctor's office. The letter from Dr Dearing lay open beside a file on which my name had been written in large letters. At the desk sat a dark-haired, clean-cut young doctor. I seated myself opposite him. No one had told me his name, and he effected no introduction.

With bored indifference, the medic asked a number of questions. At the same time he lounged back in his chair, tossing the hammer used to test reflexes into the air and catching it again, with hypnotic repetition. Each time he snatched the shaft mid-fall, contact with the palm of his hand made a small slapping sound. To my tormented senses, the small noise seemed gradually to increase in volume until each catch, like the report from a rifle, boomed in my head.

Finally he turned his attention to me and, with a hint of derision, asked how many aspirin I'd been taking daily. The man's demeanour, my aching head, and the clamour of a busy casualty ward filled me with apprehension. I swallowed, afraid that whatever answer I might give would evoke the doctor's scorn.

'Well, it has been really bad at times – like a red hot knife going through me; and I've been feeling quite ill. In fact it's made me terribly sick, so I've actually taken far more than I would normally.'

'How many?'

'Well, I suppose,' I wrinkled my brow, 'I suppose six at a time.'

Expressionlessly, the medic jotted a note on a pad. 'And how often do you take six aspirins?'

I shrugged and stammered, convinced that he would chastise me for taking more than the prescribed dose. 'Every . . . few hours.'

The doctor tossed down the pen and leaned across the desk towards me. His movement caught me unawares. I cringed in my chair.

'Mrs James,' he laid heavy emphasis on every word. 'This is a busy ward. In the course of a day, we deal with many *sick* people. May I suggest that you stop wasting everyone's time, go home and take *more* aspirin.'

It was all I could do to get out of his office without crying. I felt so small; humiliated. And the pain was so bad I thought my head would explode.

'Can't understand it,' the ambulanceman said sympathetically as I was conveyed home. 'Young woman like you; you shouldn't be needing all those aspirin.'

I vomited all over the floor of the vehicle. And felt too ill to care.

The moment I walked in, Gerry promptly rang the surgery again. I lay on the settee, beyond registering the one-sided conversation, though I saw Gerry glance at me from time to time and gathered that he'd elicited some response from the doctor.

He put down the phone, crouched on the floor beside me and took my hand in his. 'Susan, the doctor's arranging for an ambulance to take you back to hospital. Do you feel up to packing, or shall I do it for you?'

More confident in the outcome now that further action had been taken on my behalf, I rallied a little. 'I'm sure they'll soon sort out the cause and I'll be back home in no time,' I said.

'This is more upmarket. The last ambulance looked as if it had come out of the Ark,' I joked, as Gerry and the ambulanceman helped me out of Rolle Villas and into the high-speed, American-style vehicle. Aware of the gaze of anonymous neighbours who paused, curiously, to watch my departure, I was filled with a scary sort of excitement and in a strange way felt important. Gerry carried the little suitcase he had hastily packed for me out to the pavement, then stood diffidently to one side, as if overcome by a sense of helplessness.

'We're taking you to Plymouth, to Freedom Fields.' The driver helped me into the back of the ambulance and covered me with a rug. 'Now you're not to worry. Ward Two is the neurological ward and the patients there can look rather strange, even a little alarming, to a newcomer. But there's nothing to be afraid of. You understand, don't you?' His broad Devon accent and kindly face should have brought comfort, but his constant and over-anxious attempts at reassurance robbed the words of meaning. Precisely the opposite effect to that desired was evoked within me. A seed of fear was sown in the pit of my stomach.

The journey took over an hour. In my semi-somnolent state, it seemed like minutes. The ambulance drew up before a long low building which seemed to be constructed almost entirely of wood. A sign indicated that we had reached the neuro-surgery department.

The ambulanceman helped me from the vehicle, lifted out my case and escorted me, hurriedly, through long, dreary corridors, past an endless array of blank windows, until, at last, we reached Ward Two.

For a moment he paused. Glanced briefly at me. Then pushed open the double doors.

12

Freedom Fields

A grotesque array of surgical paraphernalia greeted my
eyes. Tubes! Tubes and drips. Protruding from patients;
standing sentry alongside. Bandaged heads. Shaved
heads. Heads swathed in muslin. The ward was crowded
with beds; beds filled with patients; patients lying,
patients dying. Faces were drawn and pinched; eyes
gaped vacantly.

And me! Walking through a maze of horror. I tried not
to stare. This surely wasn't *my* ward; not Ward Two? A
trickle of fear ran through me.

The ambulanceman led me to the next ward, where a
smiling nurse came forward and took my suitcase from
him. With a gesture of farewell, and a softly-spoken 'good
luck', my escort retreated. The nurse took me to one of
the beds. She drew the curtains around it to form a small
green cubicle then, armed with a clipboard, took my
particulars whilst I undressed and climbed on to the high
hospital bed.

The green curtains twitched and an older nurse stepped
into the little cubicle. 'Hello, Susan. I'm Staff Nurse.' Her
round cheerful face broke into a smile. 'We're just going
to take your temperature and blood pressure then Doctor
will do one or two other tests.' She popped a
thermometer in my mouth then reached for the pressure
pump. 'Right arm please, there's a good girl.'

Suddenly, the small space was filled with medics –
nurses and white-coated doctors. From their midst came

a voice and, in deference to its owner, the group split to allow a tall, gaunt man, in his mid-fifties, access to my bedside.

'Hello, young lady. I'm Dr Alcock, the Neurologist, and this is Mr Gossman, the Consultant Neuro-Surgeon.' He indicated another man, equally tall, but of fuller face and figure.

Mr Gossman smiled, 'We'll be carrying out a few tests later to see what we can do for you. But in the meantime, tell me about your headaches.'

The date was 20th June, 1972. And so began the longest week I could have imagined. The staff were friendly and charming, the various tests interesting, even fun – to begin with. I had little inkling as to the gravity of my condition and secretly revelled in the attention and flirted, madly, with all the doctors. I felt good!

On the first day a lumbar puncture was taken. This involved inserting a needle into my back and drawing off a sample of spinal fluid. The sample was then cultured, and the cells studied on a slide beneath a microscope.

'You'll have to lie perfectly still afterwards,' a nurse told me, 'because the test can make some people feel quite ill.'

I was concerned for Gerry, whom I'd telephoned and, throughout the 'two to four hours', which I understood was the length of this enforced rest, I was impatient for his company. At the end of four hours, I leapt to my feet and went to the toilet to comb my hair, in anticipation of his arrival.

'Oh, there you are!' A nurse poked her head around the door. 'Whatever are you doing, you naughty girl. You're supposed to be on bed-rest for twenty-four hours. The doctor's waiting to see you.'

Twenty-four hours? Sheepishly, I accompanied her back to the ward.

Mr Gossman stood by my bedside, a kindly expression

on his face. He waited until I'd climbed back under the
blankets. 'Well, Susan? How are you feeling?'

I felt fine and told him so. 'Do I really have to stay in
bed for twenty-four hours?' I wrinkled my nose.

He nodded. 'For the time being you do. We've had an
early indication from the lumbar puncture that all is not
well. Of course, it'll take a while before we get all the
results through, but it seems there's some sort of
abnormality there, so we're going to run some more
tests.'

'Not another lumbar puncture?' I asked, apprehensively.

'Not at the moment. Nurse will prepare you for a series
of X-rays.' With a reassuring smile, Mr Gossman left me.

During the next day or two, X-rays were taken,
developed, and avidly studied by one doctor after
another. Each frowned, with a puzzled expression. A
pencil was waved to and fro before my eyes; then pins
were stuck into my arms and legs. 'Can you feel that,
Susan?' I was asked. 'And this? And that?' I most
certainly could! And I made sure the doctors knew it!

More tests followed. Some were mildly unpleasant. But
everyone was so gentle, so apologetic, that I could bear
them no malice. Besides, I was convinced that there was
little the matter with me. Repeatedly, I was asked to walk
up and down the ward; up and down; up and down.
'Now I'd like you to touch your nose with your finger,'
Mr Gossman commanded. More doctors joined him. My
audience enlarged.

By the end of Day Five, they were still scratching their
heads. After dinner Mr Gossman came to see me. He sat
on the edge of the bed and looked me straight in the eye.

'We're going to have to do a rather special X-ray
tomorrow, Susan. It will necessitate injecting a cannula
of dye into your head, and may be a little uncomfortable.
But I know you'll be a brave girl, won't you?' He patted
my hand. Nurse stood nearby, a little tub in her hand.
Mr Gossman rose and left.

'Your sleeping tablets, Susan.' Nurse poured a fresh glass of water from the jug on my bedside cabinet and passed it to me, together with the pills which she tipped from the little brown tub. 'I'll be off duty tomorrow. Good luck with the X-ray.' She opened the cubicle curtains and raised a hand in farewell. There seemed to be something almost sinister in her salute, and a nodule of fear took root in my mind.

A cooked breakfast, next morning, soon restored my spirits. 'Bacon and egg – and toast!' I exclaimed, tucking in with gusto. Nurse chuckled. 'You certainly enjoy your food, Susan!'

'Always have,' I replied, candidly, 'but this morning's special. I feel like a condemned man enjoying a last hearty meal!'

After the orderlies had cleared the breakfast trays, Mr Gossman approached my bed. He was accompanied by Matron, Sister and Staff Nurse. 'Nurse tells me you're eating the hospital out of provisions,' he joked. For a moment he stood at my bedside, then drew up a chair. His expression became grave.

'Susan, last night I told you that we're going to take a special X-ray of your head.' He paused for a moment and I waited expectantly. His face grew still more solemn. 'We believe you have a large tumour in the cerebellum, that's the base of the brain, and we're going to have to operate. The usual X-rays are not showing the growth, but from the way you walk, and from other tests we've undertaken, we're pretty sure it's there – probably quite deep-seated. So we're going to take the X-ray direct on the operating table.' For the first time he smiled – a grim little twist of his lips. 'You'll have the usual pre-med, a lovely relaxing sleep, and it'll all be over in no time.'

I frowned. It all seemed too straightforward. Suspiciously so. Around me, the hustle and bustle of the ward continued as usual. An old lady on the far side rang for a bedpan. Nurse wouldn't come immediately, of course. The staff knew her of old. She was always ringing for something. Sometimes she'd even shout in the middle of the night. Right out loud! Disturbing everyone.

Reluctantly, I drew my gaze back to Mr Gossman. 'What happens if you don't operate?'

He glanced down at his hands, flexed his fingers, then looked me squarely in the eye. 'If we don't operate, you'll almost certainly go blind, and then you'll die.'

Oh? Go blind and die, will I? All very normal! Well, he might sound a little more concerned.

'It's a dangerous operation at the best of times,' the surgeon continued, his voice soft and even. 'Because we believe your tumour to be deep-seated, that makes it doubly so. You might die anyway.'

I felt choked. I didn't know what to say. There didn't seem to be much that was relevant. I tried out the words in my mind. *I've got a brain tumour and I might die.* It was unreal: something that happened to other people. Not me. Not Susan James who'd hardly had a day's illness in her life.

Mr Gossman turned to Matron. 'Have next of kin been informed?'

Matron nodded. 'We've notified the husband in Ecuador. I understand he'll be given compassionate leave to fly home.'

David? Home? If I died, he'd be sorry! But what was death? What did it mean? What was life, come to that? Wasn't it all rather like the way in which the early explorers viewed the world — a flat disc that you travelled across, and when you'd gone far enough and reached the edge, you simply fell off into oblivion? Only at twenty-nine years of age I didn't feel I'd travelled far enough! I shuddered. There was still a lot of life left in me; places I wanted to go; things I longed to do; people I wanted to love.

I remembered that day in Ecuador when David and I had sped down the wide open spaces of the Pan American Highway. How exhilarating our journey had been; a swathe cut through solid rock. And what a shock when we'd been pulled up short, our way ahead blocked by a mountain wall, utterly impenetrable, totally immovable. Just like the trauma before me now!

I looked down at my hands. I'd been twisting the sheet so that it now resembled a tourniquet, the coarse cotton threads pulled into a tight damp spiral, and I thought of how easily life can be snuffed out. And of how much I wanted to live.

When Mr Gossman and Matron left, Staff Nurse summoned one of the younger nurses and I was bathed and prepared for the operation, which was scheduled for later in the day. All the time, I kept thinking, *Susan, you're about to have an operation, and you may die. When you go into that operating theatre, you may never come out again alive.* Round and round. The words still seemed to have no relevance to my life; it was as if I were referring to someone else.

Back on the ward, I felt I'd go mad. 'Could I have something to keep me occupied, please nurse? Something to take my mind off . . . you know.'

Paper and crayons were brought for me from the children's ward. At school, my only talents had been History, English and Art, and I'd managed to achieve O levels in these subjects. So, for the rest of the day, I absorbed myself in drawing: a vase of flowers belonging to a fellow patient, and for Gerry, my favourite cartoon characters, Snoopy and Charlie Brown.

'These are very good!' One of the doctors admired my work over my shoulder. 'May I have them?' he continued. 'I'm going to Greece on holiday tonight, so I shan't see you again.'

Shan't see you again! The words had a prophetic ring of doom about them. I handed him the sketches and when he left, I resumed my task.

Suddenly, my drawing was interrupted by voices from a cubicle on the opposite side of the ward.

'No! No! Please, don't.'

'I'm so sorry. You have such lovely hair, it hurts me to have to do this.'

Sounds followed – a clatter of steel, as of a trolley loaded with instruments; the sound of scissors, their blades squeaking at the point of friction as the cutting edges honed one upon the other; then the whirr of a razor . . .

And the soft sound of crying.

With growing horror, I realised the implications; understood, instantly, that this was to be my fate too. *No! No!* Mentally, I recoiled. *Not my hair. My beautiful hair, which I'd grown long since my return from Ecuador.* Death seemed insignificant compared to the loss of my crowning glory. With trembling fingers, I reached for the bell and pushed long and hard on the button.

A nurse came running. 'What is it? What's wrong?'

'I can't . . . I can't let them do that to me,' I stammered.

Immediately, she understood and, firmly, yet sympathetically, took the situation in hand. 'Now, Susan. They can't take the X-ray through all that hair, can they? It has to be shaved. It soon grows again. Honestly.'

Still I shrank from the whole idea. 'But not here. Not for everyone to hear me and see me,' I implored.

'We'll see what we can do. Perhaps Sister will have a word with the theatre staff and they'll do it on the operating table.'

'Oh, please, nurse.' I clung to her hand. 'Please see if they will.'

Sleepy and relaxed after my pre-med, I lay on the trolley in the theatre ante-room. Particles of dust danced in a shaft of light, illusive, ethereal, as tenuous and insubstantial as life itself. Snatches of conversation wafted over my senses, like gentle breezes blowing across a desert.

I was moving, being wheeled, lifted, laid on a cold,

hard table. Above me great discs of light; around me a
small, green throng, from which subdued and
unintelligible sounds were emitted. One green figure
detached itself, leaned over me and shouted disconnected
words in my ear, ' . . . just going . . . shave . . . your
hair; inject . . . with dye'. Somewhere, a long way off,
a lawnmower was in use. Up and down. Up and down.
Whatever were They up to cutting the grass in the
hospital theatre? I giggled. Did They know?

My head felt funny. Someone had taken the lid off it
and was pouring in iced tea. The liquid was running –
all around inside the bowl of my skull. I squirmed. It
wasn't nice to pour tea in someone's head; it felt
uncomfortable. I was being moved again. ' . . . nothing
to worry about . . . we'll say heat coming . . . feel a little
warm . . .'

They were pushing me into a tube . . .

' . . . Going to have to operate immediately . . . Ready
Mr Smith? . . . anaesthetic . . .'

It's so hot, so wet. I'm in the bath. With my clothes on.
Get out of your clothes, Susan. Mummy will be cross.
Quickly! Quickly! Get your arm out. I can't. Everything's
sticking. Someone's here; stopping me, holding me
down. The water's so hot, hot. I have to get these clothes
off . . . Please . . . please . . .

I'm screaming. My throat hurts. They're pushing my
tongue down my throat with a long rod, down, inside,
it hurts, it hurts.

I'm in the school playground. A boy called Gossman is
shouting at me. He's been kicking me and pulling my
plaits and I hurt all over. I don't want to listen to him;
want to run away, to lie on the playing fields where the
sun's shining and it's warm, and I can watch the skylarks
soaring above in a wide, blue sky. But he keeps shaking
me, bullying, sticking out his tongue at me. Nasty boy!

No. No. He's telling me to put my tongue out. You shouldn't do that. It's rude. I want to tell him, but he won't listen. It's rude. Mummy wouldn't like it.

'Put out your tongue, Susan. Can you hear me? Put out your tongue if you can hear me.'

I don't like this boy shouting at me. Mummy's not here. I'm going to stick out my tongue at him. Open your mouth, Susan . . .

It's awfully funny today. There's this nice monster sitting beside me, a sort of dragon, only a tame one, and he breathes ever so loud every time I do. Only it hurts to breathe, hurts in my nose. I want a nice big, daddy-hanky, Mummy, to blow my nose. It feels as if there's a great big tube going down inside me, and it hurts, and my throat's sore.

Aunty Ann is feeding me ice-cream. It's lovely. All cold and slippery, and it runs in little trickles down my throat. Aunty Ann's awfully nice. She puts the spoon on my lip, and tells me I'm a good girl when I swallow. I like being a good girl for Aunty Ann, and Mummy and Daddy are laughing, they like me to be a good girl too.

I'm a baby. Helpless and small. Doctors in long white coats are peering down at me from a great height. I might almost be a blob under a microscope.

' . . . spastic condition . . .'

They keep muttering these strange, unintelligible sounds. I feel like crying. They keep telling me I'm spastic, and that means illegitimate. Nobody wants me. I'm an illegitimate baby.

I belong to no one.

Black. Nothing. Swirling around me. Empty. Nothing. I'm tired; want to sleep. Want to swirl in the black emptiness. Drifting. Down. Down. Down. Whirling. Upward. I'm rising from black heat, to white coolness. Beautiful music like harps, a sweet, exquisite sound, like the tinkling of a stream flows on and on . . . I am in heaven; filled with joy inexpressible, being borne downstream on a river flowing seaward.

But the sound becomes irksome, won't stop, I want to cover my ears, blot it out. My arms are heavy. I cannot lift them. Cannot reach my ears. I'm in darkness. In hell. Voices float across the darkness. My body is trapped, held down.

This is not my body. I am angry. This is the body of another. I am trapped in an alien body. I have walked into a war, and I will come away wounded. I am fighting, fighting. Tension fills the air.

The girl that I was, is no more.

'Susan? Susan? Do you know who this is?'
It's Aunty Ann. Aunty Ann's nice. I like Aunty Ann.
'Darling, do you know who I am?'
Course I do. Smile, Susan. Smile at Aunty.
'Who *am* I, Susan? Do you know who I am, darling?'
'Aunty . . . Aunty . . . Ann . . .'.
'Aunty Ann! That's right, darling. It's your Aunty Ann. Clever girl. Do you know who fed ice-cream to you? Who fed you, Susan?'
'Aunty . . . Ann.'
'Yes, darling. You're such a clever, clever girl. It was Aunty Ann who fed you.

'Hello, Molly, Bill. Susan spoke! Just a minute ago. She knows who I am, and she knows I fed her with ice-cream!'
'That's wonderful. Oh, Bill, isn't that wonderful. Susan, darling, do you know who we are. Who are we, darling?'
'Mummy . . . Daddy . . . Uncle Ricky. Dear Gerry.'
I can hear them all.
But I can see nothing.

Nothing! I had no visual concept. Never before had I experienced blackness of such intensity. It pressed in on all sides, tangible, suffocating, evoking panic as I sought to be free of its entanglement. It was terrifying to hear voices, to have a sentient knowledge of human presence, yet be totally unable to see. Ordinary sounds, once unremarkable, now took on a new dimension, at times startling me, at others beginning a bewildering chain of complex, and often erroneous, deductions. Was that footfall someone approaching me? Someone I knew? Someone watching? Only with the passing of time was I to see this new development as a blessing. Without sight, my hearing was intensified and a new level of living was to be opened up to me.

Consciousness brought, also, an awareness of my corporal condition. My body was twisted, distorted, an alien being no longer under my control. In my mind I willed, but in my limbs there was no response. Muscles refused to obey. If my nose itched, it could not be scratched by *my* hand; nor, more distressing by far, had I any power over the functions of bladder and bowel.

It was so hot. I felt stifled. Miss Savage, the physiotherapist assigned to me, asked the nurses to put my mattress on the floor next to an electric fan to relieve my distress. My body felt heavy; heavy and lifeless as I was lifted off the bed. The worst moment I had ever imagined had come to be: I was dependent, unable to do anything for myself. Weeping quietly, I recalled the small boy outside David's office in Ancon. Born with feet back to front, he'd been utterly dependent on others, and had been quite unable to get about other than in a little wheeled cart; had never, in fact, known a life where he could run and skip and dance. Dance! Would *I* ever do so again?

Gradually, over a period of days, I learned, in my more lucid moments, that the operation had been successful; the tumour had been removed. But Mr Gossman saved the best news till last.

I was paralysed and blind!

Those two factors seemed comparatively insignificant to
my parents as they sat in vigil at my bedside whilst I
fought my way back to life. Each day, Mummy brought
roses from the garden and the scent, heavy and
intoxicating, filled my nostrils. Could it be only seven
years since I'd fingered the velvet petals of my wedding
bouquet and revelled in the sweet perfume which rose
from their scarlet depths? I wondered at David's absence.
Why had he not come home on compassionate leave?
Surely my illness transcended all that had gone before:
his rejection of me in favour of another, the breakdown
of our marriage and talk of divorce?

No mention was made of him by any member of the
family. But as my health improved, details of the
operation were relayed to me. My parents sat at my
bedside and recalled, for my benefit, the missing weeks.

'We thought we'd lost you, darling.' Mummy's voice
broke. 'It was touch and go as to whether or not you'd
live. You were unconscious for well over a fortnight, and
Mr Gossman had to do an emergency tracheotomy and
put you on a respirator.'

'That's why my throat's so sore! Is the tube still there?'

'Not now. There's a big white bandage, and the doctors
say that, in time, there won't be much scarring visible.'

I wanted to see, to know how I looked; wanted, too,
to lift my hand, feel the bandage, have some physical
concept of my appearance. I swallowed down tears of
frustration and self-pity. 'I vaguely remember someone
feeding me ice-cream,' I said. 'It was so soothing.'

'That was Aunty Ann. She and Uncle Rick have been
marvellous, visiting every day. You're like a daughter to
them, darling. Most of the time you had to be fed through
a tube in your nose. Some sort of high protein liquid, I
think they said.'

'Anyway, you're on the mend now.' Daddy's tone
indicated that he would prefer not to dwell on the
gruesome details.

Later, holding my hand tight in his, Gerry gave me

further information. 'Because your temperature was so high, and you had some sort of fit, the surgeon was afraid that there might be a blood clot. The staff did another lumbar puncture and found that you had a slight infection. So they put you on penicillin and kept you heavily sedated to stop the spasms. It was dreadful! They kept telling us they had no idea whether you were going forward or standing still, nor what the outcome would be.

'When you spoke . . . and actually recognised us all, and remembered your aunt giving you the ice-cream . . . Well . . . we were all overjoyed. Oh, boy, Susan! I wouldn't want to go through all that again.'

'Neither would I,' I said.

But in the bottom of my heart, I knew that my suffering was far from over.

'It's Mummy and Daddy again, darling.'

Though my body would not respond, mentally, I turned towards the sound of their voices.

'How are you today, darling? I've brought some lovely roses, white, tinged with palest pink, and some that are heavily scented – a deep dark red, called Crimson Glory. Shall I put them on the bed for you to smell before they go in water?'

My mother laid the roses on my hands. I could feel the soft down of each petal, the coolness of each leaf. And then – amazingly – I could see them, actually distinguish colour and form!

'Mummy! Daddy! I can see! I can see the roses.'

My mother's face came into view as she crouched by the side of the bed. 'Susan! Are you sure, darling?'

'I can see you. And Daddy's legs. And the side of the cabinet, and the windows . . . I tell you, I can see.'

As if afraid that my sight might disappear as fast as it had returned, my mother urged action. 'Quickly, Bill. Go and fetch a nurse, one of the doctors. Tell them what's happened.'

Tears ran down my face and dripped from my nose.

Unable to wipe them away, I laughed, a little hysterically.
It was almost worth having been blind all those weeks, I
thought, *just to have this moment.*

Later, after my parents had departed, I thought of that
moment as being a moment of rebirth. My visual world
had become a whole new experience. Knowing, as I now
do, the wonder and love of God and of his gifts to each
one of us, I have a fresh understanding. The parallel
between my self-revelation and the moment of Spiritual
Truth, when a Christian is reborn, not of the flesh, not
of water, but of the Spirit of God has become clear. But
at that time, I was not yet ready, nor even aware, of the
existence of such a doctrine, much less that it could
become a reality for me.

With the return of my sight, it was felt by the doctors
and nursing staff that I should wear some sort of head-
covering to hide the scars on my scalp.

'Here, let's pop this on to make you feel better,' one
of the nurses said, holding up a monstrous wig of
reddish-brown colouring. She pulled it over my head and
showed me my reflection in a mirror. I hated it!
Throughout the afternoon the offensive article kept
slipping over my forehead and was absolutely the last
straw, as far as I was concerned. Anyway, who would
ever look at me again, I reasoned, though Mum and Dad
and Gerry were always loving and encouraging.

'Your shaved head looks lovely,' Gerry assured me
when he came in that evening, and he handed the wig
back to the ward sister, telling her firmly that it would
not be needed. Resentful of the whole business, I was
not yet ready to recognise God's provision in giving me
Gerry's down-to-earth approach and practical experience
of nursing sick folk.

The gradual dawning of my new situation was too
much to accept with equanimity. Why, why had this
happened to *me*? David was the one who wanted a
divorce, whereas I had wanted only to return to my home

in Quito. It was, therefore, David who was in the wrong; so why was *I* the one to suffer?

Ironically, I learned that I would have been better off had I stayed in Germany with Tom. There, medical knowledge and technology was greatly in excess of that available in England, and the equipment was far more sophisticated.

The tumour had been deeply embedded. I was told, later, that to save my life, much valuable brain tissue had had to be cut and damaged, and that this had affected the motor nerves in the brain's frontal lobe; hence the lack of muscular mobility in my arms and legs. My 'spastic condition' – those words which had featured so often in my nightmares, and seemed to be a cause of major discussion between surgeon and neurologist – had caused my hands to become two tightly clenched fists. Remembering the happy days of elegance in Ecuador, when a manicure was a weekly occurrence, I regarded them with horror. They were like two deformed paws, hideous and claw-like, and were encased in huge and hateful, pink plastic splints.

Raymond Beecroft, my first love, when I'd been only eleven years of age, had told me I had 'pianist's fingers' and that he was going to marry me when we grew up. But now? Who would ever again caress or admire my hands? Tears welled in my eyes. And then I remembered my wedding day and how impatient I'd felt with the photographer when he'd prolonged the photo session before the reception. David and I had had to stand with our hands clasped before us so that shots of the rings might be taken. How glad I was now that David had persuaded me to comply and that there was some record of the previous grace of my limbs.

There was considerable time, between visiting hours, for me to dwell on my predicament. However, when my parents were with me, I smiled for them. Beneath their cheerful façade, I could see their sadness, so to help them, I would pretend that all was well.

I knew no one with whom I could share my despair, my hurt and pain. What purpose was there for me now? Was there any hope for the rest of my life? What was the point of living? And what happened to the dancing girl of Latin America?

My whole body was inflamed with pain and heat. My visitors brought me ice-cream and fruit, crouching on the floor by my makeshift bed-roll, and taking in their stride, not only my paralysis, but also the horror of my incontinence. So these were the tubes I'd seen on first being admitted to Ward Two! How I hated the two bags into which the waste products of my body were evacuated; Gerry coped with the indignity so much better than I.

I see, now, how God provides for our times of trial. Gerry was good at nursing me, and this was a great help to the beleagured staffing levels in the hospital. Neither did he seem to mind that I was no longer the same girl with whom he had lived. But there was worse to come.

On 29th July, just one month and three days after the operation, I was transferred to Royal Devon & Exeter Hospital at Heavitree in Exeter.

'I'm afraid we need the bed here, Susan,' Mr Gossman told me, 'but you'll still be under the care of Mr Alcock in Exeter.'

What he didn't tell me was that at twenty-nine years of age I was to be placed in a Geriatric Ward!

13

Red Feather

For the next three months I was resident in the Royal Devon & Exeter Hospital. Mr Alcock, the neurologist, had hoped that I might benefit from the hydrotherapy available there but, as the expected level of movement in my limbs proved disappointing, this was not possible. A blind physiotherapist was assigned to put my legs and arms through a series of complicated and agonising manipulations designed to strengthen the muscle tone. Throughout each session, I was acutely aware of the fact that he was unable to see my face and was, therefore, oblivious of the pain he inflicted upon me.

To make matters worse, a kidney infection had caused further set-back and the drugs which were prescribed to counter the complaint made me terribly giddy. I felt as if the bed on which I lay was swirling, uncontrollably, and that at any moment I would be ejected and deposited upside down on the floor. I was terrified and cried out to the nurses who promptly put me in a cot, telling me I'd feel safer. Safer? I felt imprisoned! The bars merely reinforced my immobility.

I shared the Geriatric Ward with women nearly three times my age, and certainly too far advanced in disease and senility to be good company to a young woman not yet out of her twenties. Nor were the nurses any more forthcoming; their sour faces and bullying tactics intimidated me. And so, once over the infection, there was no alternative but for me to fall into the ward regime.

Each day I was lifted into a chair where I spent long hours staring vacantly at the wall, unable to do anything for myself. Every muscle and sinew, every tendon and joint, joined forces in an orchestration of aching torment and, gradually, during the day, my body slumped lower and slewed sideways in the chair. When my parents came to visit, they would arrange pillows around me to prop me up. But inside I felt like a rag doll whose stuffing had come out: old and bent and discarded.

The cot in which I lay by night was immediately opposite the drugs cabinet. Hour after hour, in the dim light shed from the nurses' station, I planned, with a sense of hopelessness, how I might reach its contents and thus bring release of a sort to this life of endless, empty, futility.

I suppose this existence could have gone on indefinitely. Instead, I was to see once more, though only with hindsight, the provision of God. And the purposes he was to bring into effect, were, ultimately, to secure a release for me which was both temporal and spiritual. A release I could never have dreamed of.

One day in August, when I had been in the Royal Devon & Exeter over four weeks, I learned, through my parents, that there was the possibility of my being admitted to the local Cheshire Home. Through a series of 'coincidences', which I later saw to be the hand of God, my parents had met up with the Chairman of the Management Committee.

It transpired that this had come about as an indirect result of my action some two years earlier. At that time, obeying a persistent voice in my head whilst out shopping one day, I had crossed the street, entered a solicitor's office and made a will. More recently, when my parents wanted to add a codicil to their wills, they remembered the particular firm of solicitors to whom I had been and took their business to the same place. There they met with the senior partner, Hamish Turner, and, during the course of conveying their wishes to him, my plight was revealed. In his capacity as Chairman of the Management Committee, Mr Turner suggested that my name be added to the waiting list for accommodation.

When my parents first conveyed the news to me, with great excitement, I wasn't at all sure that I wanted to be resident in a home for the disabled! Eventually, however, I realised that anything would be better than the hated Geriatric Ward in which I existed at present and, after a visit from Peter Allen, the Head of Home, I was persuaded of the advantages of such a move.

Peter Allen was a tall man with dark wavy hair, a ready wit, which I did not at first appreciate, and an utter dedication to the cause in which he was involved. He explained that the Management Committee were 'choosy and selective' about their residents, who were expected to work for two hours daily in the Occupational Therapy Room. He told me that, although I was having difficulty in reading because of my impaired sight, he hoped I might listen to tapes on the history of the Cheshire Homes. Then, in due course, I would be able to give lectures and explain to people about the Movement. By the time he left, arrangements had been put into action for me to leave the hospital and move to the Cheshire Home.

On Monday, 16th October, 1972, just sixteen weeks after my operation, I was admitted to Douglas House in Brixham.

A middle-aged woman with a pleasant, smiling face crouched on the floor to welcome me to the Home. My body was too curved to permit me to sit upright in the canvas chair into which I'd been lowered, so visitors were required to perform a contorted obeisance just to see my face.

The woman introduced herself as Joy Ford, a member of the Management Committee, and told me that I would soon come to like it there. How did she know how I felt, I thought, uncharitably, and told her, in sour tones, that

I felt like a sack of potatoes. Then I reminded myself that anything was better than the Geriatric Ward from which I'd just escaped.

Later, I wasn't so sure. Gerry had accompanied me in the ambulance from Exeter and this did not seem to please Peter Allen. Nor did the Superintendent hide his displeasure when Gerry kissed me farewell, and called, 'See you, my Sweet.' But it was the realisation that I had been sent out from the hospital without a wheelchair which was the final straw. Mr Allen's black eyebrows and swarthy countenance registered real annoyance.

'Where's your wheelchair?' he demanded, as if it were my fault that I'd been dumped in a canvas chair in the dining-room.

'I haven't got one.'

'Didn't the hospital send one?' His face darkened as I shook my head.

'Right! Let's get this sorted out.' He turned on his heel and left the room.

Moments later, through the open door, I heard him shouting into the telephone. 'Some social worker dismissed this young woman without a wheelchair. What incompetence. She can't walk, I tell you.'

I felt myself grow cold at the realisation that *I* was the cause of his anger, and the subject of his rage.

'Send a wheelchair over right away, do you hear? No, she can't walk. She can't move.'

And then, at that instant, the nature of my illness was revealed to me, terrifyingly. Something that had never dawned on me in Freedom Fields nor even in the Exeter ward: I was crippled, permanently crippled.

I listened to the squeak of wheels on linoleum, saw the shadow of chairs passing the dining-room windows.

Everyone, all of them, were in wheelchairs.

And I was one of them.

Crippled for the rest of my life.

On my arrival at Douglas House, I was unable to sit

upright, and even going to the toilet necessitated a lengthy routine of being lifted on to my bed, and thence a bedpan. Peter, and his wife Julie who was a nurse, worked tirelessly, assisting and encouraging me in a daily regime aimed at strengthening my back. In this they were helped by other nurses, Betty, Pat, Paddy, Tessa and Hilda; their young, fresh enthusiasm was in marked contrast to the dour demeanour of the Exeter hospital staff.

To begin with I shared a room with two young women who introduced themselves as Denise and Susy. Denise was beautiful and when she smiled, her face was lit with a radiance that was dazzling. She'd been a North Devon Beauty Queen, and loved to be made-up, and dressed-up to the nines. She had multiple sclerosis and, like me, was wheelchair-bound, whilst Susy, who had been disabled since birth, was a grinning youngster on a pair of crutches.

For a while it was a relief to find other young people like me in this situation, and to be cared for by young, attractive nurses. In time, however, the youth and vitality of the staff served only to remind me of what I had lost. Not knowing God as I now do, I again questioned why this should have happened to *me* when it was David who wanted to end our marriage? What miscarriage of justice had dictated that it should be I who was afflicted with a brain tumour? I didn't understand that God does not punish sin by inflicting suffering on mankind.

The drugs I was on had strange side-effects. Aided by the hallucinations they induced, I became obsessed by death. One day I would greet my mother with the news: 'Gerry has committed suicide'; next day I would be convinced that my mother, the Shah of Persia, had been assassinated by Tony Curtis. Increasingly, I became confused as to what was reality and, one night whilst I lay in bed, a voice said, quite clearly: 'I am Jesus.' For some months I endeavoured to speak to the voice, but when it disappeared I decided that it would be silly to have anything to do with something so obviously unreal.

Dreams dominated my night-life, many of them self-induced. I began to play games of fantasy, persuading the nurses to put me to bed early so that I could indulge in my make-believe world: a fall would reverse the brain-damage caused by my operation, so that I was a normal, happy, laughing girl. I would relive the sensation of what it was to sit up, to straighten both arms. Then I would re-enact what it was to stand, to get dressed. Finally, I would run down the passage and skip down the stairs to the dining-room where admiring residents would greet my recovery with cries of joy.

Dawn found me lost and saddened, a victim of my own imagination, and I was left, once more, with a bitter sense of helplessness and deformity. Who would want me now?

A real-live romance between two of the residents brought me a flicker of hope. If others could marry, who knows? Perhaps one day, someone might reach out to me in love and commitment, someone on whom I could rely, someone in whom to put my trust.

How could I have known then who that Someone was to be?

Peter Allen was a Christian, and I began to see in him, though without recognising it at the time, something of the love of Christ. There were twenty-six of us in residence and, in the evenings, Peter would read to us – amusing little tales, delivered in his broad Devonshire dialect. At other times the staff would sit and talk, play cards with us, or table tennis. Even for the disabled, life could be fun, I discovered, though not in all respects.

From ten o'clock each morning, after breakfast was cleared, the dining-room became a therapy centre. One woman made lovely jewellery. Other residents eagerly embraced basketwork and a variety of crafts. I found it boring! With one hand too shaky to do any detailed work, all I could achieve was the stringing together of pieces of chamois leather to make cleaners for windows and cars.

Peter Allen found me a physiotherapist, a domiciliary who would treat me in the Home. An attractive and vivacious woman by the name of Miss Broad, she made the exercises and manipulations a time of fun and lively conversation. Consequently, I regained a degree of control over my limbs and, though my left arm remained paralysed, despite the wearing of splints and a later operation to straighten the fingers, I gradually developed the ability to use my right hand. This became very flexible and by using my hand in conjunction with my teeth, I was able to open and tear certain items. She encouraged me to take care of my appearance and to shed my self-imposed uniform of trousers and smocks which covered my calipers and denied any hint of femininity in me. With endless patience, Peter encouraged me too, to fend for myself once more – feeding myself, combing my hair, putting on lipstick.

Mid-way through November, Miss Broad arrived for our session in a state of great excitement and told me that I was to have my own room, that it had a 'monster' in one corner and that she'd never seen anything like it.

I'd grown used to the routine with Denise and Susy and enjoyed their company, though there was little privacy in the cramped quarters when visitors called. A room of my own was not to be lightly dismissed.

Miss Broad grabbed the handles of my wheelchair and pushed me down the corridor. She stopped outside a door marked BRIXHAM, so named after the Brixham Support Group, then flung it wide to permit our entrance. A spacious room, overlooking the garden and aviary, greeted my eyes. In one corner stood my very own wash-basin and a vanitory unit, whilst opposite was a large wardrobe. It was wonderful! All this to myself, and privacy too!

'And there's the monster,' Miss Broad proclaimed in theatrical fashion.

I stared. It was indeed a monster! An antiquated orthopaedic bed, built like a huge chrome four-poster,

dominated the room. From it hung the most peculiar
collection of ropes, weights, pulleys and slings. Miss
Broad explained that my special need of such a bed had
won me the privilege of my own room. She seemed
highly delighted whereas I thought it hideous! My mind
was filled with thoughts of what Gerry would say when
he next came down from London to visit me.

I felt so much had happened to impair his perception
of me and that this monster bed would be a further
reminder of my disability. When I'd been in hospital my
paralysis had been terrible enough. However, that had
been as nothing compared to the humiliation of having
had the man who had once caressed my body, actually
dealing with my incontinence, handling and emptying
the catheter bag which had swung beneath the bed.

Now, five months on, experimentation with my drugs
had eliminated the need for a bag, and though
suppositories were still a twice-weekly necessity, there
was the possibility that these, too, could become a thing
of the past. Grudgingly, I realised that a room of my own
with toilet just across the corridor was a great
improvement on what had been.

Even so, I wanted to obliterate the more unpleasant
aspects of my illness from Gerry's mind and wished that
the bed was not a necessity. I was anxious to please him,
to impress this man with whom I had lived and slept and
by whom I'd been known so intimately. I longed to
restore the image of being 'his girl', of being female in
every sense, of attracting him in the old, familiar way.

A few weeks later my wish was granted – at least in
part. Miss Broad discovered that the apparatus festooned
from my giant bed was just *too* antiquated, and she sent
the monster back whence it had come. A new, ordinary
bed took its place. And I was left with a room of my own!

As a special treat I was allowed home for my thirtieth
birthday. I travelled in a friend's car which was loaded
to the roof with all my paraphernalia, including a big, red

commode which stood upright in the open boot for all to see! It was the first of several visits and I spent Christmas, too, in the centre of a happy family gathering.

New Year, however, began bleakly. There was talk of an operation on my left foot which drooped and was causing immense pain. Subsequent corrective surgery and the wearing of a caliper enabled me to walk with the aid of a physiotherapist and tripod, but pain eventually made me give up and drove me back to my wheelchair.

Also in January, my father was taken ill and an enforced period of rest was prescribed. Obviously, this meant that neither he nor my mother would be able to visit so often, but my feelings on that score were overshadowed by news which I found far more painful, emotionally.

On 3rd February, 1973, I received a letter from my solicitors informing me that David had filed for divorce. I found it difficult to keep the bitterness from my voice as I conveyed the news to my parents. It was now two years since David and I had lived together and the suit would be brought on the grounds of irretrievable breakdown.

Daddy sat on the end of my bed in Douglas House and looked across at me in my wheelchair. 'I suppose that'll be less harrowing for you than on grounds of adultery,' he said.

'It will certainly make it easier on David,' I said with a degree of rancour. Then, guiltily, I remembered: what about me with Greg! I wondered how my parents would react if that came out. Daddy was right. Breakdown would be less harrowing than adultery.

5th April was a Thursday and the Watergate scandal was causing as ill a wind as the seasonably blustery weather. I clutched my jacket around me as Peter Allen wheeled me towards the Torquay Court. Then he and the young voluntary worker who had accompanied us lifted me in the wheelchair and staggered up the stone staircase which led into the building.

'These steps are a bit hazardous if you're a criminal trying to make an escape,' I joked. 'Hope access to the cells is good for wheelchairs.' Relentlessly, I cracked jokes in an effort to subdue the fear within me whilst we waited in the vestibule for my solicitor's arrival.

It had been a shock when I'd learned, some weeks ago, that, because David had returned to live in Ecuador, I would have to be the one to go to court. It seemed so unfair! Once again the guilty spectre of Greg rose in my mind – our meetings in Quito, in London, and our fond, though reluctant, farewell. Well, he certainly wouldn't want me now that I was disabled, any more than David did. Full of hurt, I turned to Peter Allen.

'The church where I married was just along the road from here,' I said caustically. 'They pulled it down and built another – just like my marriage. Strange, really. I met David on the tennis court at the back of this building, and now I'm to be divorced from him in *this* court. My life seems to be like a vicious circle; back to the beginning again.'

Peter squeezed my shoulder in a gesture of understanding then, as my solicitor joined us, pushed me forward through the doors. The court room was crowded and it was evident that another case was in session. Together with my little entourage, I entered in time to see a woman who was standing in the dock, take a Bible in her hand as requested and swear, on oath, to tell the truth, the whole truth and nothing but the truth. The woman looked hard, and brash, the Judge stern and frightening. Lawyers flitted between bench and pews, their black gowns fluttering and curled wigs hooding their faces in a grim reminder of the vultures which had perched outside my home in Ancon. Mesmerised by the proceedings, I looked from one to the other.

Then it was over. The woman's case was granted. The Judge turned as an usher motioned me forward. Peter pushed me to the front, and a large, black testament was held out to me.

'Take the Bible in your left hand . . .'

This was terrible! 'I . . . I . . . can't use my left hand.'
I began to cry.

The Judge leaned forward from the Bench. He
conferred with my lawyer, who then turned to me: 'His
Honour wants to know if you'd rather come back another
day?'

Another day? I glanced behind me. At the back of the
court three or four court officials from the previous case
had closed in on the hard-faced woman. Only she was
hard no longer. Her expression had crumpled and she
seemed to have been swallowed up by those who pressed
around her. The black-gowned figures hemmed her in
and the grey wigs wagged up and down as they picked
over the remaining details of the case.

'No! Oh, no!' I was horrified at the prospect of drawing
out the tension still further.

'You'd like to proceed then?'

I nodded.

My lawyer approached the Bench and spoke in soft
tones. Again the Judge leaned forward, his wig slipping
slightly askew as he did so. He glanced at me; smiled.
Suddenly, he looked human. Human and friendly.

Mr Turner returned to my side, produced a crisp white
handkerchief from his pocket and passed it to me. 'His
Honour says to tell you that he's ready when you are.
And you're not to worry; he's not going to eat you.'

I smiled through my tears, dried my eyes and pulled
myself together. The solicitor who was about to bring
about a divorce I did not want, I reminded myself, was
none other than the man who had procured my release
from the hated Exeter hospital.

Physically I was stronger each day, and with the divorce
behind me, I gained in confidence. My parents seemed
happier. Gerry visited a little less frequently.

When he did come, we dined at the Berry Head Hotel.
The dining-room overlooked the sea — and Torquay, on

the far side of the bay, looked especially beautiful at night. Gerry would assist me in and out of the front seat of the car, and seemed to enjoy each evening as much as I, though he was certainly not as tender as I remembered him.

Shortly before I'd moved to Douglas House, when the therapy had partially restored the use of my right hand and given me some mobility on one side, Gerry had been instrumental in an important aspect of my rehabilitation. He'd arrived at the Royal Devon and Exeter hospital one day, with a beaming smile and his hands full of packages. 'Now, my Sweet,' he'd said, 'We're going to learn how to write again.'

He'd taken out a big brown hardboard folder and a brown paper packet in which was a ream of plain paper. Taking a ruler from his briefcase, he'd ruled lines from top to bottom and I'd teasingly passed comment on how well organised he was. He'd smiled, and ruffled the tufts of hair sprouting from my shaved head telling me he loved me and that what we were about to do would be fun.

The nurses had sat me at the side of my cot that day, and Gerry had pulled a small table alongside and pushed my armchair up to it. He'd taken a pencil and placed it in the fingers of my right hand. Then, with his hand over mine, together we'd written a large, lopsided SUSAN. It was a beginning, and later, at Douglas House, as my hand had strengthened, we'd advanced from capitals to little letters; and finally to signing my name in joined-up writing! Gerry had been exultant.

Suddenly now, a few months on, Gerry changed. He was working successfully, and had bought a car. Where once he had assured me of the unimportance of my wheelchair, it now loomed large in his thinking as something which would damage the paintwork of his shiny, new vehicle. I was so hurt.

Occasionally, other able-bodied men told me I was still beautiful, but there was no escaping the chair: it was a barrier to any normal encounter. When I went out to the shops or restaurants, I felt that people stared above me and behaved as if I did not exist. On the rare occasions that anyone did speak to me, they did so as if I were an imbecile, or shouted as if I were deaf.

One spring afternoon, I was sitting in the dining-room with one of the residents, a dark-haired, good-looking young man by the name of John Bennett. Although only twenty-six years of age, John was very much a recluse. He had broken his neck as a result of a surfing accident in California, and the injury had put paid to his hopes of entering the Air Force, and had terminated his engagement to be married.

Suddenly, as we were chatting, the room became hazy, my eyes blurred and all went dark. I was terrified.

'John! John! I can't see.'

John called a member of staff, and in due course Dr Jowitt arrived to examine my eyes.

'I'm sorry,' the doctor said, 'it's not unusual for post-operative problems to occur.'

It was bad enough to have lost my sight after the operation; to do so again now was more than I could bear.

I was reminded of an occasion in Ancon when our neighbours, an English girl and her Ecuadorian husband, had to dispose of their cat. Despite numerous attempts on their part to discipline him, the animal constantly clawed and spat at anyone approaching it. Following the advice of the *Sanidad* Department, they put the wretched creature in a sack, tied the neck securely and drove fifteen miles into the desert. There, amongst the straggly scrub, they left the struggling, heaving little heap and drove home.

Some two weeks later there was a cry outside the servants' quarters one night. The cat had returned. Secretly, I'd been full of admiration for its tenacity and determined to champion such a resourceful spirit. Though its disposition showed no signs of improvement, the cat was allowed to stay. But I had often pondered, since, how it must have felt in the black, hot, unknown depths of darkness when it was tied into the sack.

After my operation, and again now, I thought I knew. For I, too, was experiencing that same dreaded claustrophobia for myself. But my condition was only temporary and, in due course, some vision returned to my eyes.

'Your illness is following a pattern, Susan,' Mr Alcock told me on my next check-up. 'These set-backs are to be expected, I'm afraid. I'd like you to wear an eye patch on your left eye for the time being.'

With the patch in place I felt hideous, and was extremely distressed. Back at Douglas House I conveyed the strength of my feeling to my mother. 'I feel like Long John Silver and I'm sure I must look absolutely ridiculous.'

Without a word to me, she took the offending article home that night and stitched shiny green sequins all over it. When she returned it next day I peered at it in dismay. I didn't know which was worse, the patch or the sequins!

Within a few weeks my sight was fully restored, though with double vision. Dark glasses were prescribed to protect the retina from light. But there were problems other than my sight with which to contend. My left foot became so painful that I was unable to wear the caliper designed to straighten my leg and further investigation revealed poisonous sores which had to be lanced and drained. My left hand, too, needed further attention and once again a splint was fitted to open the fingers from the palm. Bitterly, I reflected on how complacent I had been about my health and wholeness and how much I had taken for granted my beautiful slim hands and slender tapering fingers.

In an attempt to broaden the horizons of my focus and in accordance with his original plan, Peter Allen began initiating me in the art of public speaking and tutoring me in the history and aims of the Cheshire Homes Movement.

At the heart of the Cheshire Foundation is a Red Feather. The symbol is emblazoned on the façade of its buildings, its vehicles, its stationery. Group Captain Leonard Cheshire, founder of the Movement, had a great love of the Far East and, as red is symbolic of joy to the Chinese, and a feather meant hope and happiness in Korea, he chose these components to convey the essence of his objectives.

Leonard's vision was of real homes in the heart of the local community for those suffering physical handicap, whose disabilities would otherwise have forced them to live on the boundary of society. To this end, he was able to purchase, on easy terms, a house and farmland which had belonged to an aunt. The house was called Le Court and was in the heart of Hampshire.

He began putting his plan into operation in a very small way in May, 1948, when he took in a cancer patient by the name of Arthur Dykes – though the name 'Cheshire Home' did not come into being until June, 1950, some years after Arthur's death. In the meantime, however, other chronically ill and terminal patients began making approaches to Leonard Cheshire in the hope that they, too, might experience the security of a home – a place of their very own, albeit one room.

From the first, Leonard Cheshire determined not to worry about finance. Residents paid what they could; hospital schemes, local donations and the sale of flowers and vegetables from Le Court made up the shortfall. The staff, such as they were, scoured local dustbins and dumps in search of any household items which were lacking, and residents were put to work according to their ability. Even 'Granny', as one resident was affectionately known – well into her nineties and severely incapacitated – was set to peeling potatoes from her bed.

Eventually, the Foundation spread its nets overseas, to the Third World, India, South America, the Philippines,

North America, Singapore – anywhere and everywhere that a need existed. By 1976 there were nearly seventy Cheshire Homes in the United Kingdom, and over one hundred in thirty-two overseas countries.

Dutifully, urged on by Peter Allen's zeal, I learned all that I could of the Movement.

And then, in 1979, when I had been a resident of Douglas House for seven years, life changed abruptly. Peter Allen found it necessary to leave his post as Head of Home. Two men attended interviews for his position and, with a complete disregard for the opinions of the residents, the Management Committee made an appointment. It seemed that even the most concerned individuals submitted to the generally held point of view that, once in a wheelchair, human beings were deemed to have no valid discernment, or ability to make sound judgements.

With such blatant disregard for my point of view and that of fellow residents, and under a new management of which we did not approve, I found myself becoming increasingly bitter.

Within a few months of Peter Allen's departure, a depression took hold of me from which I could not shake free. Convinced that I was friendless, unloved and uncared for, the days ahead looked bleak and empty. I was deprived of all that the Red Feather symbolised, without joy, without happiness, without hope and the true nature of my life hit home. I was a hemiplegic. Wheelchair bound. Utterly dependent. Without hope of ever knowing anything better in life.

14

A Motorised Bed

Throughout the seven years of my residence in Douglas House, Peter Allen had been not only Head of Home but also my friend and mentor. He and his wife Julie had done much to encourage me, physically and mentally, so that in every sense I was now a far stronger person than the enfeebled girl with suicidal tendencies who had first entered the Cheshire Home on that October afternoon so long ago. At that time the curve of my body, slumped in a borrowed canvas chair, had resembled a question mark. But if dedicated physiotherapy and skilled surgery had now largely straightened my frame, there still remained the question which hovered in my mind – and that was not to be easily answered. Why?

When, in 1979, Peter Allen departed suddenly I was bereft, and for a time lost all sense of direction. Eventually, however, Tom Fallon replaced Peter as Head of Home, a man as different from Peter as the proverbial chalk is from cheese. Tom was Irish, with a native easy-going charm and blarney humour. In no time his more relaxed attitudes made themselves felt in Douglas House, with the bending of rules and abolition of uniforms.

In need of a break after Peter's departure, I was encouraged by Tom to take a holiday. Later in the summer, when I was invited by Patsy Lee, a Chinese Ecuadorian friend, to visit her in Spain, I gladly accepted. She was now happily married to a Spanish doctor by the name of Dario de Salazar, who was Medical

Superintendent of Santander. He, therefore, had at his finger-tips all the facilities I would need should a medical emergency arise. Nevertheless, an escort was obviously necessary for my sea voyage on the SS *Patricia* and I took with me a girl on the Care Staff of Douglas House, together with her boyfriend. Both were extremely young and seemed to spend much of their time absorbed in their own romance, rather than in my welfare. My heart ached with loneliness for a love of my own; but who would look at a partially-sighted, disabled girl with only one functioning arm?

With the beach and pavement cafés of Santander so reminiscent of our shared Ecuadorian experience, Patsy and I spent many happy hours poring over memories of parties and friends. She and her Chinese family had lived in the nearby port of La Lubertad when David was working on the Ancon oilfield and she had kept in touch with friends from the Peninsula. Greg, Patsy told me, was still in Ecuador with his wife, Clare. Marie, David's girlfriend, had returned to her husband Steve when David had refused to visit me in hospital, and David was now married to a wealthy Ecuadorian who had given him two fine sons. Jealousy ate into me, a jealousy which no amount of rationalising would eradicate. Oh yes, I enlightened my friend, I too had had news of David. As well as the maintenance which he sent faithfully every month, each Christmas a cheque would arrive, along with a card which read: *Hope you and your parents are well.*

During the early days of life in Ancon, Patsy had been responsible for the gift of Goliat, my precious collie dog. A tragedy had occurred, she informed me; Goliat had escaped from the house in Quito when David had been living there alone soon after my return to England. He was the victim of a road traffic accident and, sadly, had died. I was overcome with grief, and found it difficult not to blame David. Yet in a sense it was easier to know that my beloved dog did not have a new mistress. I realised also that, even had I still been living in Ecuador, it would have been impossible for me to take him for the long walks we had both enjoyed along Ancon's white sandy beaches.

Nevertheless, such knowledge did little to appease my perpetual state of frustration. How I hated my dependence! In all that I did, even the most basic functions of going to bed, to the lavatory, taking a bath or a 'walk' in my wheelchair, I was utterly reliant on the whims and availability of others.

After the experience with my two young escorts, I made sure of a more mature companion on my next visit to Santander. Val was also on the Care Staff, a compassionate woman with two children, who talked often of my going to live with her at home, telling me in vivid terms of the way in which she would look after me. It was a wonderful dream, a dream which, after the holiday, was shattered, leaving me very embittered. For, during our stay in Santander, Val changed in her attitudes towards me and, on our return to the Home, she never again mentioned my moving in with her.

Concerned for my state of mind Tom arranged for me to see one of the Care Advisors for the Cheshire Foundation. In his early forties, he was a dark-haired man of medium build, by the name of Hugh Bryant. Hugh made periodic visits to the Home and on each occasion I poured myself out to him, telling him of my feelings of loneliness, the periods of depression and the utter lack of purpose in my life. Tears accompanied the telling of my tale of woe, welling up uncontrollably from the aching emptiness at the centre of my being. Though Hugh would always produce a hanky for me to mop them up, I felt that my tears annoyed him and that he felt uncomfortable and embarrassed with the sight of my red and swollen eyes.

Tom Fallon also lost patience with my constant blubbering and told me, in his usual kindly fashion, that he couldn't bear to see a woman cry. I liked Tom and was full of remorse for causing his discomfort, but still the tears kept coming.

Tom now continued the work of Peter Allen in attempting to redirect the focus of my thinking away from myself. Under his direction and encouragement I was launched into a career of sorts, albeit in an unpaid capacity, whereby I represented the goals, aspirations and financial needs of Douglas House to the general public.

Each individual House in the group of Cheshire Homes scattered about the world was fully autonomous in its day-to-day running, as well as in raising funds. From the moment of its inception, right through the building work, furnishing, equipping, staffing, and all subsequent running costs, the Homes relied on the generosity of public donations and benefactors to meet requirements. To this end, Support Groups held charitable fund-raising events, in addition to the gifts and legacies made by caring individuals and organisations.

Schools, Rotary Clubs, Women's Institutes – any and every group and organisation who might require a speaker – they all became a platform for the sort of information I had been groomed to convey. Nor had my coaching been confined to the actual ideas I was to present. Both Peter and Tom had seen to it that the messenger was as attractive as the message itself and I now had a more than passing interest in my appearance. Despite my disability, I had learned how to dress and use cosmetics to full advantage.

Life began to revolve around my talks on behalf of the Cheshire Home.

It would be foolish to pretend that I did not enjoy the opportunities that came my way or suggest that I was not fully aware of the way in which my talks opened up a new world to me, a world denied to many of the residents of Douglas House. Travel, meeting local dignitaries – and the very real concern and compassion of many ordinary folk, were all part of the spin-off. Somewhere, deep within, however, lurked that same sense of futility, of emptiness, of questioning the realities of life which had dogged me even in the sophisticated days of Quito.

In addition to the talks I gave on behalf of Cheshire Homes, my quest for the reasons to my existence, for some sort of purpose in life, led me also into other ventures: the setting up and running of a Greetings Card Shop at Douglas House, taking French lessons, and a very active part in the Resident's Association. The Association had started in Peter Allen's time, and was a body of residents nominated and elected in a democratic way to have a voice in the policies of the Home, its social functions and fund-raising activities. At various times I was Secretary and Chairman.

Then in May, 1982, ten years all but a month since my operation, my dear dad died. It seemed that he'd suddenly been taken ill and had passed away in hospital.

Just ten months previously, in the spring of 1981, he and Mum had given a lively party to celebrate their Golden Wedding. They'd both looked frail, I recalled, yet utterly devoted to one another. I'd been conscious, at the time, of the toll which so many tragedies had taken on their health and happiness: the quarrels between them during my childhood following Janet's death, then later, the upsets of my rebellious teenage years, and finally the double trauma of my divorce and brain tumour. Though unable ever to express my feelings, deep down I thought my parents wonderful; and now my dad was dead!

A Union Jack covered the coffin at the Crematorium, and I felt both proud and sad as I watched my mother, now so little without the big tall man at her side. I wept for the loss of my father and I wept for myself, for the fear that was in my heart, the fear that when Mum followed him I'd be utterly alone.

With the funeral now behind her, my mother put the house on the market and, once it was sold, made her home in a warden-controlled development for the elderly.

Poundsgate Close was a well-laid-out area with tiny bungalows set amidst bordered gardens, and had the added advantage of being quite close to Douglas House. Even so, it was too far for me to be pushed in my manual wheelchair, and I was thrilled when the authorities decided to supply me with my very own electric chair so that I could visit Mum without recourse to friends or staff.

But where, I questioned on first seeing the complex, were the ramps and wide doorways? Surely elderly people needed wheelchair facilities, I asked, indignantly? I could not believe that disablement was a tragedy confined only to the young.

I had grown used to viewing buildings from a different stance. The previous year, 1981, had been the International Year of the Disabled when architects, planners and councils had declared a passionate intention to give priority to certain aspects of building; to provide, at the outset, ramps, wider doorways with lower handles and special toilet facilities. Tremendous publicity had been given to the subject, speakers had fervently supported the cause, pretty stamps had even been issued to commemorate the occasion. A few authorities had complied, stressing the importance of access for the disabled, particularly in public areas, then – nothing! My mother's new home, part of a government sponsored scheme, did not even give lip-service to such planning; to add insult to injury, even the Community Room was upstairs!

Such lack of foresight denied me access to my mother's home and conversation was, therefore, limited to that which could be held on the doorstep. In the early days, tea-parties, to which all the residents were invited, were held on my mother's back lawn. However, eventually a ramp was built at the back of the house so that I could drive up it and through the patio doors, straight into Mum's lounge.

Over the next few months my mother slowly deteriorated. With an operation for a serious heart condition only recently behind her, she became increasingly frail. Unable to stand for long, she neglected to cook for herself. Meals on Wheels were organised to make deliveries; but she detested the very idea and toyed with the food on her plate, eating little of substance. Gradually she became thinner, weaker, spending most of her days in an armchair staring at the hedge around her small, neat garden, and at the sparrows that pecked away on the ramp.

I felt sure that my mother's days were limited and, selfishly, thought only of myself, alone and friendless.

My battery-operated chair gave me access to places undreamed of and brought spontaneity of sorts back into my life. To be able to go where I wanted, when I wanted was a miracle, and I revelled in the opportunities created: visits to Mum; shopping in Brixham alone; spending as long as I liked choosing a lipstick colour without being conscious of a friend or escort waiting patiently by.

Mobility also brought escape: relief from the noise of the Home and its many residents. With the little 'joy-stick' of my motorised chair between the fingers of my right hand I was able to trundle down the road and along a path which took me right on to the huge limestone clifftop of Berry Head, overlooking St Mary's Bay, where nesting herring gulls mewed plaintively and kittiwakes uttered the sweet, haunting sound of their namesake. Berry Head became my sanctuary, a special, private place to which I could retreat to indulge my self-pity and let the tears fall unseen.

It was in just such a frame of mind that I sat in my wheelchair one day in the summer of 1983 in my usual spot hidden from view and hemmed in by a clump of prickly gorsebushes. Behind me a broad tarmacadamed pathway ran between the ramparts of a Napoleonic fort. The huge, limestone blocks hewn from the promontory upon which they'd stood for centuries, cast heavy shadows, deep and foreboding. Before me, battalions of pink Valerian, bowed by the sea-breeze, plunged down the cliff face, attractive enough to look at, but exuding a pungent odour when crushed. And beyond, far beyond, a lone dinghy lay like a discarded toy on the hard shiny surface of the sea, its white sail a tiny speck almost lost to sight in the vast, empty, sweep of ocean.

'Jesus Christ died for your sins. God loves you and sent His Son to die for your redemption!'

The words came unexpectedly, as if from nowhere, disturbing my usual bitter contemplation. I looked up, feeling an unreasonable and unidentified surge of anger. An elderly, dark-haired man stood before me, dressed in, of all things, given the heat of the day, a smart city suit. In contrast to his surroundings he looked utterly alien.

'Go away!' I rasped. 'I don't want to know. How dare you talk to me about things like that.'

A sudden flurry of gulls flew from the cliffs of St Mary's Bay and gave vent to a high, shrill screech. The man, whoever he was, turned and walked away.

Jesus! I thought. *As if I need to hear about him!*

But an inexplicable disquiet lay beneath my burning resentment. And, in the days to come, I was to know no peace.

But peace was the hallmark of Geoffrey James!

Geoffrey James was one of the residents of Douglas House. He'd been confined to bed from the age of nine when he'd contracted muscular dystrophy at school in Hartland, North Devon. Quite unable to sit, he'd been bed-ridden ever since. When Douglas House was officially opened in 1973 by Leonard Cheshire, Geoffrey was one of the first to move in. Some years later he had been given a motorised bed.

Geoffrey James could drive! It was a wonderful sight! By manipulating a tiny hand control that engaged a battery-driven motor, he could bowl down the corridor, manoeuvre into the lift, and make his way to the garden.

But the garden was not the limit of Geoffrey James and his motorised bed; his excursions took him to London and Ireland. He even went to Ascot in his bed!

Everyone loved Geoffrey. His face beamed from the pillows, and his blue eyes sparkled when he talked. And talk he did. Into every conversation Geoffrey brought the subject of God. But because it was Geoffrey and because he was so popular, nobody minded. People constantly sought his company.

One afternoon, soon after the incident on Berry Head, I parked my chair in Geoffrey's room, close to his motorised bed with its green and white striped cotton bedcover. Noise drifted through the half-open door from the busy corridor outside: the squeak of rubber on linoleum from the passage of wheelchairs, chattering staff, and the overriding and insistent call of the intercom system. Inside the neat, square room, all was tranquil; an air of peace prevailed.

'God is so good. I have so much to thank him for.'

I stared at Geoffrey in amazement, at his prostrate body, twisted and ravaged with disease. What could Geoffrey possibly have to be thankful for?

'I don't believe in God.' I spoke mildly, aware that I felt none of the resentment of my conversation with the stranger on the clifftop.

Geoffrey ignored me. 'Sometimes I think this room is like a little bit of heaven.'

This was becoming ridiculous! Geoffrey's room might be a haven compared with the cacophony of the corridor, but to describe in such glowing terms a tiny, cramped, institutionalised room dominated by a motorised bed in which you lay crippled was going too far.

'I don't believe in heaven.' I surprised myself by my lack of vehemence. Geoffrey looked incredulous, but apparently for different reasons. When he spoke again his voice was rapturous, and his face shone beatifically.

'You don't believe in heaven? Susan, you don't know what you're missing. It's something to look forward to;

something that makes sense of the here-and-now,
something that gives a purpose to life. Just think! All that
wonderful eternity ahead of me . . .'

A knock came at the door; it slid open and someone
entered the room. The conversation ended.

But the words lived on in my mind.

And in my heart dwelt the gentle memory of Geoffrey's
shining face.

A few weeks later I was working on the Reception Desk
of the Cheshire Home, as I did every Tuesday, when
Geoffrey returned from a visit to his mother, Hilda. She
lived locally in Brixham and Geoffrey was a regular
visitor. On this particular morning he looked pinched and
chilled as he drove through the doorway and stopped for
a moment to chat.

'A new entrance is having to be made into my mother's
house and I was outside in my bed for longer than I
expected,' he told me. 'I felt so cold . . .' He shivered,
engaged the tiny lever which operated his bed, and set
off down the corridor.

Geoffrey stayed in his room all that day and all the
following day. On Thursday we heard that he had
pneumonia.

'I'm afraid he's really very ill,' one of the nursing staff
confided to me when I made enquiries.

The following day the news we all dreaded hit the
Home. 'Geoffrey James is dead.'

A heavy silence hung like a shroud over staff and
residents alike. It was terrible. So many lovely people had
died since my entry into the Cheshire Home and the
memory of each was a sweet reminder of the private
battle with disability in which each had engaged, of
courage in the face of suffering, of tears, of joys, of death.
But those memories, however poignant, were as nothing
compared with the impact of Geoffrey's passing;
Geoffrey with his homespun philosophy, his twinkling
eyes and ever present sense of humour which had

softened his intellect and staggering knowledge of wild life, history, the arts, politics and religion. Life had abounded in Geoffrey's crippled body. How could death have won the day?

Over and over in my mind came the words of Geoffrey's profession: *God is so good. I have so much to thank him for.* Tumbling in disarray, they were like pieces of jigsaw thrown into the air, senseless in isolation, yet together making a whole, perfect picture. But not for me, not yet for me. Somewhere, I knew, there must be a key, the central piece upon which all else pivoted. With anguish, with despair too profound to be plumbed, I twisted and turned in my effort to grasp at the Truth of Geoffrey's God.

15

Geoffrey's God

*'I am the resurrection, and the life: he that believeth in me,
though he were dead, yet shall he live: And whosoever liveth
and believeth in me shall never die.'*[1]

The ancient words that had rung down through the
centuries brought comfort to those who crowded into
Brixham Methodist Church that day in May, 1984. The
little stone-walled chapel, which nestled against the
hillside in the heart of town, was filled with folk who had
known and loved Geoffrey. They packed the pews and
overflowed into the aisles. Wheelchairs and their
occupants were also evident in abundance. They lined
a platform which had been specially constructed some
years ago to accommodate Geoffrey's motorised bed.

I'd entered the chapel via the wooden ramp and
widened doorway that led to the platform. I'd expected
to find grief and mourning for the loss of Geoffrey's life
with its pleasure and pains and, sure enough, these
emotions were present. But there was no sign of anguish
or desolation amongst the congregation. Overall, joy
predominated. Incomprehensible! I gazed from face to
face noting, with amazement, the radiance that shone
from each.

Despite the diversity of origin and creeds, the
congregation stood as a single entity whilst the coffin was
solemnly conveyed up the aisle. Seated in my wheelchair
at the rear of the congregation, I watched and listened.

'For God so loved the world that he gave his only Son,

that whoever believes in him should not perish but have eternal life.'2

Eternal life! How the words seared into me! An image of Geoffrey's countenance, sublime above his powerless body, rose in my mind. Suddenly, his faith made sense: all that he'd said; all that he'd embodied. Right there and then, as I sat in Geoffrey's church, the understanding of my heart was illuminated. Gone was grief and sorrow; in its place peace and a strange excitement filled my breast. *Geoffrey was not dead. The Geoff I had loved so well, the real Geoff, contained within the broken shell of his body, was incorruptible, imperishable, undefiled and unfading.* In an instant, comprehension swept away my doubts and I *knew*. Knew that because of Geoffrey's belief in God, he would *never* die! Knew that, even now, he lived and was loved. The thought was staggering!

Yet was this not the Truth to which Geoffrey had alluded that afternoon in his room? *All that eternity ahead . . .*

Music filled the air around me – and in that moment realisation was born within me: an, as yet, dimly recognised conception that here was the answer to all of life's questions. This was the key to all the bewilderment of my youth; the missing piece in the puzzle of my adult years, the undiscovered purpose, the central pivot around which all else moved. The God of whom Geoffrey had spoken was Someone *I* wanted to know. The search was on. Somewhere, somehow, God was to be found, of that I was certain. I had only to look. And I determined that I would do all in my power to hunt him out.

It never occurred to me that, throughout the years, God had been involved in finding me: that he, not I, had instigated the action. Nor did it cross my mind that, having found me, he was even now alongside, waiting quietly until I should turn to him. My sights were still set on a remote and far-flung horizon. In reality I did not need to look so far into the distance. All that I lacked was right beneath my nose.

For years I'd nursed a vague awareness of the vacuous nature of my life. I'd longed to discover some meaning, some substance that had always eluded me. Now I knew, with absolute certainty, that Geoffrey had possessed that knowledge, that his life had had point and purpose, and that what he had known, I wanted for myself. Geoffrey's God was to be my God.

Convinced of this truth, I began my quest in the most obvious place. On the first Sunday after his funeral, I attended Geoffrey's church. Peter Crew, the Minister, was young and vital with a great love for the lost and the lonely and the hurting, hungry souls who crossed his path. That love, coupled with his enthusiasm and wisdom, exerted an influence on others which was life-changing. Under his ministry, I began to see the sophisticated and affluent lifestyle I had led in Ecuador as empty and futile, the years of bitterness since I had been struck down by illness as self-centred and introverted. I was filled with regret for all the wasted years, years when I could have been looking outward, to God and to others.

In other respects, too, I was convicted of sin, of the ways in which I had fallen short of God's glory. Memories of my wedding service filled me with remorse. I had wanted only ceremony, tradition and finery. Vows made before God to love, honour, cherish and obey had meant nothing to me and there had been little in the way of understanding or sincerity on my part that what I had undertaken was a lifelong commitment. Hot shame flooded through me when I remembered my love affairs.

Each Sunday, following Morning Service, a number of folk from the congregation would meet for coffee in the Community Centre opposite the church. It was a time of lively conversation and informal chatter, but though I was now ostensibly on the inside, I still felt like an outsider. I lacked assurance and was convinced that there was more to discover. Much more!

It was from the Centre, one Sunday, that I was set on the pathway to find the Truth I sought.

'Are you going to Ashton Gate?' One of the young women from church interrupted my brooding and handed me a cup of coffee.

Ashton Gate? Isn't that a football ground?'

The woman smiled. 'That's right. Billy Graham's going to be there. Mission England?'

I shrugged. I didn't know what she was talking about.

'Think about it,' she persisted. 'There are still some seats left on the coach.' She turned away and continued handing out coffees.

Billy Graham? A poster in the window of the Centre displayed his name, emblazoned beneath a picture of a kindly, smiling face. I sat for a moment and studied it. As far as I knew, the man was an American evangelist in Britain to make converts. Peter Crew had made some reference to him during service that morning, and had detailed the church's involvement. But it had never occurred to me to consider going to Bristol to hear him.

Until now! Suddenly, the prospect filled me with excitement. I was hungry for God. I longed to find out all I could about him. And where better to do so than at a Mission England Rally? If Billy Graham didn't have the sort of knowledge I required, then nobody did. Without delay, I booked a seat on the coach to take me to Ashton Gate.

And one step nearer to Geoffrey's God.

Thousands, literally thousands, of people milled around the entrance of the Ashton Gate football ground that Monday, 18th June. Tens of thousands filled the stadium. A thrill of anticipation ran through me: confirmation that I was on the right path to find Geoffrey's God.

'All these people are here for one purpose!' Incredulously, I kept saying this over and over to my friends from Brixham.

From the grandstand, assorted choirs sang choruses

which only in the future were to become familiar to me.
They sang of Jesus, of knowing him, of loving him. They
sang of the lamb that was slain, of his Majesty, of his
'touch upon my life'. And from all around me the same
theme swelled in a great tidal wave that swept me onward
and upward, turning my sight to the Almighty, to his
glory and splendour.

It was so moving – like nothing I had ever experienced
before. Tears welled in my eyes and an all-consuming
passion rose in my breast.

Billy Graham walked on to the rostrum which was set
out on the pitch before the grandstand. God is holy, he
explained simply yet clearly. He yearns for the children
of his creation to be brought into a relationship with him,
to be sons and daughters, to know him as Father. But
sin stands in the way; our sin separates us from God.
In his holiness, God cannot look upon sin, cannot be in
relationship with sinners.

Again I was convicted of my unworthiness and knew
a burning desire to be right before God, to enter into a
relationship with him. I listened, intently.

We only love because God first loved us, Billy Graham
continued, and he demonstrates his love that whilst we
were yet sinners he sent his son, Jesus Christ, to die for
our sin. Only through the sinless sacrifice of Jesus, who
gave himself for the iniquities of mankind, can we be
brought into fellowship with God. *'For God so loved the
world, that he gave his only begotten Son, that whosoever
believeth in him should not perish, but have everlasting life.'*[3]
There it was again! The same verse I'd heard at Geoffrey's
funeral.

Rapturous silence lay upon the people. Around the
arena, tens of thousands of ears tuned in to the Word
that is Life; and the eyes of all fixed upon the figure of
one ordinary man – a man with no great oratory skill
– whom God had chosen to favour as his mouthpiece.
Beneath the high blue dome of heaven, the vision of row
upon row of individuals from miles and miles around

blurred and faded into insignificance. Billy Graham's voice rang out in the stadium, echoing and re-echoing. For me. For me alone.

There is no condemnation for those in Christ Jesus. No condemnation . . . no condemnation . . .

The grass took on a greener hue. A gentle breeze, warm, like the breath of God, caressed my bare arms. Above me, a lone cloud, which had momentarily darkened the sky, dissipated in the sun's rays and dispersed into the stratosphere.

Then I heard it: the voice in my heart! *'Jesus loves you and died for you – for YOU, for YOU, FOR YOU!'*

Why had nobody ever spoken to me of this before? This, the most important thing: the infinite love of God, forgiving me, redeeming me through his Son, making me his daughter and bringing me into everlasting life. *He loves me. He loves me!* But this was Love as I had never known it – free and unconditional, liberating and fulfilling.

By comparison, the love affairs of my past life were empty, clanging vessels which had left me hollow and incomplete. Far from satisfying my needs, those relationships had merely increased my craving for meaning and purpose in my life.

I'd managed for years to silence my conscience, to cast it from me. More recently that had proved impossible. Shame, like a cruel gaoler, had stalked my mind and guilt had shackled me as if with clanking chains. Imprisoned by my own transgressions, and filled with remorse, I felt soiled and sullied.

But now – now I could be free. Free and washed clean. Cut loose from all that had ensnared me. A new creation in Christ Jesus.

'Majesty, worship his majesty; unto Jesus be glory, honour and praise . . .'

I sang the words and in my heart I bowed to the Kingship of Jesus. Repeating Billy Graham's prayer of repentance, acknowledging my sinful nature and turning away from sinful acts of self-will, I asked God to forgive me and thrilled at the knowledge of his acceptance. In utter humility, I asked Jesus into my life to reign there as my Saviour and my Lord.

The voices of massed choirs lifted to the heavens. And in heaven itself, they were joined by the voices of angels. And great was their rejoicing. Geoffrey's God had become my God.

Immediately, upon my return to Brixham, I set about making Geoffrey's church my church too. Peter Crew, the young minister, led me through the steps of confirmation and, in due course, I was accepted into membership of the Methodist chapel.

During those weeks of instruction, I began to understand that faith was less a question of believing than of a daily walk, hand in hand, with the Lord. In this way, through prayer, Bible reading, and fellowship with other members of his family, I became involved in him and in his kingdom. The Bible tells us that unless we become like little children we cannot know God (Matt. 18:3). It was only through childlike dependency on the Father that I was able to see how his purposes had led me to this moment, to discern, little by little, his plans for the future.

In this respect, counselling sessions with Hugh Bryant became a thing of the past. Though he had been endlessly patient in his endeavours to help me overcome my problems of loneliness, unhappiness, lack of purpose and bitterness, came the day when I was able to think that now I was a Christian I would no longer require his services. Far from being put-out, he was delighted at my new-found liberty, and wished me well. As I sat in my wheelchair and watched him walk down the corridor away from me, I knew the most amazing and transforming effect on my spirit. I delighted in the knowledge that I no longer needed the advice of Man. From now on I had the power of the Holy Spirit at my disposal, as my Comforter, my Guide, my Counsellor, my Friend.

However, despite having become a member of the Methodist church, I felt that God wanted more of me. After attending the baptisms of several friends at the local Baptist church, I was convinced by Jesus' own command that I, too, should follow him into the waters. This was not part of Methodist tradition, but no objection was raised to my taking part in a baptismal service at my friends' church and, after going forward during an appeal at one of the services, my own baptism was arranged for the following November.

From the moment of decision, it was almost as if some outside agent was intent upon putting me off. One day, whilst on an outing in the grounds of a nearby stately home, one of the boys from Douglas House took the back of my chair to assist me down a slope which led to a large lake. As we drew near, for some unknown reason, the young man let go. My chair gathered speed, took off on the descent and careered headlong towards the water. The spectre of dark, unfathomable depths, and choking memories of water closing overhead, loomed before me. Gripped with fear, I clung to the armrests of my chair.

Then, just as I reached the brink, miraculously, an unknown man saw my predicament, darted forward and grabbed the handles of my chair, averting almost certain disaster. Shaking, I thanked my deliverer and, to cover my emotion, joked that, without his intervention, the battery of my chair would have been ruined. But in truth, I'd been terrified, and thanked God for his hand upon me and for keeping me safe.

For weeks after, snatches of conversation overheard in the dining-room of Douglas House haunted my mind. 'Susan being baptised?' said one resident to another. 'You mean she'll go completely under? She must be crazy!' Others nodded. 'Crazy,' they agreed, tapping their temples, sagely.

Was I crazy, I wondered? What madness had possessed me to think that I, a severely disabled young woman, could possibly undertake such a dangerous procedure?

Baptism was, after all, only a symbol — an outward sign of an inner conviction. And why was I doing it? God, who sees the hearts of men and women, knew the extent of my commitment; knew that Jesus was my Saviour and Lord. So I reasoned; and in my mind, fear fought with faith.

Shortly after, one of the residents came to my room for an evening coffee. When she left, I flipped on the hot tap at my basin in order to wash the cups. On the dresser, were two dirty mugs from earlier in the day and, not wanting to waste the lovely sudsy washing-up water, I trundled, in my wheelchair, to collect them from the far side of the room. I felt most domesticated! Then, out of the corner of my eye, I saw white foam erupting, like a mini volcano, from the washbasin. At any moment it threatened to run, lava-like, down the sides of my vanitory unit. In a panic, I swivelled my chair and shot forward to avert the disaster.

Halfway across the room, I stopped abruptly. I had no hope of reaching the taps without filling my lap with hot soapy water. And to do so would imperil my safety. For if my chair battery was flooded, I might be electrocuted!

Even as the thought flitted through my mind, suds poured over the basin's sides and streamed across the freshly shampooed carpet towards me. Mesmerised, I watched as the water acted upon residue foam in the carpet and rose, as if inflated, with ever-increasing volume.

I pulled myself together, turned and made for the bell to summon aid. To my intense frustration I discovered someone had looped it out of reach above my bed. Everything took on the slow-motion action of a nightmare in a bad film.

'So I did what any Spirit-filled Christian should do,' I later told a friend. 'I yelled "Help!" Fortunately my neighbour heard and summoned the Care Staff to the rescue.'

But, despite the retrospective jocularity, I *was*

concerned. 'Are you trying to tell me something, Lord?'
I prayed. 'There seems to be too much water involved
in my life at present. Is there some significance?'

Friends reassured me. 'If God wants something of you,
Susan,' they said, 'then you can be sure the Enemy will
try to prevent it.'

Past experiences had induced in me a great deal of fear
of water. Desperately, I prayed that I would not lose heart
before the day of my baptism arrived.

The Baptist church was undergoing an interregnum.
In the absence of a regular minister my baptism was to
be conducted by three deacons, two of whom were local
general practitioners. Brian Caunter was the third man.

'I want to *walk* into the water,' I told Dr David Langley.
'Do you think that would be possible?'

A recent stay at Mary Marlborough Lodge – a
rehabilitation centre – had given me a strong desire for
independence, and if it was at all feasible just this once,
I wanted to demonstrate my determination on this special
occasion.

After consideration it was felt that, with the physical
support of the three men, my wishes could be fulfilled.
A rehearsal was duly scheduled for the evening before
the actual service.

When we met, after supper that night, I could see at
a glance that Brian, like so many lay people, was acutely
nervous about my disability; he responded gamely,
however, to Dr Langley's instructions.

'We've worked out a plan of campaign,' David told me.
'Dr Wood, Brian and I will hold on to one another to form
a ring around you so that you'll be supported on all sides.
And we'll come with you right into the water.'

'This evening, though, is only a dry-run,' Dr Wood
reminded us. 'We'll fill the pool tomorrow.'

'Hope it's going to be warm,' I joked, apprehensively.

'Positively hot,' David Langley assured me. 'Right,
shall we make a start?'

The rehearsal began.

At first all went well. Supported by the three men, I stepped towards the baptismal pool and slowly, like a giant octopus, the four of us inched our way down the steps. Then suddenly, I slipped. The three men, caught completely unawares, staggered under my dead-weight, lost balance and, in a tangle of arms and legs, collapsed with me on to the floor of the pool. Laughter exploded from us all. Shaking with mirth, we disentangled our various limbs and squatted in the small, dry, blue plastic tub with tears rolling down our faces. Our merriment saved the day and a potentially embarrassing situation was averted. Later, however, a niggling doubt remained with me: how come that this, one of the most sacred moments of my life, had been reduced by such outrageous hilarity?

Convinced by now that the whole event would be an utter disaster, I prayed even more fervently, and approached the great day with considerable trepidation. My fears were unfounded.

I was to give a brief testimony before my baptism. Until that November evening, I had never thought of my life in South America without a gnawing nostalgia and sense of loss and sorrow. On this occasion, however, I heard myself speaking of my previous life – the huge house in Ecuador, servants, parties and social standing – as of no significance compared with all that I had gained in Christ. What had seemed so vital then, seemed trivial now. God was saying to me, '*Fix your thoughts not on what is seen, but on what is unseen. For what is seen is temporary, yet what is unseen is eternal.*'[4]

With gentlemanly support, I stepped into the pool and, for the first time in my life, went under the water without fear or discomfort. The symbolism of cleansing from sin, the burial of self-will and rising again from the grave, clothed in the righteousness of Christ Jesus, moved me as nothing else had before. I was, truly, a new creation.

'Be not ashamed of the gospel of Christ,' David Langley

said as I stood before him, 'for it is the power of God until salvation.'[5]

Baptism over, I struggled, with the help of my two friends, Margaret and Beryl, to remove my long white baptismal robe and under-shift. In the interests of modesty, both were weighted at the hem and tied around my ankles. In addition, the whole operation was rendered even more difficult by my paralysed left arm, and the way the wet fabric clung to my body. Because I needed to be out front once more to witness the other baptisms, speed and silence were essential. But as our antics became ever more frenzied, the three of us were convulsed with giggles, and it was with a good deal of mirth that we eventually rejoined the congregation. Again, I marvelled that, even in the most solemn moments of my life, God could bring laughter and happiness in such abundance.

As I took my place once more in the body of the church, Dr David Wood moved towards me. 'My daughter,' he prophesied, 'My love is upon you. If you sit with me in the heavenlies, I will sit with you on earth.'

I wept at the beauty of the words, and the way they portrayed the depths of God's love for me.

In the following weeks, I relived the events of that evening. Something had happened to me. From that night on, I was aware of change at the deepest level of my being. No longer did I feel I must hide my Christian books and tapes. My faith was strengthened. And in my heart I understood the power that trauma and tragedy had played in my life – my divorce, the loss of my home, even my disablement – and the way that, in God's hands, those events could be used to encourage, to comfort and to guide others. God's plan and his timing are perfect. Disability was not a thing to be hidden, but to be used for the glory of God. For his strength is made perfect in weakness.

In the course of the next three years that conviction

became ever stronger. Under the ministries of Luis Palau,
Eric Delve, Spring Harvest and other people and events,
my sight was turned outward, away from self, towards
the needs of others.

After three years in membership at the Methodist
church, I felt led to support the tiny congregation at the
Church of the Nazarene. Whilst there, I was invited to
give my testimony, and when the BBC decided, later in
the year, to focus upon the fishing town of Brixham for
one of the *Songs of Praise* programmes, I was asked to
feature in the film.

Me! On TV! I could hardly believe it. First a researcher
came to interview me in my room at Douglas House.
Skilfully he extracted my lifestory from me. Then he
asked the strangest question: *'Tell me, what do you think
of the old Chinese conundrum: Are there wheelchairs in
heaven?'* I stared at him, trying to fathom what lay behind
his question. Did he not know the war I'd waged to come
to terms with life in a wheelchair I wondered?

Filming was to commence on Berry Head and my
wheelchair had to be anchored by large stones to prevent
my taking off down the slope and over the clifftop.
Behind and beneath me, the might of the ocean reined
in, undulating towards the cliffs' foot and spreading a
train of white, fold upon fold. On the headland, tufts of
pink sea thrift, spangled with golden bird's-foot, formed
small round footstools set on a carpet of wiry grasses.
Pam Rhodes had been seconded from Anglia TV to
interview me. I'd quenched my disappointment on
learning that it was not be someone really well-known
like Cliff Michelmore or Roger Royle but when I saw her
pretty face and calm serene manner, I had no regrets. I
was instantly at ease in her company and felt quite
composed before the camera.

Later, on the Quay, surrounded by the townspeople
of Brixham, we sang the hymn I had chosen: 'The Servant
King'. The haunting melody and beautiful words,
rendered almost perfect by massed choirs and

congregations, drifted across harbour and bay. My paralysed hand, still twisted despite numerous operations, lay in my lap. I glanced down and couldn't help but regret that my favourite verse, which speaks of Christ's hands being surrendered to cruel nails as a sacrifice for our sins, had had to be omitted due to the lack of time.

The programme went on air in September and in no time, it seemed, my story was renowned. Correspondence flooded in – from a man in Australia who sent gifts periodically; a man in Fife who carved a pair of praying hands set on a plaque which read, 'Prayer changes things'. Then there was a letter from a young girl in Wales who wanted to take me on holiday, another from Belgium and yet another from a nun in Ireland. One epistle arrived with the envelope boldly addressed: TO THE LADY IN THE WHEELCHAIR ON BERRY HEAD, BRIXHAM. An enlightened postman delivered it with pride. When I shopped in town, or sat on Berry Head, holiday-makers called to one another, 'There goes the lady from *Songs of Praise*' and one, a farmer's wife from Wales, brought me a sun hat and an ice cream.

But fame is not without its discomforts. Though initially I was flattered by being in the public eye, eventually I found the constant attention an embarrassment and was relieved when the time came that I could once again venture out without being accosted by well-wishers. Besides, the stories shared by my correspondents had inspired me to begin writing poetry in praise of God and, through my friend, Rev Peter Lorkin, they were edited, printed and bound. I named the book *Rainbow Through The Rain* and, as part of my tithe to the Lord, advertised it in various magazines. The first five hundred copies soon sold and repeat orders flowed in. That little book is now in its fourth reprint, still selling well and, I believe, bringing glory to God.

In the autumn following transmission of *Songs of Praise*,

I found the Lord leading me down new and exciting paths. Margaret Gould, wife of one of the local doctors, asked me to join the local committee of Christian Viewpoint, whose aims I had recently begun supporting. This was a national organisation which had come into being in the sixties, primarily to bring the Gospel to women who would not attend a church or conventional mission, an objective subsequently widened and diversified. I was delighted to be granted an opportunity to become involved in something so worthwhile and told Margaret I'd be glad to accept her offer.

Some months later, quite out of the blue, I was asked to share my testimony with another Christian Viewpoint group. A letter arrived inviting me to speak at New Milton, near Bournemouth. I remembered a DAMAS meeting in Quito – the first time I'd ever been asked to address an audience. How I'd quaked while delivering that simple Vote of Thanks! And now – here I was being asked to join the Christian Viewpoint Speakers' List!

Nervously, I contemplated the practical problems that would surely face me: who would drive me to Bournemouth? Would an overnight stay be necessary, in which case who would wash me, dress me, help me to the toilet? Would I be able to use my electric wheelchair, and would there be steps? My disability loomed large, making me more aware than ever of my dependence on others.

There were other problems, too – more personal, more subtle. I worried about whether I would have enough to say; how embarrassing it would be if I ran out of steam halfway through! Then there was the matter of what I should wear and whether it would be possible for Ruth, my hairdresser, to give me a shampoo and set prior to the meeting? Trivial though these matters might be, the level of my confidence depended upon knowing that, despite the wheelchair, I looked good – especially when surrounded by able-bodied women. Furthermore, I knew that such confidence would free me to concentrate on the really important issue: would God use my talk to bring someone to Christ? I prayed, fervently, for his power to be released in me and through me.

Priscilla Gurney offered to be my driver and carer. She was a fellow committee member who, having previously taken me to Spring Harvest, knew the ropes. On arrival in New Milton, we discovered that entry to the venue was via several steps. But that proved no problem to the ladies of the committee, who galvanised their husbands into action. Priscilla discovered a wicker chair and once I was installed in it, I was borne aloft by the gentlemen, and arrived at the meeting feeling like the Queen of Sheba – an auspicious start to my new ministry!

Nor was the end of my first speaking engagement any less eventful. In answer to my prayers, an American lady, in desperate straits, shared her problems with us and later came to know the love of Jesus.

God was using me in a way I would never have thought possible. And it seemed that the more I made myself available to him, the greater became his power within. My second talk, in Salisbury, was attended by one of the editors of Hodder & Stoughton, and she asked, afterwards, if I had ever thought of writing a book? Heady stuff! But the seed was sown. And in God's time it would grow.

Aware of a need for greater freedom in worship, and an easier journey to and from services, I left the Nazarene church in 1987 and joined the Community Church just up the hill. The natural exuberance of its pentecostal origins better suited my personality. Besides, gifts of the Spirit were practised and healing services held regularly. Again, it was as if God were leading me to the right place at the right time and, in this way, I was to know his healing in my own life.

It was a Saturday afternoon and I had a hospital appointment scheduled for the following week. My left leg, which had drooped since my operation in 1972, was causing considerable alarm. The colour was terrible and, with circulation an additional problem, there was a strong possibility of gangrene setting in. Inevitably this would result in my losing the limb.

I felt a new nighty was in order for my hospital visit and rushed down to town before closing time. I could not believe my eyes as I turned the corner to the Co-Op. There, on the window, was a notice: CLOSED: MOVING PREMISES. Behind the glass, tantalisingly inaccessible, was a display of nighties.

Dejection filled me. So much had seemed to be against me that week. My precious computer, my only means of writing, had broken down and, though only three years old, was out of production. Moreover, spare parts were unavailable. And now this! I would have to go into hospital with only my shabby old nighty to wear. A sudden squall whipped up a miniature dust storm and sent it scurrying along the pavement.

'What's the trouble, Susan?' A friendly voice startled me out of my disappointment. Tim was a great friend from the Pentecostal church. Both he and another man called Andrew had prayed with me from time to time and, as I began to share with Tim my need for a new nighty, as if on cue, Andrew appeared on the scene. Without further ado, the two young men laid hands on me and, right there and then, with Saturday shoppers dodging around us on the pavement outside the Co-Op, they prayed for my healing.

Warmth radiated through my shoulders where both had laid their hands, my dejection lifted and I felt, suddenly, overwhelmed with joy and happiness. The Bible tells us that where two or three agree on earth, that shall be done in heaven. Before we parted, we agreed in faith that the Lord would heal my leg and that there would be no need for a new nighty. In a very different frame of mind I waved my farewells and, gaily singing choruses, set off for Douglas House. My chair fairly flew up the hill.

A day or two later, after examining me, the doctor told me he felt confident that an operation would not be necessary. In the early days at Douglas House, the dropped foot condition had been so severe that other residents had constantly, though unwittingly, run over my poor limb with their wheelchairs. Numerous operations later, adjustment of tendons and ligaments had resulted in the foot being set in a more respectable position. No one, however, in all that time, had ever suggested prayer for healing!

A subsequent visit to the specialist convinced not only me of the power of prayer. Following a lengthy examination of the 'faulty' arteries which had been causing such concern, he gave his diagnosis with puzzled amazement. 'Perfect!' he pronounced. 'And not only the leg. Blood pressure on both the good side and paralysed side of your body is identical. Excellent, in fact.'

The Nighty Episode became legend. And the relating of the story was an encouragement to all who heard it – to my loving, praying friends at church, to friends at the Home and those who had witnessed our prayer meeting outside the Co-Op and, not least, to me. I had no need to buy a new nighty!

Nevertheless, the incident posed questions in my mind. Had I been limiting God's power? Could it be possible that, since my conversion, I'd adopted phrases like 'it must be God's purpose for me to glorify him through my wheelchair' only as a 'cop-out'? Moreover, was there still unforgiveness in my own heart which prevented God's power working in me?

The answer seemed to come during a day of meditation and silence which was held at Brunel Manor, a Christian Conference Centre in Torquay. Shortly before lunch, a tall regal woman bore down on me, 'I have a word from God for you: "It is the Sword, the Sword that sets you free." '

The woman left and I turned, with my companion, to

join the others for lunch in the gardens. There, in the warm sunshine, I looked back at the façade of the Manor, its mellow sandstone and granite infill monument to some of the finest masonry work of Victorian Gothic architecture. And I reflected upon the author and instigator of this building: Isambard Kingdom Brunel, bridge builder par excellence who had designed the house as his own home. How fitting that I should receive this Word from the Lord in this place of retreat. For if I had been concerned about limiting God's power in my life, His Word – a two-edged Sword – had surely set me free by pointing me towards the One who is the greatest bridge builder of all, the One who had bridged the gulf between my sin and God's holiness – Christ Jesus himself.

16

Healed Within

Nervously, I re-applied my lipstick; it wasn't often you had a personal interview with a celebrity like Joni Eareckson Tada, nor the privilege of a TV film crew to record it. In fact, the whole trip to America had taken on miracle status in the manner that God had provided. My fare had been raised by gifts of money from the Cheshire Home Foundation and friends; the power of prayer had secured a place on the plane for my electric wheelchair when airline officials had initially refused to allow an acid-filled battery on board; then a delay in schedule had made my dreams come true. In my initial planning I'd had to forgo a longed-for stopover in Chicago, due to a shortage of funds. However, because of the rescheduling of my flight and the nature of my disability, the airline had provided overnight accommodation free of charge, for my Japanese escort and me, in the Chicago Hilton. What style! Instead of 'slumming it' with other passengers, I'd slept in air-conditioned luxury in a kingsize bed.

I reflected on all that had led up to this moment. I suppose my initial interest in disability in the context of Christian faith had been sparked off a year or two before when a friend had given me a copy of Joni Eareckson's autobiography. When I'd read of her diving accident and subsequent struggle to equate quadriplegia and depression with belief in an all-loving, all-powerful God, I'd readily identified with her plight. I'd later learned that Joni had eventually initiated a support group called 'Joni and Friends', an idea that had inspired me to launch a small Christian Fellowship at Douglas House.

In the meantime, the publishing firm of Hodder & Stoughton had again approached me and, with the help of a professional writer, my story was to be turned into a book. Next, Jim Wiltshire, a freelance film director, heard my testimony and asked if he could make a documentary — hence the presence of the men around me. From them and others I learned that 'Joni and Friends' was now a huge, international concern with various offshoots. And when I heard, a few months later, that the 1990 Church and Disabled Congress was to take place at Calvin College, Grand Rapids — an event that would draw together disabled folk from all over the world — I never dreamed that my longing to be one of the delegates would be transformed into a reality. But on Monday 28th June, accompanied by Jim Wiltshire and Sayuri Arikawa, who was on the Care Staff at Douglas House, I flew out to Michigan and joined the eight hundred or so members of the congress.

Blindness, mental handicap and deafness were among the topics that were presented and explored at the congressional sessions, sometimes in the form of straight discussions, on other occasions by inspirational ministries. Silent Touch was one — a group of deaf youngsters who used the media of song and dance to portray their affliction. In addition, those who lived in chronic pain and those with environmental allergies and diseases such as AIDS, shared their own peculiar suffering. Awareness and compassion were heightened by our universal agreement on the need to reach out in love, however risky, to those who did not yet know the love of Jesus. The whole experience of being in close Christian fellowship with hundreds of disabled people of many nationalities and from such diverse walks of life was one I will always treasure.

And now, here I was a few days after the congress had finished, at Inspiration Centre, Walworth, Wisconsin, at a retreat sponsored by Joni and Friends and the Christian League for the Handicapped, awaiting my meeting with Joni herself.

Rain beat against the windows of the log cabin and wind moaned softly in the chimney breast. The elements, however, served merely to heighten the warmth and security of the cabin's interior. Heat and flickering orange light radiated from a huge log fire in a great stone hearth and around me the pine walls glistened with a mellow iridescence that reminded me of honey.

Joni's presence, when she entered the room, was magnetic. Now aged forty, she looked little changed from the photograph which graced the front of her first book. She'd been seventeen when her accident had occurred, but her thick, corn-coloured hair showed no signs of fading and her pretty, snub-nosed face was still unlined. Seated in her wheelchair, splints on both arms, she had a natural radiance that eclipsed her disability and, bubbling beneath the suave confidence and cool detachment of a professional, was the infectious effervescence and freshness of a child.

We greeted each other and took up positions on either side of the log fire. The filming team made ready, one crewman holding a huge silvery screen to reflect light into our faces, another crouching at our feet with a microphone. Jim Wiltshire, the director, gave final instructions then indicated to the cameraman to start the shoot. I glanced across at Joni and nervously asked my first question.

'At what point after your accident did life become worth living again?'

'Oh boy! That is a tough question.' Joni shook her head. 'I suppose it was important that I go through a lot of questions, a lot of struggling, a lot of anger. I had to go down into the depths of all my depression and I had to experience that pain before I could rise above it.'

Joni's expression changed to register incredulity. 'I do not understand these people who never get depressed.

I knew people when I was in the hospital that never cried. They never opened their hearts to anyone else. They never had a box of tissues by their bedside. I could not relate to them. I could not identify with them.

'I identified with the people who grieved the loss of a body that no longer was working, or the loss of a heart that was numb, or maybe the loss of a mind that could think clearly, that could feel hope. These were the people I identified with when I got down to the depths of all that pain and depression – I mean to the point when I was begging my friends to slit my wrists with a razor, begging my friends to push pills down my throat.

'After I went through that – and it was so important that I go through it – then I was able to look up and I will never forget when it happened.

'I was sitting in Occupational Therapy one day and this young ventilator-dependent quadriplegic, far more disabled than me, was there. He had a breathing machine attached to his throat, a ventilator. As this point I did not want to write with my mouth, type with my mouth, talk to anybody. I watched him. He was so kind to everyone and he seemed so hopeful and when he talked to the occupational therapists he did what they told him to do. He started learning to write and type with the pencil between his teeth and when I saw him and his face and his positive attitude and his desire to grow, I said I can do it.

'If he can do it, far more paralysed than me, then I have hope. I can find faith. I can believe in someone far bigger, someone far greater, and I think that is when my life began to take on meaning. When I saw that after the questions, I could move the arm of depression and look at inspiring examples of other people who had faith in God, who had faith in the future and who looked at life as a kind of challenge, that inspired me to go on.'

I could identify with Joni's response to the inspiration of others since she, herself, had so fired my enthusiasm through her writing, speaking and painting.

My next question was on the nature of anger. Joni's reply indicated that anger was just self-pity turned outward on others − all the inside turmoil, hurt and disappointment, the self-absorption and introspection that poisons your own life loaded on to another person.

'There comes a point when it kind of explodes out of your mouth in a lot of hot words and your anger begins to sting and poison the lives of other people around you,' she continued.

Then she went on to point out that the Bible provides an incredibly comprehensive guide for these kinds of questions, and quoted from Hebrews 12:15: 'See to it that no one misses the grace of God and that no bitter root grows up to cause trouble and defile many.'

'The answer to anger is to clean it up and grab hold of faith,' she concluded. 'Grab hold of saying *Yes* to the future and *Yes* to bright promises, *Yes* to God.'

On the question of why God allows tragedy to touch lives, Joni felt able to answer only on a personal level. With simple humility she acknowledged that what she had to say might sound a little pious or 'canned', but she went on to state that she believed God had allowed her paralysis in order to change her for the better, to increase her capacity to open up to God himself, and to identify with others. She acknowledged, too, that her focus had moved away from the passing material trappings of this world on to the 'heavenly glories above'.

'Now I know that is a lot of religious language,' she said, 'but basically we are saying that there is the life after this one. I am convinced that the best things in this life are only a foreshadowing, a sneak preview of even greater things yet to come.

'I can see the wisdom of the Bible when it says all flesh is as grass,' she continued. 'It fades and withers under the heat of the summer sun. I mean all that I have to do, all that you have to do is look down at our bodies. They are wasting away, our paralysis is creeping up on us. But Susan, I am convinced that you and I and people like us know, almost intuitively, that there has got to be a better life – a life beyond.'

A log settled in the grate and sparks leapt up the chimney. I watched for a moment then turned back to Joni.

'Have you ever tried faith healing? How do you feel when people pray for healing?'

'Early on in my journey with disability I went to all kinds of tent meetings, revivals. I went to churches. I was annointed with oil. I had Elders lay hands on me. I prayed believingly. Come on! I prayed to the point where I was wearing my faith on my sleeve, you know. I would call my friends up on the telephone and say, ''next time you guys see me I am going to be on my feet. You had better believe along with me!''

'Well, that is not only being a fool for Christ – right? I believed with a capital B, yet my fingers and my feet were not getting the message. My head was saying ''move'' and my heart was saying ''move'' but my body just did not sink in.'

Joni went on to describe the struggle she'd had – wondering if her faith were insufficient, or if she had more sins to confess. She admitted that she had been catapulted into a horrible period of spiritual depression before she began to realise that we are only required to have faith the size of a mustard seed, and that the work that God had in mind may not be the big, explosive miracle of physical healing. When Jesus was paralysed on the cross he was challenged by the rulers and elders to 'call up a legion of angels' to save him.

'But I think Jesus on his cross knew that even if the angels had delivered him right then and there, his challengers would not believe. We always think a miracle is going to convince us, but we are not supposed to walk by sight. We are supposed to walk by faith. I think you and I, Susan, have had a much more dramatic, a much more exciting, healing in that God has healed us on the inside. And I think that is what really counts.'

There was no doubting the wholeness, joy and peace

that shone from Joni's face as she sat in the flickering firelight of that log cabin in Wisconsin and smiled across at me. And I knew, as I returned her smile, that she spoke Truth, that what God had done in her life and mine, and in the lives of others like us, was no less a miracle than Jesus' death on the cross and his rising to new life.

God has healed us on the inside. And that's what really counts.

The 'high' which had filled me during my sojourn in America began to evaporate as I touched down in England, and a sense of anti-climax pervaded my return to Brixham. As I disembarked from the Cheshire Home mini-bus and passed through the double doors of the Home, it occurred to me that I simply did not want to be there. For the first time since my arrival seventeen years ago, Douglas House seemed an alien place. I no longer felt that I belonged.

'I feel sure that God is telling me that my time here is drawing to a close,' I later told a friend. Over the next few days, jet-lagged and generally fatigued, I tried to analyse my emotions, my thinking.

Back in Wisconsin I'd felt completely liberated. Faith there had a tangible quality; though unseen of itself it was visible by the life it imbued. I'd tasted of its Life-giving manna, drunk at its well and known the nourishment of sustaining prayer.

It seemed to me that at the congress and Inspiration Centre, faith's power had been evident throughout. It was present in the exaltation that exuded from people who, by the world's standards, should have been cowed and broken. And it was demonstrated in the fruit of their lives – that fruit of the spirit of which Galatians speaks: love, joy, peace, patience, kindness, goodness, faithfulness, gentleness and self-control. Steeped in God's spirit, I'd felt the cloying excesses of the world melt away, and with them the all-pervading numbness of spirit which they imparted.

Now that I was home, however, peace eluded me. Home? Where *was* home I asked myself? For seventeen years I'd thought of Douglas House as home, but as I prepared for bed that first night back, I began to wonder. What did God want of me? Had his purposes in my life changed? If they remained the same, was there a change in the manner in which those purposes were to be achieved?

The staff at the Home were as loving and attentive as always and interested in hearing of my exploits. But something was missing. I longed to be elsewhere, far from the intrusive noise and strife of secular institutionalised living, to have peace and quiet to hear God's voice speaking into my life.

Within a few days of my return I was acutely aware of an overwhelming need to escape, to know once more that quality of liberation I'd found in America. One place, only, had the ability to impart the peace that I sought. A few days later, in pursuit of answers, I set off for Berry Head.

Unseasonal June weather chilled my flesh and northerly winds cut into my bones. Grey lowering skies pressed upon the earth's surface and clung to its contours and, below − far below the clifftop − the sea spread before me − vast and impenetrable as polished marble.

Again and again in life I had encountered that same feeling. Dark days of emptiness − in my affluence, my marriage, my illness and disability − were symbolised in the seascape before me.

But God had seen my plight and, throughout those dark chilling days, I had never been out of his sight. Succour had come to me in the form of Jesus and my helplessness, my hopelessness, had been the very means by which he had reached out to rescue me. Over and over again he had shown me that in my weakness his strength is made perfect.

'I will lift up mine eyes to the hills, from whence cometh my help,'[1] writes the psalmist.

I lifted my head. Frail and feeble though my body might be, I was, nevertheless, elevated above my infirmity. Held aloft and supported by a mighty mass of rock that, for thousands of years, had withstood the erosion of sea-winds and torrential rains, I was lifted out of reach of the crashing waves which might break a man or a woman to pieces against the cliffs, or suck them under into darkness.

No matter where life took me, no matter what troubles were thrown against me, Jesus was my Rock. The gates of hell could not prevail against him. He would bear me aloft, high above the elements, my frailty hidden in his fortification, my deficiencies in his durability.

Neither here in England nor abroad in America could God's Kingdom be contained. It was boundless, to be found both here and now in my own life, but sweeping, also, beyond my vision, without parameters, infinity shimmering in a haze of human limitation.

I'd sought answers to mundane questions: was I to remain in Douglas House, eking out what sometimes seemed an unexciting life of trivia, or was I to be part of some exhilarating new venture similar to the Christian League for the Handicapped in Wisconsin? Would God use me to champion the causes of the disabled, to influence society, to take on governments in a quest for Independent Living which would enable those with disabilities to move into the community?

Even as I pondered the questions, I knew that God was affirming that I did not have to Do anything, I simply had to Be.

Berry Head: this was where it had all begun, with the angel on the clifftop — a man dressed in a suit on a hot summer's day six years ago, who'd told me that Jesus loved me. I hadn't wanted to know. How things had changed! God had refused to take 'no' for an answer. He'd sought me out. He'd made me his own. He'd saved me, primarily, to be his child, to know him and love him in an intimate relationship. The natural outworking of his love for me was that I should be his hands, his feet, his love.

I was part of a greater whole.

My focus was not to be taken up with the work that God required of me, but with the Lord himself. I'd asked Joni, 'How do you do more for God? How did you begin your life's work?'

Her reply had made eminent sense. 'We all want to do more for God. We all want to be used by God. I often pray "Lord, please use me", but the Bible tells me that he already wants to use us. I think the issue is "God make us more usable".'

Joni had gone on to explain that purifying our hearts, opening our minds, reading his Word and living by his guidelines were the means of becoming more usable. 'When we make ourselves available to him and abandoned to him, then God is going to use us.'

'When . . . then . . .' And I'd been asking 'how?'

I raised my eyes. Faint iridescence shimmered on the distant sea. God's purposes may sometimes seem obscure. But _he_ is always to hand. Frequently only a glimmer on the far horizon under a leaden English sky; occasionally a brilliant Ecuadorian sunset that sets the seas ablaze. Rays shed by the same sun – the radiation of a greater light: the Light of the World.

From a wheelchair there's only one way to perceive that Light.

I will lift up mine eyes . . . from whence cometh my help.
And be healed, as I am, on the inside.

Postscript

In November 1979 Susan formed a Christian Fellowship in the Cheshire Home. Today this is still flourishing with Bible study, prayer and worship, testimonies and outside speakers.

Since Susan's visit to America, her desire to be involved in the Christian League for the Handicapped has taken up a new slant. She corresponds with folk all over the world, has had her story published in a magazine in New Zealand and has been instrumental in obtaining a wheelchair for a disabled Christian in Malawi and an amputee in Kingswear, Devon.

Susan is also writing her second poetry book, *Footsteps in the Sea.*

Bible References

Chapter 15

Chapter 16